FRENCH IN THE PRIMARY SCHOOL
Attitudes and Achievement

FRENCH IN THE PRIMARY SCHOOL

Attitudes and Achievement

Clare Burstall
Senior research officer, NFER

National Foundation
for Educational
Research in
England and Wales

Published by the National Foundation for Educational Research
in England and Wales

The Mere, Upton Park, Slough, Bucks
and at 79 Wimpole Street, London, W1M 8EA

First Published 1970

© *National Foundation for Educational Research*
in England and Wales

SBN   901225   59   2

Cover Design by
PETER GAULD, FSIA

Printed in Great Britain by
KING, THORNE & STACE LTD., SCHOOL ROAD, HOVE SUSSEX

Foreword

THIS report represents the 'half-way mark' in the NFER evaluation of the Pilot Scheme for the teaching of French in primary schools. The research described in this report was carried out between the spring of 1967 and the autumn of 1969 and spans the transition between the primary and secondary stages of the experiment. The report is primarily concerned with the achievement in French of the pupils in the experimental sample, at both the primary and the secondary level, and with the relationship between level of achievement in French and attitudes towards teaching and learning the language. The results reported are derived from a longitudinal study of two experimental year-groups or 'cohorts' of pupils: those who began to learn French from the age of eight in 1964 and in 1965. Mention is occasionally made in the text of a third cohort: this cohort consists of approximately 6,000 primary school pupils who began to learn French from the age of eight in 1968. The Schools Council agreed in 1968 to sponsor the extension of the NFER evaluation of the Pilot Scheme to a third cohort, so that the results obtained from the study of the first two cohorts could be amplified and extended and an opportunity provided to pursue promising lines of inquiry suggested by the early findings of the main project.

Since the research project now encompasses a 10-year period, the interim nature of the present report must be emphasized and the findings interpreted with caution. As in any long-term investigation, results yet to be obtained may modify earlier emphases and define more closely the limits of interpretation.

It will be clear to the reader that the work of the research team has been greatly facilitated by the generous assistance of all those who have taken part in the experiment. Research which has to be carried out within the normal school environment can only be accomplished with considerable assistance from the heads and teaching staff of the schools concerned and with the co-operation of the Local Education Authority. The members of the research team would particularly like to express their gratitude to the heads and teaching staff of the 'experimental' and 'control' schools, who gallantly bore the brunt of the fieldwork, to the members of HM Inspectorate, whose reports provided a major contribution to the evaluation, and to the staff of the Local Education Authorities, who did much to smooth the path of the project.

C.B.

Contents

Contents

List of Tables

List of Tables

List of tables in the appendices

Appendix One

List of Tables

11

List of Tables

12

List of Tables

List of Figures (Appendices Two and Six)

SECTION ONE

General Attainment in the Primary School

THE evaluation of the Pilot Scheme for the teaching of French in primary schools includes an investigation of the effect on general attainment of the introduction of French at the primary stage. Since the provision of daily French lessons would inevitably reduce the time available for other school activities, the possibility arose that the children's mastery of the basic skills might in the long run be adversely affected by the introduction of French. It was equally possible that the stimulus of learning a second language might serve to increase the children's understanding of their own language, and so exert a beneficial influence on the development of verbal skills. In order to investigate these possibilities, it was necessary to assess the general level of attainment in the Pilot Scheme classes both at the outset of the experiment and at the end of the primary stage. It was also necessary to establish appropriate control groups in classes where the pupils would not be taught French during their primary school career, so that the level of attainment in these classes could serve as a basis for comparison. If the introduction of French affected general attainment either positively or negatively, a comparison of the test scores of the experimental and control groups at the end of the primary stage would reveal this effect.

The Pilot Scheme schools had been assigned to one of three experimental groups, on the basis of their size, type, and history of French teaching, and the establishment of appropriate controls entailed different problems for each experimental group. Group 1 schools, for example, were large primary schools in which there had been no French teaching to the school population in existence in September 1964, although in some cases French had been taught in the past to selected groups of pupils, on a short-term basis. In this group of schools, the teaching of French was to be confined to second-year juniors during the first year of the experiment, and thereafter extended to succeeding year-groups. Since the third- and fourth-year pupils were not to be taught French during their primary school career, they were able to serve as internal controls. In the second group of schools, on the other hand, differing circumstances necessitated the establishment of external controls. Group 2 schools were similar in size and type to those in Group 1 and differed from them only in regard to their history of French teaching. In Group 2 schools, the teaching of French was either well-established before the introduction of the Pilot Scheme or else had previously been restricted to certain year-groups, but was to be extended to the whole junior age-range from September 1964 onwards. This precluded any possibility of setting up internal control groups. External control groups were therefore established in the fourth-year classes of junior schools similar in size and type to Group 2 schools, but in which no French was taught. A different system of controls had to be adopted for the schools in the third experimental group. The schools assigned to Group 3 were all small rural schools with fewer than three junior classes. Some of the Group 3 schools had a brief history of French teaching prior to the introduction of the Pilot Scheme, but no French had been taught to the school population in existence in September 1964. Since many of the schools in this group had only one class for the whole of the junior age-range, it was impossible to select groups of pupils to act as internal controls and equally impossible to use fourth-year pupils in other junior schools as external controls. Each school in Group 3 was therefore individually matched with a control school which resembled the experimental school as closely as possible, but in which no French was taught. All pupils who fell within the experimental age-range in the Group 3 schools and in the matching control schools would thus be given the general attainment battery at the beginning of the experiment and would subsequently be re-tested for general attainment before transferring to the secondary school.

The general attainment battery consisted of the following five tests: Primary Verbal, Reading, English, Mechanical Arithmetic and Problem Arithmetic. These tests were standardized by the NFER for use in the investigation into the effects of streaming in the primary school, and were used in the present inquiry because the test-retest design demanded a test battery suitable for use with the whole junior age-range.[1] The maximum score obtainable for each test is as follows: Primary Verbal: 85; Reading: 48; English: 66; Mechanical Arithmetic: 44; Problem Arithmetic: 30. The general attainment battery was initially administered to the first experimental cohort in October

---

[1] For further information about the tests making up the general attainment battery, see: BARKER-LUNN, J. C. (1970). *Streaming in the Primary School.* Slough: NFER.

1964 and to the second in October 1965. The first cohort comprised all pupils in Group 1 and Group 2 schools who fell within the age-range 8.0—8.11 on 1 September 1964, and all pupils in Group 3 schools who fell within the age-range 8.0—9.11 on that date. A wider age-range was selected for study in Group 3 schools in view of the extensive age-range obtaining in junior classes in this group of schools. Pupils in Group 3 schools were not therefore represented in the second experimental cohort, which comprised all pupils in Group 1 and Group 2 schools who fell within the age-range 8.0—8.11 on 1 September 1965. For each cohort, age of pupil was the sole criterion of selection. The results obtained from the initial administration of the general attainment battery to Cohorts 1 and 2 and from the final administration of the test battery to the Cohort 1 pupils in Group 3 schools in June 1966 have already been reported[1]. Cohort 1 pupils in Group 1 and Group 2 schools were retested for general attainment at the end of the primary stage in June 1967. Cohort 2 pupils in the same schools were retested in June 1968. The results obtained on each occasion are summarized below.

Final administration of general attainment battery: summary of results.

A detailed breakdown of the general attainment test scores is presented in Tables 1.1 to 1.10 in Appendix 1. Tables 1.1 to 1.5 show mean scores for the experimental and control groups on each of the general attainment tests, distributed by school group and parental occupation catgeory. Five categories of parental occupation have been discerned: 'professional' and 'clerical', 'skilled', 'semi-skilled', and 'unskilled'. The 'professional', 'clerical' categories have been combined for purposes of analysis and are presented as a single category in all tables showing the distribution of test scores. Tables 1.6 to 1.10 show mean scores for the experimental sample on each of the general attainment tests, distributed by cohort, school group, sex of pupil, and parental occupation category. The data presented in Tables 1.6 to 1.10 refer only to those pupils in the experimental sample who were present for both the initial and the final administration of the general attainment test battery.

The results obtained from the final administration of the general attainment battery may be summarized as follows:

[1] BURSTALL, C. (1968). *French From Eight: A National Experiment.* Slough: NFER.

1. *Comparison of Experimental and Control Groups*

When the general attainment test scores obtained by the pupils in the experimental groups at the end of their primary school career are compared with those obtained by the pupils in the control groups, there is no indication of a major trend in either a positive or a negative direction. There are minor variations in test performance, but these are usually associated with variations in the social composition of the groups concerned. In the Group 1 schools, for instance, Cohort 1 pupils in the 'semi-skilled' parental occupation category tend to obtain higher mean scores that those obtained by the control pupils in this category, but, when the parental occupation categories are combined, the differences between the mean scores of the experimental and control groups are very slight. Cohort 2 pupils in the 'professional and clerical' parental occupation category in Group 1 schools tend to obtain lower mean scores than those obtained by the control pupils in the same category, but, when parental occupation categories are combined, the differences between the mean scores of the experimental and control groups are again very slight. Furthermore, the Cohort 2 sample contains proportionately fewer pupils in the 'professional and clerical' category and proportionately more pupils in the 'unskilled' category than the control sample does: this difference in the social composition of the two groups is probably sufficient to account for the variation in test performance. Similarly, the pupils in Group 2 schools tend to obtain higher mean scores than those obtained by the pupils in the external control groups, but significant differences between mean scores in favour of the experimental sample tend to be concentrated in the higher-status parental occupation categories, and the experimental sample contains proportionately more pupils in the 'professional and clerical' category and proportionately fewer pupils in the 'unskilled' category than the external control groups do. Pupils in Group 3 schools, on the other hand, tend to obtain slightly lower mean scores on the general attainment battery than those obtained by pupils in the matching control schools, but differences between mean scores in favour of the control schools only reach statistical significance in the case of pupils in the 'unskilled' category. With all parental occupation categories combined, differences between the mean scores obtained by pupils in the experimental and control schools do not reach a significant level.

These results are shown in summary form in Table 1 and presented in greater detail in Tables 1.1 to 1.5 in Appendix 1. Table 1 shows the mean scores obtained by the pupils in the experimental and control groups on each of the general attainment tests, distributed by school

TABLE 1: *General attainment. Comparison of experimental and control groups: mean scores by school group*

School Group		Primary Verbal	Mechanical Arithmetic	Reading	Problem Arithmetic	English
Group 1 (Cohort 1)	N	1129	1133	1163	1152	1153
	x̄	66·89	25·78	32·85	19·48	42·32
	SD	15·53	9·84	7·93	5·99	14·59
Group 1 (Cohort 2)	N	1226	1233	1219	1228	1216
	x̄	65·69	24·36	32·41	19·10	41·21
	SD	15·76	9·73	8·25	5·98	14·91
Group 1 Controls	N	2922	1442	2933	2935	2914
	x̄	65·68	25·53	32·28	19·72	42·67
	SD	17·26	7·80	8·97	6·52	16·11
Group 2 (Cohort 1)	N	2724	2721	2731	2726	2738
	x̄	66·59	25·08	32·44	19·45	41·20
	SD	16·45	10·38	8·59	6·27	15·59
Group 2 (Cohort 2)	N	2890	2890	2874	2874	2850
	x̄	66·74	24·32	32·38	19·20	41·40
	SD	15·89	10·14	8·22	6·18	14·99
Group 2 Controls	N	1709	1701	1699	1636	1706
	x̄	62·93	23·68	31·50	18·95	40·43
	SD	18·29	7·99	9·15	6·64	16·17
Group 3	N	497	493	491	491	487
	x̄	62·61	21·94	29·74	17·27	37·82
	SD	17·62	10·01	9·03	6·51	16·48
Group 3 Controls	N	554	554	551	549	547
	x̄	64·29	22·62	30·01	17·83	38·86
	SD	17·06	9·84	8·75	6·64	16·04

group, but with scores for pupils of both sexes and in each parental occupation category combined.

The test performance of the pupils in the experimental and control groups does not indicate that the level of general attainment in the primary school is significantly affected by the introduction of French. The evidence does not support the view that the introduction of a second language at the primary stage depresses the level of general attainment; neither does it encourage the view that instruction in French promotes the development of fluency in the mother tongue.

It must be emphasized, however, that these findings are specific to the battery of tests used in the inquiry and cannot be generalized to other subject areas.

2. Sex Differences

The differences between the sexes with regard to test performance are less marked than they were on the first occasion of testing, when the girls in the sample obtained significantly higher mean scores than the boys on all tests except the Problem Arithmetic test. By the end of the primary stage, the only test on which the girls' scores are markedly higher than the boys' is the English test, although the girls still tend to obtain slightly higher mean scores than the boys on the Primary Verbal test and the Mechanical Arithmetic test. On the Reading test and the Problem Arithmetic test, the performance of the girls in the sample differs little from that of the boys. Mean scores for each test, by cohort and sex of pupil, but with school groups and parental occupation categories combined, are shown in Table 2. These results are presented in greater detail in Tables 1.6 to 1.10 in Appendix 1.

3. Parental Occupation

There is a linear relationship between test score and parental occupation: for both boys and girls in each school group and cohort,

TABLE 2: *General attainment. Mean scores by cohort and sex of pupil*

COHORT SEX OF PUPIL		PRIMARY VERBAL	MECHANICAL ARITHMETIC	READING	PROBLEM ARITHMETIC	ENGLISH
Cohort 1	N	1939	1937	1970	1961	1985
Boys	x̄	65·06	24·62	32·15	19·53	39·04
	SD	17·52	10·34	9·04	6·34	15·80
Cohort 1	N	1914	1917	1924	1917	1906
Girls	x̄	68·31	25·96	32·99	19·39	44·13
	SD	14·53	10·07	7·65	6·03	14·33
Cohort 2	N	2046	2053	2032	2034	2023
Boys	x̄	65·14	23·79	32·16	19·19	38·79
	SD	17·00	10·25	8·81	6·28	15·67
Cohort 2	N	2070	2070	2061	2068	2043
Girls	x̄	67·70	24·86	32·62	19·15	43·87
	SD	14·54	9·75	7·61	5·96	13·77

TABLE 3: *General attainment. Mean scores by cohort and parental occupation*

COHORT TEST		Professional and Clerical	Skilled	Semi-skilled	Unskilled	TOTAL
		PARENTAL OCCUPATION				
Cohort 1 Primary Verbal	N	862	1220	1187	584	3853
	x̄	75·02	69·54	63·24	55·35	66·68
	SD	9·85	13·52	16·06	20·17	16·19
Cohort 2 Primary Verbal	N	946	1447	1173	550	4116
	x̄	73·52	68·59	62·70	56·45	66·42
	SD	11·77	13·49	16·77	18·37	15·86
Cohort 1 Mechanical Arithmetic	N	861	1220	1187	586	3854
	x̄	30·93	26·76	22·51	19·56	25·29
	SD	8·92	9·57	9·68	9·53	10·23
Cohort 2 Mechanical Arithmetic	N	950	1454	1167	552	4123
	x̄	29·07	25·16	21·99	18·91	24·33
	SD	9·43	9·60	9·54	8·93	10·02
Cohort 1 Reading	N	868	1240	1195	591	3894
	x̄	37·32	33·74	30·58	27·13	32·56
	SD	6·03	7·41	8·10	9·47	8·40
Cohort 2 Reading	N	935	1433	1175	550	4093
	x̄	36·44	33·48	30·13	27·48	32·39
	SD	6·69	7·19	8·37	8·83	8·23
Cohort 1 Problem Arithmetic	N	868	1234	1189	587	3878
	x̄	22·88	20·21	17·96	15·85	19·46
	SD	5·11	5·66	5·90	6·37	6·19
Cohort 2 Problem Arithmetic	N	934	1440	1176	552	4102
	x̄	22·05	19·84	17·66	15·77	19·17
	SD	5·30	5·65	6·04	6·17	6·12
Cohort 1 English	N	877	1244	1188	582	3891
	x̄	50·56	43·67	37·53	31·54	41·53
	SD	11·22	13·68	14·65	16·56	15·31
Cohort 2 English	N	942	1420	1161	543	4066
	x̄	48·86	43·10	37·38	32·20	41·35
	SD	11·93	13·54	15·08	15·52	14·97

high mean scores coincide with high-status parental occupation and low mean scores with low-status parental occupation. This finding applies equally to each test in the general attainment battery. Mean scores for each test, by cohort and parental occupation, but with scores for pupils of both sexes and in both school groups combined, are shown in Table 3. These results are presented in greater detail in Tables 1.6 to 1.10 in Appendix 1.

4. *Cohort and School Group*

Taking the sample as a whole, there are no significant differences between the mean scores obtained by the pupils in Cohort 1 and those obtained by the pupils in Cohort 2 on the Primary Verbal test, the Reading test, and the English test. With the scores for all pupils in each cohort combined, mean scores for Cohort 1 pupils are, however, significantly higher than those for Cohort 2 pupils on the Mechanical

TABLE 4: *General attainment. Mean scores by cohort and school group*

COHORT SCHOOL GROUP		PRIMARY VERBAL	MECHANICAL ARITHMETIC	READING	PROBLEM ARITHMETIC	ENGLISH
Cohort 1	N	1129	1133	1163	1152	1153
Group 1	x̄	66·89	25·78	32·85	19·48	42·32
	SD	15·53	9·84	7·93	5·99	14·59
Cohort 1	N	2724	2721	2731	2726	2738
Group 2	x̄	66·59	25·08	32·44	19·45	41·20
	SD	16·45	10·38	8·58	6·27	15·59
Cohort 1	N	3853	3854	3894	3878	3891
Groups 1 and 2	x̄	66·68	25·29	32·56	19·46	41·53
	SD	16·19	10·23	8·40	6·19	15·31
Cohort 2	N	1226	1233	1219	1228	1216
Group 1	x̄	65·69	24·36	32·41	19·10	41·21
	SD	15·76	9·73	8·25	5·98	14·91
Cohort 2	N	2890	2890	2874	2874	2850
Group 2	x̄	66·74	24·32	32·38	19·20	41·40
	SD	15·89	10·14	8·22	6·18	14·99
Cohort 2	N	4116	4123	4093	4102	4066
Groups 1 and 2	x̄	66·42	24·33	32·39	19·17	41·35
	SD	15·86	10·02	8·23	6·12	14·97

Arithmetic test and the Problem Arithmetic test. In each case, significant differences between mean scores in favour of Cohort 1 pupils are concentrated in the higher-status parental occupation categories. This finding could be indicative of the trend away from the more traditional methods of teaching arithmetic. By the time the Cohort 2 pupils were retested for general attainment in the summer of 1968, most of the primary schools in the experimental sample had abandoned the traditional approach to the teaching of computational skills and, in consequence, the arithmetic tests used in the general attainment battery no longer provided an adequate reflection of classroom practice.

Mean scores for each test, by cohort and school group, but with scores for pupils of both sexes and in each parental occupation category combined are shown in Table 4. These results are presented in greater detail in Tables 1.6 to 1.10 in Appendix 1.

In each cohort, the test performance of pupils in Group 1 schools differs little from that of pupils in Group 2 schools. These two groups of schools were differentiated solely on the basis of their history of French teaching: the schools within each group are otherwise similar in size, type and social composition.

SECTION TWO

Achievement in French in the Primary School

IT was originally anticipated that the assessment of achievement in French at the end of the primary stage would include a measure of the pupils' ability to write in French. As the pupils in the first experimental cohort approached their final term in the primary school, however, it became clear that very few of them would have had any experience of writing in French, apart from simple copy-writing, before transferring to the secondary school. The administration of a writing test to the first cohort was therefore postponed until the secondary stage of the experiment. Consequently, the only French test administered to these pupils in their final term of primary school was Test RCA, a group test of reading comprehension. This test, developed during 1966-1967, had been devised for the pupils in the experimental sample, with specific reference to the French teaching materials in use in the Pilot Scheme schools. The construction of test items was preceded by a content analysis of the teaching materials used in the third-year French classes and by extensive classroom observation of the methods used to introduce reading in French. The first draft of the test was given pre-pilot classroom trials in February 1967. The draft test was revised in the light of classroom experience and then subjected to a full schedule of pilot-testing in primary schools outside the Pilot Scheme areas. After item analysis and revision, the final version of Test RCA was produced in May 1967. This version of the test carries a maximum score of 50 and is in three sections. Each section of the test is preceded by printed instructions in English and by appropriate practice examples, to familiarize the pupil with the type of item contained in that section. The content of the test items in each section reflects the common content of the audio-visual French courses in use in the schools taking part in the experiment. The first section of Test RCA contains 20 multiple-choice items. Each item in this section consists of a sentence in French printed in bold-face type, beneath a set of four pictures in the pupil's test booklet. The pupil is required to examine each set of four pictures and to select the picture which corresponds to the printed item. He then indicates his choice by marking his test booklet

24

appropriately: no ability to write in French is required. This type of item was developed from that used originally to test listening comprehension in French and has been described more fully in an earlier report[1]. The second section of Test RCA contains 20 multiple-choice sentence-completion items. Each item consists of a sentence in French which needs one word to complete it. In each instance, the pupil is given four words to choose from, and is simply required to identify the missing word and to place a tick beside it. He has only to recognize the correct word, not to copy it: the task involves no element of writing ability. The final section of the test consists of a passage of dialogue, followed by 10 multiple-choice questions designed to test the pupil's understanding of the content of the passage. As before, the pupil indicates his answer to each question by marking his test-booklet appropriately: he is not required to write in French.

The final version of Test RCA was administered to 3,790 first cohort pupils in June 1967. Pupils in three permanent remedial classes, who had not been introduced to reading in French, were excluded from the test programme. The results obtained from the administration of Test RCA are summarized below.

Administration of Test RCA: summary of results.

A detailed breakdown of the test scores is presented in Table 2.1 in Appendix 2. This table shows mean scores for Test RCA, distributed by school group, sex of pupil, and parental occupation. As before, the 'professional' and 'clerical' parental occupation categories

TABLE 5: *Test RCA. Mean scores by sex of pupil and parental occupation*

SEX OF PUPIL		Professional and Clerical	Skilled	Semi-skilled	Unskilled	TOTAL
		PARENTAL OCCUPATION				
Boys	N	420	611	588	302	1921
	x̄	30·50	26·49	23·46	19·99	25·42
	SD	9·12	8·93	8·98	9·22	9·66
Girls	N	438	591	576	264	1869
	x̄	34·55	31·13	27·22	24·42	29·78
	SD	8·39	9·66	9·58	9·64	9·97

[1] Burstall, C. op cit.

have been combined to form a single category. The results obtained from the administration of Test RCA may be summarized as follows:

1. Sex Differences

The girls in the first cohort score consistently higher than the boys on Test RCA. In both groups of schools and within each parental occupation category, the girls obtain significantly higher mean scores than the boys. Differences between mean scores in favour of the girls are significant at the 0.1 per cent level. Mean scores by sex of pupil and parental occupation, but with school groups combined, are shown in Table 5.

2. Parental Occupation

There is a linear relationship between test score and parental occupation: for both boys and girls in each school group, high mean scores on Test RCA coincide with high-status parental occupation and low mean scores with low-status parental occupation. Differences between mean scores are significant at the 0.1 per cent level. The distribution of RCA scores for Cohort 1 pupils within each parental occupation category, but with scores for pupils of both sexes combined, is shown in graphic form in Figure 2.1 in Appendix 2.

3. School Group

The test performance of Cohort 1 pupils in Group 1 schools differs little from that of Cohort 1 pupils in Group 2 schools. In Group 1

TABLE 6: *Test RCA. Mean scores by school group and parental occupation*

SCHOOL GROUP		Professional and Clerical	Skilled	Semi-skilled	Unskilled	TOTAL
		PARENTAL OCCUPATION				
Group 1	N	214	353	368	183	1118
	x̄	33·37	29·12	26·45	22·25	27·93
	SD	8·95	9·48	9·01	8·88	9·77
Group 2	N	644	849	796	383	2672
	x̄	32·31	28·63	24·80	21·97	27·42
	SD	8·98	9·62	9·63	10·03	10·17
Combined Groups	N	858	1202	1164	566	3790
	x̄	32·57	28·77	25·32	22·06	27·57
	SD	8·98	9·58	9·47	9·67	10·06

schools, girls in the 'semi-skilled' parental occupation category tend to obtain slightly higher mean scores than girls in the same category in Group 2 schools, but this is the sole instance of a significant difference between the mean scores obtained by Cohort 1 pupils in the two groups of schools. Mean scores by school group and parental occupation, but with the scores for pupils of both sexes combined, are shown in Table 6.

4. *Correlations Between General Attainment and French Test Scores*

The scores obtained by the pupils in the first cohort on Test RCA were correlated with those previously obtained by the same pupils on Test LCA and on the general attainment battery. The extent to which scores on the different tests correlate with one another is shown in Table 7. The French test scores correlate fairly highly with one another (0·74) and scores on Test RCA correlate to a similar extent (0·75) with the English test scores. The French test scores do not otherwise correlate highly with the general attainment test scores, although each of the French tests correlates more highly with those tests in the general attainment battery which demand verbal skills (Primary Verbal, Reading, English) than with those with which require mathematical ability (Mechanical Arithmetic, Problem Arithmetic). Test RCA correlates more highly with the general attainment tests than does Test LCA. This is not unexpected, since Test RCA is designed to measure ability to understand the written forms of language, an ability also demanded by the general attainment tests.

To judge both from the test results and from the pupils' own comments, the introduction of reading constitutes a critical period in the language-learning process. For some pupils, it provides a welcome return to a familiar medium of achievement; for others, it presents an almost insuperable obstacle to further progress. Pupils accustomed to a high level of achievement in their written work are often frustrated and uneasy during the purely oral phase of learning French and press for the earlier introduction of reading and writing. It is significant that, of the 96 high-achieving pupils in the first cohort whose performance on Test LCA fell below the average for their group, all but 17 scored well above the group average on Test RCA a year later. Every high-achieving pupil who scored above the average for his group on Test LCA subsequently scored well above the average on Test RCA also. Pupils whose general level of achievement is low, on the other hand, and who experience serious difficulties during the oral phase of learning French, are unlikely to welcome the intro- duction of reading. All but four of the 181 low-achieving pupils who

TABLE 7: *Cohort 1. Correlations between general attainment test scores and French group test scores*

TEST	PRIMARY VERBAL	MECHANICAL ARITHMETIC	READING	PROBLEM ARITHMETIC	ENGLISH	LCA	RCA
Primary Verbal	1·00	—	—	—	—	—	—
Mechanical Arithmetic.. ..	0·72	1·00	—	—	—	—	—
Reading	0·87	0·68	1·00	—	—	—	—
Problem Arithmetic	0·77	0·86	0·74	1·00	—	—	—
English	0·88	0·76	0·86	0·77	1·00	—	—
LCA	0·54	0·51	0·52	0·50	0·58	1·00	—
RCA	0·68	0·65	0·69	0·63	0·75	0·74	1·00

Note: The correlations shown in Table 7 are based on 3,304 cases.

scored below the average for their group on Test LCA subsequently scored well below the average on Test RCA. For some low-achieving pupils, success during the oral phase of learning French did lead to further achievement once reading had been introduced, but these pupils were in the minority. Of the 114 low-achieving pupils who scored above the average for their group on Test LCA, only 22 subsequently maintained an above-average performance on Test RCA. The remainder scored well below the average for their group.

Unlike the pupils in the first cohort, the majority of pupils in the second cohort (approximately 70 per cent of the sample) were introduced to writing in French, other than simple copy-writing, before their final term in primary school. It was therefore possible to administer a full battery of French tests (Battery 1) to the second cohort pupils in the summer of 1968, before they transferred to secondary school. Battery 1 contains three group tests, designed to measure listening comprehension, reading comprehension, and ability to write in French, and one individually-administered test of ability to speak in French. The tests which make up Battery I will only be described in outline at the present time, since the security requirements of the experiment are still in force. The construction of the tests will be described in detail in a later report, when all the pupils taking part in the experiment have completed the primary stage.

The Battery 1 Listening test contains 40 multiple-choice picture-items, similar to those developed for Test LCA, but of a higher level of difficulty. Each item consists of a sentence or sentences, tape-recorded in French, describing one of a series of four pictures printed in the pupil's test booklet. The pupil's task is to select the picture which he hears described and to mark his test booklet appropriately. The test does not therefore require any ability to read or write in French. All instructions for the test are given in English and appropriate practice examples are provided, to familiarize the pupil with the test procedure. The Listening test is paced by the master-tape and takes less than 20 minutes to administer. It carries a maximum score of 40.

The Battery 1 Reading test is in two parts and carries a maximum score of 60. The first part of the test contains 30 multiple-choice picture-items, similar to those developed for the Listening test, but with the test items printed beneath the picture-sets instead of recorded on tape. The second part of the test contains 12 prose passages, followed by a total of 30 multiple-choice comprehension items in French, designed to test the pupil's understanding of the

29

content of the passages. In each part of the test, the pupil has only to indicate his response by marking his test booklet appropriately: he is not required to write in French. All instructions for the Reading test are given in English and appropriate practice examples are provided. The maximum time allowance for the test is 35 minutes.

The Battery 1 Writing test is in two parts and carries a maximum score of 70. The first part of the test contains 27 picture items. Each item consists of a pair of pictures, with a short sentence in French printed beneath the first picture of the pair. The pupil is required to provide a similar sentence in French, describing the second of the two pictures. For example, the first picture of a pair might show a boy eating an ice-cream and have printed beneath it the sentence: 'Il mange une glace'. The second picture of the pair might then show a girl eating an ice-cream: the pupil would be expected to supply a sentence such as 'Elle mange une glace' or 'La petite fille mange une glace'. The second part of the Writing test contains 15 sentence-completion items. Each item consists of a sentence in French from which one word has been omitted. The pupil is expected to complete the sentence by supplying the missing word. All instructions for the test are given in English and suitable practice examples are provided. The maximum time allowance for the test is 35 minutes.

The Battery 1 Speaking test contains 14 items and carries a maximum score of 84. Each item is in the form of a simple question referring to a black and white illustration in the pupil's test booklet. The pupil is expected to respond in French to each question. For example, a picture might show a boy eating a meal and the pupil might be asked the question: 'Que fait le garçon?'. The pupil would be expected to supply a response such as 'Le garçon mange' or 'Il mange'. Throughout the Speaking test the pupil's responses are recorded on magnetic tape. All instructions for the test are given in English and appropriate practice examples precede the test items. There is no maximum time allowance for the Speaking test, since each pupil is encouraged to work at his own speed.

The Battery 1 French tests were administered in 1968, not only to the pupils in the second cohort, but also, for comparison purposes, to two other groups of pupils: pupils in small primary schools and pupils in comprehensive schools. The small primary schools are not represented in the second cohort sample, since the first cohort sample encompassed a two-year age-range in the small schools. However, in view of the high level of achievement in French observed earlier in the small rural schools, it was considered desirable to include pupils from the small schools in the Battery 1 sample. All the small schools which had previously contained first cohort pupils were therefore from the small schools in the Battery 1 sample. All the small schools which had previously contained first cohort pupils were therefore contacted and permission was obtained to administer Battery 1 to those pupils who fell within the same age-range as the pupils in the second cohort and who had also been learning French for an equal period. Pupils in 22 small schools fulfilled these requirements: this group of schools constitutes the 'small primary school' sample.

Since differences between pupils in Group 1 and Group 2 schools had proved minimal with regard to test performance, it was no longer considered necessary to treat the second cohort pupils in these two groups of schools separately: the schools containing second cohort pupils have therefore been grouped together to form the 'large primary school' sample.

The comprehensive school pupils were included in the Battery 1 sample so that it would be possible to compare the test performance of pupils who were of different ages at the time of testing, but who had nevertheless received an equivalent amount of instruction in French. At the time of testing, the pupils in the two groups of primary schools were of the same age: the average age of the large school sample was 11 years 2 months; that of the small school sample was 11 years 1 month. The pupils in each group of schools had been learning French for three years. The average age of the comprehensive school sample at the time of testing was 13 years 2 months. The pupils concerned had been learning French for two years. In terms of actual teaching time, however, the comprehensive school pupils had been learning French for approximately the same number of hours as the primary school pupils, since French lessons in the primary school are shorter than those in the secondary school. No account could be taken of the variable amounts of time devoted to homework in French by the comprehensive school pupils but, since all the classes involved were using audio-visual materials, written homework assignments did not feature prominently in the French programme. Since the second cohort contains pupils of all abilities, only those comprehensive schools which cater for the whole ability range and which provide all pupils with instruction in French were included in the final sample of 17 schools.

The Battery 1 Listening and Reading tests were administered to all pupils in each of the three groups of schools in the summer of 1968. The Battery 1 Writing test was administered to all comprehensive school pupils and to all primary school pupils who had been introduced to writing in French before the test period. The Speaking test was administered to a sub-sample of pupils (one in five in the large primary schools and in the comprehensive schools; one in three in the small primary schools, because of the limited number of pupils available) from which had been excluded all pupils with a known speech defect, all pupils considered by their teachers to be psychologically unsuited for individual testing, and any pupil who had been absent for any of the group tests. The results of the administration of Battery 1 are summarized below.

Administration of Battery 1: summary of results

A detailed breakdown of the Battery 1 test scores is presented in Tables 2.2 to 2.5 in Appendix 2. These tables show mean scores for each French test, distributed by type of school, sex of pupil, and parental occupation. As before, the 'professional' and 'clerical' parental occupation categories have been combined to form a single category. The results obtained from the administration of Battery 1 may be summarized as follows:

1. *Sex Differences*

In all types of school, girls score significantly higher than boys on each of the three group tests. On the Listening, Reading, and Writing tests, differences between mean scores in favour of the girls are significant at the 0·1 per cent level. Girls also tend to obtain higher mean scores than boys on the individually-administered Speaking test, but significant differences between mean scores in favour of the girls occur less frequently than on the group tests. In the large primary schools, for example, girls tend to obtain higher mean scores than boys, but differences between mean scores only reach significance in the 'professional and clerical' parental occupation category and when all parental occupation categories are combined. In the comprehensive schools also, girls tend to obtain higher mean scores than boys: the most significant difference between mean scores in favour of the girls occurs in the 'skilled' parental occupation category. In the small primary schools there are no significant differences between the mean scores of boys and girls in the 'professional and clerical' and 'skilled' parental occupation categories, but, in the 'semi-skilled' and 'unskilled' categories, and when all parental occupation categories are combined, the boys tend to obtain higher mean scores than the girls. It must be emphasized, however, that the sample size in this instance is extremely small.

2. *Parental Occupation*

The pattern of results obtained from each of the group tests points to a linear relationship between test score and parental occupation. For pupils of both sexes and in each type of school, high mean scores on the Listening, Reading, and Writing tests coincide with high-status parental occupation and low mean scores on each of these tests with low-status parental occupation. The Speaking test results follow a similar but less consistent pattern. When Speaking test scores for pupils of both sexes are combined, there is a tendency in each group of schools for high mean scores to coincide with high-status parental occupation and for low mean scores to coincide with low-status parental occupation, but this tendency is not always apparent when scores for boys and girls are considered separately. In the small primary schools, for example, mean scores obtained by boys in the 'skilled', 'semi-skilled' and 'unskilled' parental occupation categories do not differ significantly from one another. However, it must again be emphasized that the sample size in this instance is extremely small: in general, the Speaking test results follow a pattern similar to that of the group tests.

The association between parental occupation and test score is illustrated in Figures 2.2 to 2.5 in Appendix 2. These figures show the distribution of Battery 1 test scores for Cohort 2 pupils within each parental occupation category, but with scores for pupils of both sexes combined.

3. *School Group*

Pupils in the three different groups of schools differ markedly from one another in their test performance. Since the Battery 1 results indicate an association between parental occupation and test score, it is important to consider test performance in relation to the social composition of the three groups of schools. Table 2.6 in Appendix 2 shows the distribution of the sample by type of school, sex of pupil, and parental occupation. The small primary schools contain proportionately fewer pupils in the 'professional and clerical' parental occupation category and proportionately more pupils in the 'semi-skilled' and 'unskilled' categories than do either the large primary schools or the comprehensive schools. The social composition of the large primary schools is similar to that of the comprehensive schools.

The results for each of the Battery 1 French tests will be considered separately:

(i) *Speaking test.* Mean scores for pupils in the small primary schools are significantly higher than those for pupils in the comprehensive schools. Taking the sample as a whole, the differences between mean scores for both boys and girls are significant at the 0·1 per cent level. Significant differences between mean scores in favour of the pupils in the small primary schools also occur within each separate parental occupation category. Mean scores for pupils in the small primary schools are significantly higher than those for pupils in the large primary schools. With all parental occupation categories combined, differences between mean scores for both boys and girls are significant at the 0·1 per cent level. Within parental occupation categories, significant differences in favour of the pupils in the small primary schools occur in the 'professional and clerical', 'semi-skilled' and 'unskilled' categories for boys and in the 'skilled' category for girls. Differences between mean scores in the remaining parental occupation groups do not reach a significant level but, in each case, mean scores for pupils in the small primary schools are higher than those for pupils in the large primary schools. Taking the sample as a whole, mean scores for pupils in the large primary schools are significantly higher than those for pupils in the comprehensive schools. Significant differences between mean scores in favour of the primary school pupils are concentrated in the higher-status parental occupation categories: there are no significant differences between mean scores for pupils in the 'semi-skilled' and 'unskilled' categories.

TABLE 8: *Battery 1 Speaking Test. Mean scores by type of school and parental occupation*

| TYPE OF SCHOOL | | PARENTAL OCCUPATION | | | | TOTAL |
		Professional and Clerical	*Skilled*	*Semi-skilled*	*Unskilled*	
Large Primary	N	301	354	214	119	988
	x̄	34·17	28·80	22·27	18·58	27·79
	SD	20·30	18·20	16·32	15·05	18·95
Small Primary	N	13	30	29	12	84
	x̄	48·38	37·73	33·51	32·83	37·22
	SD	16·98	12·07	14·27	12·62	14·72
Comprehensive	N	95	153	73	42	363
	x̄	31·07	25·56	22·63	21·48	25·94
	SD	18·28	17·46	18·89	18·85	18·45

Achievement in French in the Primary School

These results are shown in summary form in Table 8 and presented in greater detail in Table 2.2 in Appendix 2. They are also illustrated in graphic form in Figure 2.6 in Appendix 2.

(ii) *Listening test.* Mean scores for pupils in the small primary schools are significantly higher than those for pupils in the comprehensive schools. With all parental occupation categories combined, differences between mean scores in favour of the primary school pupils are significant at the 0·1 per cent level for both boys and girls. Significant differences between mean scores in favour of the pupils in the small primary schools also occur within each separate parental occupation category. Mean scores for pupils in the small primary schools are significantly higher than those for pupils in the large primary schools. With all parental occupation categories combined, differences between mean scores in favour of pupils in the small primary schools are significant at the 0·1 per cent level for both boys and girls. Significant differences in favour of the pupils in the small schools also occur within each parental occupation category, but are most marked in the 'skilled' and 'semi-skilled' categories. Taking the sample as a whole, the mean scores obtained by pupils in the large primary schools do not differ significantly from those obtained by pupils in the comprehensive schools.

These results are shown in summary form in Table 9 and presented in greater detail in Table 2.3 in Appendix 2. They are also illustrated in graphic form in Figure 2.7 in Appendix 2.

TABLE 9: *Battery 1 Listening Test. Mean scores by type of school and parental occupation*

		PARENTAL OCCUPATION				
TYPE OF SCHOOL		*Professional and Clerical*	*Skilled*	*Semi-skilled*	*Unskilled*	TOTAL
Large Primary	N	1435	1787	1228	662	5112
	x̄	24·39	22·18	19·77	17·92	21·67
	SD	7·88	7·72	7·17	6·88	7·85
Small Primary	N	23	67	62	28	180
	x̄	29·86	27·97	26·91	22·60	27·01
	SD	6·49	5·61	7·04	6·44	6·71
Comprehensive	N	510	766	514	274	2064
	x̄	24·69	21·92	20·59	18·45	21·81
	SD	7·92	7·82	8·21	7·17	8·11

(iii) *Reading test.* Mean scores for pupils in the comprehensive schools are significantly higher than those for pupils in either the large or the small primary schools. The mean scores of pupils in the large primary schools and those of pupils in the comprehensive schools differ significantly in favour of the comprehensive school pupils at the 0·1 per cent level for both boys and girls within each parental occupation category. With all parental occupation categories combined, the mean scores of pupils in the small primary schools and those of pupils in the comprehensive schools also differ significantly in favour of the latter at the 0.1 per cent level for both boys and girls. Within the separate parental occupation categories, however, significant differences in favour of the comprehensive school pupils occur only in the 'skilled' and 'unskilled' categories: there are no significant differences between mean scores for pupils in the 'professional and clerical' and 'semi-skilled' categories. Mean scores for pupils in the small primary schools are significantly higher than those for pupils in the large primary schools. With all parental occupation categories combined, differences between mean scores in favour of the pupils in the small schools are significant at the 0·1 per cent level for both boys and girls. Significant differences between mean scores in favour of the pupils in the small schools also occur within each parental occupation category, but tend to be less marked in the 'professional and clerical' category than in the other categories.

TABLE 10: *Battery 1 Reading Test. Mean scores by type of school and parental occupation*

| | | PARENTAL OCCUPATION | | | | |
TYPE OF SCHOOL		*Professional and Clerical*	*Skilled*	*Semi-skilled*	*Unskilled*	TOTAL
Large Primary	N	1429	1766	1211	650	5056
	x̄	31·88	27·72	24·61	21·57	27·36
	SD	11·68	10·86	9·89	8·71	11·18
Small Primary	N	23	67	61	28	179
	x̄	39·78	34·07	32·47	27·42	33·22
	SD	11·62	10·11	10·86	8·45	10·87
Comprehensive	N	505	734	509	257	2005
	x̄	42·05	39·14	34·59	30·96	37·67
	SD	11·72	11·61	12·72	12·11	12·55

These results are shown in summary form in Table 10 and presented in greater detail in Table 2.4 in Appendix 2. They are also illustrated in graphic form in Figure 2.8 in Appendix 2.

(iv) *Writing test*. Mean scores for pupils in the comprehensive schools are significantly higher than those for pupils in either the large or the small primary schools. With all parental occupation categories combined, and within each separate category, differences between mean scores in favour of the comprehensive school pupils are significant at the 0.1 per cent level for both boys and girls. There are few significant differences between the mean scores obtained by the pupils in the two groups of primary schools. Significant differences between mean scores in favour of the pupils in the small schools occur only in the 'professional and clerical' category for both boys and girls, in the 'skilled' category for girls and in the 'unskilled' category for boys. There are no other significant differences between mean scores, but the level of performance in the Writing test is generally higher in the small schools than in the large schools.

These results are shown in summary form in Table 11 and presented in greater detail in Table 2.5 in Appendix 2. They are also illustrated in graphic form in Figure 2.9 in Appendix 2.

TABLE 11: *Battery 1 Writing Test. Mean scores by type of school and parental occupation*

		PARENTAL OCCUPATION				
TYPE OF SCHOOL		*Professional and Clerical*	*Skilled*	*Semi-skilled*	*Unskilled*	TOTAL
Large Primary	N	1123	1340	797	336	3596
	x̄	22·66	18·83	16·16	14·13	18·99
	SD	10·78	9·97	9·52	9·08	10·46
Small Primary	N	15	30	36	19	100
	x̄	31·06	23·56	18·66	17·15	21·71
	SD	10·90	9·09	10·11	6·61	10·45
Comprehensive	N	512	770	523	275	2080
	x̄	37·80	34·36	28·94	24·85	32·59
	SD	14·90	14·64	15·20	14·52	15·46

The Writing test was not administered to all second cohort pupils, but only to those who had been introduced to writing in French before their final term in primary school. After the administration of the Writing test, it was found that 65 per cent of the second cohort pupils had taken the test, six per cent had been absent on the day of testing, and 29 per cent had not been entered for the test because they had not been introduced to writing in French before the test period. Further examination of the sample revealed that the percentage of pupils entered for the test increased with social status: high-status parental occupation tended to be associated with an increasing percentage of pupils taking the Writing test and low-status parental occupation with a decreasing percentage of pupils taking the test. Low-status parental occupation was therefore correspondingly associated with an increasing percentage of pupils not introduced to writing in French before transferring to secondary school. The percentage of second cohort pupils who took the Writing test, were absent on the day of testing, or were not entered for the test, is shown in Table 2.7 in Appendix 2. In each instance, the percentage of pupils is shown distributed by the French course followed and by parental occupation category.

4. *Correlations Between General Attainment and French Test Scores.*

The scores obtained by the pupils in the second cohort on the Battery 1 French tests were correlated with those previously obtained by the same pupils on the general attainment battery. The extent to which the different test scores correlate with one another is shown in Table 12. All the French tests correlate more highly with those tests in the general attainment battery which demand verbal ability than with those which require mathematical skills. The Battery 1 group tests correlate more highly with the general attainment tests than the individual Speaking test does: of the Battery 1 group tests, the Reading test correlates most highly with the tests in the general attainment battery. Each of the Battery 1 tests correlates more highly with the English test than with any other general attainment test. The Battery 1 Writing test, for example, correlates 0·57 with the Reading test, 0·59 with the Primary Verbal test, and 0·66 with the English test; the Battery 1 Reading test correlates 0·62 with both the Primary and the Reading tests, but correlates 0·69 with the English test. The French tests all correlate fairly highly with one another. The highest correlations are those between the Reading and Listening test scores (0·81) and between the Reading and Writing test scores (0·79). The lowest correlations are those between the Speaking and Reading test scores (0·69) and between the Speaking and Writing test scores (0·70). The Speaking test correlates more highly with the

TABLE 12: *Cohort 2. Correlations between general attainment test scores and French test scores*

TEST	PRIMARY VERBAL	MECHANICAL ARITHMETIC	READING	PROBLEM ARITHMETIC	ENGLISH	BATTERY 1 SPEAKING	BATTERY 1 LISTENING	BATTERY 1 READING	BATTERY 1 WRITING
Primary Verbal	1·00	—	—	—	—	—	—	—	—
Mechanical Arithmetic	0·71	1·00	—	—	—	—	—	—	—
Reading	0·79	0·62	1·00	—	—	—	—	—	—
Problem Arithmetic	0·74	0·85	0·67	1·00	—	—	—	—	—
English	0·84	0·71	0·81	0·73	1·00	—	—	—	—
Battery 1 Speaking	0·39	0·37	0·36	0·37	0·44	1·00	—	—	—
Battery 1 Listening	0·53	0·49	0·50	0·50	0·57	0·73	1·00	—	—
Battery 1 Reading	0·62	0·60	0·62	0·60	0·69	0·69	0·81	1·00	—
Battery 1 Writing	0·59	0·56	0·57	0·56	0·66	0·70	0·73	0·79	1·00

Note: The correlations shown in Table 12 are based on 648 cases (i.e. those pupils who were included in the Speaking test sub-sample).

Listening test (0·73) than with either of the other group tests. This finding may possibly result from the oral nature of the Speaking and Listening tests, since neither test requires any ability to understand the written forms of the language, but the fact that the Listening test correlates equally highly with the Writing test (0·73) and more highly with the Reading test (0·81) is less easily interpreted. A possible explanation for those findings may lie in the fact that the Reading and Listening tests both make use of a multiple-choice technique in which the pupil selects his responses from among the response-alternatives offered, whereas the Writing and Speaking tests employ only supply-type items, which require the pupil himself to provide each response.

The assessment of achievement in French in the primary school is continuing with a third cohort of pupils. The fieldwork of the study will not reach completion until the final administration of Battery 1 in the summer of 1971, when the pupils concerned reach the end of their primary school career. The analysis of the Battery 1 results, to be carried out during 1971—1972, will conclude this phase of the evaluation.

SECTION THREE

Pupils' Attitudes Towards Learning French in the Primary School

B EFORE the pupils in the first experimental cohort left their primary schools in the summer of 1967, they were asked to complete anonymously a questionnaire relating to their attitudes towards learning French. The questionnaire contained a number of general statements, such as: 'I would like to speak many languages'; 'Learning French is a waste of time'; 'My parents are pleased that I am learning French'; 'I would like to meet some French people', and so on. The questionnaire also included statements relating to specific aspects of learning French, such as: 'It is more difficult to understand the tape-recorder than the teacher'; 'If I see a French word written down, it helps me to say it'; 'I am afraid to speak French', etc. There were 34 such statements in the questionnaire and the pupils were simply asked to indicate whether they agreed or disagreed with each statement. The attitude statements were followed by a free-response section, in which pupils were asked to complete sentences such as: 'I like French because . . .'; 'I don't like French because . . .'. In addition, pupils were encouraged to comment freely on any aspect of learning French which was not specifically covered by the questionnaire items.

The questionnaires were completed in class. Each child was given an envelope with his copy of the questionnaire, so that he could place the completed questionnaire in the envelope and seal it himself, without revealing what he had written to his teacher or his classmates. This procedure was adopted in order to encourage the free expression of opinion and to minimize the production of responses intended primarily to please the teacher or impress other members of the class. For the same reasons, the questionnaires were completed under conditions of anonymity. This proved to be an unnecessary precaution, however, since most pupils wrote their name (and often their address!) at the end of the questionnaire, even though no space had been provided for this purpose.

Approximately 5,000 completed questionnaires were returned to the NFER before the end of the 1967 summer term. The questionnaire data were processed and analysed and, in the light of the results of

41

this analysis, a slightly revised version of the questionnaire, containing 38 items, was produced and administered in the summer of 1968 to the second experimental cohort, before the pupils concerned completed their final term in primary school. Approximately 5,000 pupils completed the revised version of the questionnaire in 1968. On this occasion, however, pupils were instructed to write their name on the questionnaire before filling it in, so that it would eventually be possible to compare pupils' attitudes towards learning French (as evidenced by their responses to the questionnaire items) with their level of achievement in French (as demonstrated by their performance on the Battery 1 French tests). It had not been possible to analyse the results obtained from the first cohort in this way, since the pupils concerned completed the questionnaire anonymously and, furthermore, were unable to attempt the full battery of French tests during their final junior term. It is, however, of some interest to note that the results obtained from the administration of the attitude questionnaire were essentially the same for both cohorts. Taking the sample as a whole, the responses obtained from the second cohort confirmed, both in general and in particular, those obtained anonymously from the first cohort. Since the data obtained from the second cohort offered the possibility of analysis by sex and social background, as well as by achievement in French, they will be utilized in preference to those obtained from the first cohort, whenever such factors are at issue. When more general features of pupils' attitudes towards learning French are under discussion, however, the data obtained from both cohorts will be drawn on.

All pupils completing the questionnaire were initially required to state whether they like learning French or not. This initial statement was then used to classify all further responses. It was found that, in both cohorts, the pupils concerned were almost equally divided as to whether they liked learning French or not. In the first cohort, 47 per cent of the pupils stated that they liked learning French, whereas 53 per cent stated that they did not. In the second cohort, 54 per cent of the pupils like learning French, compared with 46 per cent who did not. Girls had a more favourable attitude towards learning French than boys: 65 per cent of the girls in the second cohort stated that they liked learning French, but only 44 per cent of the boys did so. The second cohort's responses to the questionnaire items are shown in full in Tables 3.1 to 3.38 in Appendix 3. These tables show the percentage of pupils who agree with each item statement, distributed by pupils' sex and general attitude towards learning French.

Taking the sample as a whole, pupils with a favourable attitude towards learning French tend also to have a favourable attitude towards learning other foreign languages. This is particularly true of girls. In the second cohort, for example, more than 83 per cent of the girls who enjoy learning French state that they would also like to learn other foreign languages. Their motivation for further language learning stems primarily from their desire to communicate with people who speak the language in question. As one girl wrote: 'I have always wanted to learn the ways of foreign people and join in with them'. Most of the pupils who like French state that they would also like to learn German, Spanish, Italian or Russian, although a minority argue strongly in favour of the introduction of Latin at the primary level. 'Latin is the basis of most European languages', explained one girl. 'If we learned Latin, we would be able to speak French, Italian, Spanish and other languages'.

Except for a minority of pupils, a hostile attitude towards learning French does not necessarily imply a rejection of all further language learning. Over 60 per cent of those who dislike learning French would nevertheless like to have learnt a language other than French, taking the view that there are more important languages than French to learn. This point of view is more frequently expressed by boys than by girls and tends to be associated with particular areas of the country. Pupils in the North of England, for example, tend to feel that they are geographically distant from France but close to Scandinavia, and consequently press for the introduction of Norwegian, Swedish, or Icelandic. As one boy wrote: 'I hate French. I think we should learn Norwegian because Norway is closer to Northumberland'. It terms of actual distance, Norway is not, of course, closer to Northumberland than France is, but there are effective sea and air links between Scandinavia and the North of England, which are possibly more familiar to the children than the routes which lead to France. Scandinavia may be physically distant, but it is nevertheless psychologically close to those children who live in the North, very few of whom expect to go to France. 'If you never go to France, what is the use of learning French?', asked one Northumbrian schoolboy. 'Half of us will never go', agreed another. 'Learning French is a waste of time if you never want to go to France', concluded a third. Children who live in the South of England, on the other hand, tend to stress the importance of French as the language of 'our nearest neighbour' and to regard travel in France as the logical outcome of learning French. 'I think it is essential to learn French, as France is so near to us', wrote one girl. 'If you have learnt

French and you don't go to France, the lessons will have been wasted,' explained another. Regional differences in attitude towards learning French are not, of course, determined solely by distance from France. In Monmouthshire, for example, loyalty to Wales can produce hostility towards learning French and a corresponding desire to learn Welsh. A point of view frequently encountered is that of the Monmouthshire schoolboy who wrote: 'I think it is stupid for a Welsh boy to learn French. Why can't we learn Welsh?'

In a minority of cases, an unfavourable attitude towards learning French entails hostility towards all foreign language learning. This is particularly true of boys: more than 38 per cent of those boys who dislike learning French state that they have no interest in learning foreign languages. This point of view is usually associated with a highly ethnocentric attitude. 'England is good enough for me'; 'This is the country we come from—England—so why don't we keep to English?'; 'I can't imagine anyone wanting to go to France'; 'I don't like foreigners',—such comments typify the narrowly patriotic 'Little England' attitude adopted by this group of pupils, most of whom take the view that the French should be learning English, not the reverse.

More than 80 per cent of the total sample, whether they like learning French or not, agree that they would like to go to France, meet French people and make friends with French children. This percentage includes significantly more girls than boys. Most girls feel strongly that the primary objective of learning French is to be able to communicate with French-speaking people. Very few children in the sample had actually been to France (less than nine per cent of each cohort), but most agreed that they would like to go there, preferably on a school visit. 'I would like to go to France with the school and then I would have a chance of talking to French people', wrote one girl. 'I would very much like to go to France on an educational tour and actually speak to French people', agreed another. Many children comment on the fact that they have never heard a 'real' French person talk, 'except on a tape-recorder', and are eager to try out their French in a real-life situation.

The majority of those who do not want to visit France are boys who dislike learning French. Some of them are afraid of speaking French ('I would be too scared to say the words'), some maintain a generally parochial attitude ('There is nothing there, only the Eiffel Tower, and that is just like Blackpool Tower'), and others express anxiety about travelling away from home. One boy wrote: 'The ship might sink, the plane might crash and, when I got there, I would not like the food'. Another wrote: 'The country would be strange. The journey would be too long. I would not like to leave my family. I would be homesick'. One boy wrote simply: 'It would be too big.'

Despite the fact that few of them had ever had any personal contact with France or with French people, many of the children in the sample had definite views about the French and their way of life. French adults were generally considered polite, comfort-loving, optimistic, talkative, boastful, quick-tempered and emotional. French children, on the other hand, were considered 'more disciplined and obedient' than their English counterparts. French schools were usually seen as rather repressive establishments, where it was obligatory to 'stay to tea' and essential to behave in a 'prim and proper' way, since punishment swiftly followed any attempt to 'move about' or 'be jolly'. Most children expressed fear of the French police and felt that the least infringement of the law would bring a shouting, gesticulating, gun-waving policeman, ready to exact immediate punishment. Fear of the traffic in France was also common. As one boy wrote: 'It is dangerous even to step outside the door. The traffic is much too fast'. It was generally agreed that there were more road accidents in France than in England and 'more crimes committed'. Fears about French cooking were also frequently expressed. The view that the staple French diet consists of frogs' legs, snails and octopus, 'smothered in garlic and cooking oil', obviously dies hard. Equally resistant to the passage of time is the stereotype of the Frenchman, in beret and 'bleus de travail', bicycling off to work carrying a loaf of bread and a litre of red wine. The children are not necessarily entrenched in these beliefs, however: most of them admit of a certain scepticism and are anxious to go to France 'to see what it is really like' or 'to see whether what I have been told is really true'.

Children's attitudes towards learning French appear also to be influenced by those of their parents. Girls, for example, who tend to have more favourable attitudes towards learning French than boys and to reach a higher level of achievement in French, also appear to benefit more from parental encouragement to learn French. Although more than 75 per cent of the total sample believe that their parents are pleased that they are learning French at school, significantly more girls than boys are represented in this number. Girls also give frequent instances of parental support and encouragement; boys rarely do. Boys who comment at all on their parents' response tend to report either apathy or mild hostility: learning French is considered 'silly', 'a waste of time', or 'all right for girls'. As one boy wrote: 'My parents do not mind me learning French, but they do not think that it will be any use to me'. Girls tend to report a much more positive response from their parents. The following comments, all made by girls, suggest the effect of active parental encouragement on children's motivation to learn French: 'I enjoy speaking French and often do so at home with my parents, who both know French'; 'My mother and father are glad that I am learning French. I learn some French at home, by having conversations with my mother'; 'My mum teaches me French at home, in addition to the French I learn at school'; 'My parents are very pleased that I am learning French, so I will try my best at it'; 'I like French very much and Mummy tests me on it at home'; 'My parents think it is very good that I am learning French, because they did not have a chance until they were much older', and so on. The general impression produced by the children's comments is that many parents perceive French as a subject eminently suitable for girls, but of more doubtful value for boys,—a response which may well reflect parents' expectations regarding the future employment of their sons and daughters.

The pupils themselves undoubtedly assess the value of learning French partly in terms of their employment prospects. This is true of both sexes, but particularly true of girls. The majority of girls, whether they like learning French or not (91 per cent of those who like French and 64 per cent of those who do not) anticipate that French will be useful to them when they leave school. Those who dislike learning French usually express this expectation in fairly vague terms: 'You can get a better job if you know a language well' or 'It will help you to get a job when the manager asks what kind of education you had'. Those who like learning French more frequently state that they expect to earn their living in occupations which specifically require a knowledge of French. Most of these girls hope to become air-hostesses, secretaries or French teachers, but others plan to be ballet dancers ('You have to say the steps in French'), pop singers ('You may have to sing in French') or dress designers ('I would like to open a boutique in Paris,—that is why I want to speak French'). Only a third of the girls who dislike learning French feel that French will be of no use to them when they leave school. This is usually because they consider that they are unlikely ever to go to France ('Some of us are too poor to go.') or to find employment which would make use of their knowledge of French. As one girl explained: 'Only about one third of our class will ever get the opportunity to use French. It won't be any use to me when I leave school.' A similar point of view is common among boys who dislike learning French ('Why do we learn French? What good is it to us

46

when we leave school? Unless we go there, it's a waste of time'.), but, like the girls, the great majority of boys (92 per cent of those who like French, 61 per cent of those who do not) expect French to be useful to them after they leave school. Boys seem to be more aware of current political events than girls and frequently cite Britain's prospective entry into the Common Market as a sufficient reason for learning French. As one boy put it: 'French is a very good language to learn because we may enter the Common Market and, if we do, it will become very handy indeed'. Boys tend to take a somewhat larger view than girls and to instance entry into the Common Market or the building of the Channel Tunnel as examples of the potential usefulness of French, rather than to stress the relevance of French to a particular occupation. There is also less agreement among boys regarding the types of employment which might require a knowledge of French. Intending businessmen, aircraft designers, couriers, soldiers and sailors expect to make some use of their knowledge of French, but the area in which French is seen to have the most direct relevance to future employment is undoubtedly that of the catering trade. Intending chefs ('Most courses come in French in big hotels'.) and waiters ('I like French very much. I would like to be a posh waiter who tells the cook in French what he wants'.) expect to make practical use of the French that they have learnt, as soon as they leave school.

Although the majority of pupils think that French will be useful to them when they leave school, they do not necessarily advocate that French should be taught to everyone. Approximately 50 per cent of the pupils in the first cohort and 60 per cent of those in the second cohort agree with the statement that everyone should learn French in school. Significantly more girls than boys agree with this statement, as do significantly more pupils who themselves like learning French. Pupils who like learning French, but who do not agree that everyone should be taught French in school, usually base their argument on the irrelevance of French to certain occupations: 'Some people do not need to know French in their jobs when they grow up'. For this reason, some pupils feel that it would be advisable to postpone the introduction of French until the secondary school, 'because then they will have an idea of what job they will do. If they are only capable of being a dustman, French would be a waste of time for them'. The children completed the attitude questionnaires when they were in their final junior term, so their transfer to secondary schools was imminent. At that time, the majority of those with a favourable attitude towards learning French were satisfied with the progress which they had already made and were looking forward to continuing French in secondary school. Eighty-nine per cent of these pupils agreed that they had already learnt 'a great deal of French' and were eager to extend their knowledge. 'I would like to go on learning French at my senior school and learn other languages as well', wrote one boy. 'I feel good knowing a different language', wrote another.

Not all children were able to share this sense of achievement, however. More than a third of the total sample felt that learning French had become increasingly difficult and viewed the prospect of continuing French in their secondary schools with some apprehension. As one girl wrote: 'Now that we are going to our new school we will have harder French, and I cannot do it,—even my mum agrees that it is a complete waste of time.' 'Why do we have to go on with it?', asked a boy, adding: 'I know that I am a dunce and cannot learn French'. Another boy wrote: 'I am not very intelligent and I am no good at French. It's a waste of time for my teacher.' The pupils in this group—particularly the boys—maintain that learning French is a waste of time as far as they are concerned and that there are other, more important, subjects which they need to learn. In particular, they stress that it is more important for them to learn 'proper English' than French,—a view not infrequently shared by their parents and teachers. 'French is a waste of time when we could be learning how to speak proper English', wrote one boy. 'What's the point of learning French when some people cannot even speak proper English?', asked another. 'My mum thinks it is silly to learn French when half the British people don't know how to speak proper English', commented a third. A view commonly expressed by this group of pupils is that only those who are good at English should be expected to learn French,—a view not shared by the majority of the sample. Most pupils tend to reject the view that achievement in French is related to achievement in English. As one girl wrote: 'If a child is no good at English, it might be wise to try him on French. To some people, French may be easier to learn than English', French is not generally considered to be an 'easy' subject, however. Only 21 per cent of the sample, containing a significantly higher proportion of girls than boys, find French easier than other school subjects; only 25 per cent of those who like French consider that their level of achievement in French is higher than in other subjects. The majority of those who do so are girls. French is not given a very high priority by the majority of the sample when considered in relation to the rest of the curriculum. Eighty per cent of the sample (71 per cent of those who like French and 91 per cent of those who dislike French) agree that there are more important subjects to learn in school than French notably English and Mathematics. This view is particularly common among boys.

For pupils of both sexes, level of achievement in French appears to be closely associated with attitudes towards learning French. There are highly significant differences between mean scores for both boys and girls on each of the Battery 1 French tests, according to the pupils' favourable or unfavourable attitudes towards learning French. Mean scores for pupils who like French are significantly higher than those for pupils who dislike French. Significant differences between mean scores are particularly marked in the case of pupils whose fathers' occupations fall within the 'professional', 'clerical' and 'skilled' categories. Mean scores on each of the Battery 1 French tests, distributed by pupils' attitude towards French and by parental occupation category, are shown in Table 13.

These results are presented in full in Tables 3.39—3.42 in Appendix 3, which show the mean scores for each of the Battery 1 French tests, distributed by pupils' sex, attitude towards French, and parental occupation category. The Speaking test results, shown in full in Table 3.39, demonstrate the association between attitude and achievement most clearly. Significant differences between the mean scores of pupils with favourable or unfavourable attitudes towards learning French tend to be concentrated in the higher parental occupation categories. In the 'professional and clerical' category, for example, girls who like French obtain a mean score of 40·95, whereas those who dislike French obtain a mean score of 29·54. Within the same parental occupation category, boys who like French obtain a mean score of 35·70, whereas those who dislike French obtain a mean score of 27.84. The results for the three group tests follow a similar pattern. On the Listening test, for instance, girls in the 'professional and clerical' parental occupation category who like French obtain a mean score of 28·06; those who dislike French obtain a mean score of 24·96. Boys in the same parental occupation category who like French obtain a mean score of 27·04 on the Listening test; those who dislike French obtain a mean score of 22·19. These results are shown in full in Table 3.40. On the Reading test also, high scores are associated with a favourable attitude towards learning French and low scores with an unfavourable one. Again, significant differences between mean scores are particularly marked in the higher parental occupation categories. In the 'professional and clerical' category, for example, the mean Reading test score for girls who like French is 37·22; the mean score for those who dislike French is 32. For boys in the same parental occupation category, the mean score for those who like French is 35·11, compared with a mean score of 27·25 for those who dislike French. These results are shown in full in Table 3.41. The Writing test results conform to a similar pattern. The mean Writing test score for girls in the 'professional and clerical' category who like French is 26·63; for those who dislike French the mean

TABLE 13: *Battery 1 French Tests. Mean scores by pupils' attitudes towards French and parental occupation category*

FRENCH TEST ATTITUDE TO FRENCH		Professional and Clerical	Skilled	Semi-skilled	Unskilled	TOTAL
		PARENTAL OCCUPATION				
Speaking Test:	N	138	152	103	52	445
Pupils who like	x̄	38·78	33·01	25·36	19·40	31·44
French	SD	11·43	9·85	9·77	10·39	11·10
Speaking Test:	N	96	111	63	35	305
Pupils who dislike	x̄	28·50	23·42	18·77	19·94	23·66
French	SD	9·81	8·96	7·82	9·85	9·29
Listening Test:	N	529	660	479	236	1904
Pupils who like	x̄	27·64	24·68	21·62	19·56	24·10
French	SD	7·19	7·35	7·07	7·44	7·76
Listening Test:	N	466	575	396	204	1641
Pupils who dislike	x̄	23·29	20·78	18·81	17·90	20·66
French	SD	7·26	7·17	6·32	6·74	7·21
Reading Test:	N	531	642	473	231	1877
Pupils who like	x̄	36·36	30·67	26·73	23·62	30·42
French	SD	11·23	11·47	10·23	9·36	11·70
Reading Test:	N	460	573	387	203	1623
Pupils who dislike	x̄	29·14	25·80	23·49	21·76	25·69
French	SD	11·22	9·84	8·80	8·29	10·17
Writing Test:	N	401	476	285	109	1271
Pupils who like	x̄	25·28	21·05	18·20	16·68	21·37
French	SD	10·62	10·00	9·63	9·33	10·51
Writing Test:	N	364	410	258	108	1140
Pupils who dislike	x̄	20·21	16·18	15·21	13·75	17·25
French	SD	10·31	9·21	8·95	8·31	9·70

score is 23·40. The mean score for boys in the same category who like French is 23·30, whereas for those who dislike French the mean score is 17·93. These results are shown in full in Table 3.42.

The relationship between pupils' attitudes towards learning French and their level of achievement is most clearly demonstrated with reference to the Speaking test results. From the children's response to the attitude questionnaire, it is evident that the majority consider the ability to speak French as the most important aspect of learning the language. As one girl wrote, expressing the general view: 'It is great to learn French, because you will be able to talk to French people'. Seventy-six per cent of the total sample agree that it is more important to be able to speak French than to read and write it; 72 per cent also agree that speaking French is easier than reading and writing French. In each instance, significantly more pupils who like learning French are in agreement than are those who dislike learning French. Of those who dislike French, 25 per cent admit that they feel afraid to speak in French. 'I am scared to say the French words in case they are wrong' wrote one girl. 'In French I am too nervous to speak', admitted another, adding: 'I can do it all right when I am saying it with other people. I can sing better in French than speak it'. 'I get very worried in French lessons', wrote a boy. 'I see everyone putting up their hand and I do not, because I am scared of not knowing the answers'. Another boy wrote: 'I am afraid of French because if the teacher says anything to me I am afraid I cannot say it.' 'I am scared to say the words', agreed another. 'Whenever I know that French is coming the next lesson, I dread it.'

The difficulties experienced by these pupils in speaking French stem partly from their inability to understand much of what is said to them in French. Sixty-two per cent of those who dislike French admit that they find the French lesson difficult to understand. This is particularly true of boys. As one boy wrote: 'French is the hardest lesson of all'. It is clear that for some pupils the pace of the French lesson is too fast. 'If only we had a teacher who had a lot of patience and who did not go from one lesson to another so quickly', wrote one girl. 'I think I would learn more French if the teacher went slower', wrote another. 'French would be better if we had a patient teacher', agreed another. A boy wrote: 'If we didn't go so fast and the teacher didn't shout so, I think I might like French'. Most of the pupils in this group comment on their inability to understand what is being said to them in French and feel that they are given insufficient explanation. 'French would be easier to learn if we were told the meaning in English'; 'The teacher tells us the French words, but

51

does not tell us what they mean'; 'I think that the French teacher should tell you what some of the words mean, as it gets very tiring with the teacher carrying on in French and I not knowing what it means',—such comments illustrate the difficulties experienced by some of the children. Even those who like French report that they do not always understand what they are saying when they speak in French, but are simply repeating meaningless sounds. This is true of 68 per cent of the sample: 62 per cent of those who like French and 75 per cent of those who do not like French. 'It would be better if the teacher told us what we are saying', wrote one boy. 'They should tell us what the words mean', agreed another. One girl, after nearly three years of learning French, made the following comment: 'Most of the time I don't know what I am saying. Some words like 'Pardon, Madame' I understand, but 'Pardon, Madame' and my name 'Thérèse', in French, are the only words I know'. She went on: 'My mummy said that she learned French by saying "Elle est: she is", and I would like to learn French like that'.

Many children report that they find particular difficulty in understanding spoken French when they hear it on the tape-recorder. Over 75 per cent of the total sample agree that it is more difficult to understand the tape-recorder than their teacher. This is equally true of those who like French and those who dislike French, and applies to pupils of both sexes in each cohort. 'I cannot understand the tape-recorder'; 'The tape goes too fast. I cannot hear the words clearly'; 'I cannot get hold of the words when the teacher uses the tape-recorder'; 'When you hear the tape-recorder, the words run into each other and you cannot tell who is speaking. The French teacher tells you more clearly'; 'I do not like French with the tape-recorder. It would be better for just the teacher to speak to us',—such comments illustrate the majority opinion. Most of the pupils express an active dislike of the tape-recorded sections of the French lesson and stress the boredom induced by the frequent repetition of tape-recorded material. As one boy wrote: 'French is very boring when you have to listen to the tape-recorder over and over again. It is much easier to learn when your teacher says it through for you'. The general preference for 'live' situations and active participation is well illustrated by the following comment: 'People say that French is boring, but I think it is the tape-recorder that makes it boring, for when our class does "situations" we are always interested, whereas, when the tape-recorder is going, we know that it will be just the same as all the other French lessons,—recording, repeating, recording, repeating'. The only situation in which pupils appear to enjoy working with taped material is when they are given the opportunity to work individually in a language laboratory. Those pupils who had experience of working in a language laboratory were unanimous in their approval: 'I like going to the language laboratory for French'; 'I like it in the language laboratory listening on the ear-phones'; 'I like learning French with the ear-phones best, because you don't have to listen to everyone else'. Only a small minority of those learning French have access to a language laboratory, however.

The introduction of reading and writing in French provides a welcome stimulus for some pupils and constitutes a stumbling-block for others. High-achieving children tend to welcome the introduction of the written script: this is particularly true of girls. 'It is much easier to learn French when reading and writing it, rather than just repeating it all the time', wrote one girl. 'When I started French I used to hate it, but now I like it because we are reading and writing', wrote another. 'When I first started French I found it boring, repeating all the time, but, now that we are learning to read and write, I like it', explained a third. Although the sample as a whole is almost equally divided on the question of whether both spoken and written aspects of the language should be taught simultaneously, those who support the simultaneous introduction of skills tend to be drawn from the ranks of the high-achievers. As one such pupil wrote: 'I believe that you should learn to read and write French the same time as you speak it. I find French much more interesting since we started to read and write it. Before, I was bored stiff and hated it'. Pupils who are accustomed to a high level of achievement in written work frequently comment on their sense of boredom and frustration during the early stages of learning French, before the introduction of the written script. Many high-achieving children would welcome the earlier introduction of reading and writing. They press for 'homework in French', 'spelling tests', 'proper revision', 'a French dictionary', 'a book to learn from', 'written papers to take home and learn', and so on. A number of teachers have reported cases of high-achieving pupils who have attempted to shorten the purely oral phase of learning French by making up their own phonetic script and secretly writing down all the French that they could remember. For these pupils the written script is the familiar medium of achievement: they do not find it easy to adjust to total reliance on the spoken word and their interest in learning French is not really kindled until they are given an opportunity to demonstrate their written skills. 'I think that we should learn to read and write French more quickly, so that we could write essays in French, which would be much more interesting', wrote one such pupil. 'French lessons should be longer, with more reading and writing', agreed another. 'Repetition is a bad way of learning French, because it bores people and results in them taking no interest. I would much rather learn out of a book', concluded a third.

For some pupils, however, the introduction of reading and writing comes too soon, and a sometimes precarious foothold is lost. 'Before, I was struggling along. Now I cannot understand it at all', wrote one child. 'I thought it was lovely at first, but now I dread the French lesson', wrote another. In their third year of learning French, over 38 per cent of those who dislike French regard French as too difficult for them to learn. The greatest difficulties are those caused by the complexity of the written script and the discovery of orthographical subtleties imperceptible in the spoken form of the language. 'There are too many he's and she's and I get mixed up', wrote one boy. 'All the males and females, they mix me up', wrote another. The most common errors are those which arise when the spoken form of a word gives no indication of its different written forms. A child who wishes to write 'il marche' has to discriminate between 'il marche', 'ils marche', 'il marchent' and 'ils marchent': the words are aurally familiar to him, but this provides no assistance when he attempts to select an appropriate written form. In addition, the introduction to the written script reveals 'all the little accents that you have to remember'.

The introduction of reading appears to create far less anxiety than does the introduction of writing. The majority of pupils, even those who are experiencing difficulty with French, agree that once they have seen a French word written down, it is easier for them to pronounce it. This is true of 61 per cent of the sample: 64 per cent of those who like French and 57 per cent of those who do not. This may be an indication of the proportion of children in the sample who rely on visual rather than auditory imagery. Many children complain that they cannot remember words unless they see them written down and, consequently, experience considerable difficulty during the oral phase of learning French. Only 35 per cent of the sample (45 per cent of those who like French and 24 per cent of those who do not) claim that they can remember a word easily once they have heard it. The majority prefer some form of visual support. Some pupils find it difficult to cope with 'look and say' reading methods in French. They become familiar with the 'shape' of certain sentence patterns, but are unable to recognize the separate components of the pattern, if they are encountered in a different setting. As one girl wrote:

'I do not think that we are told what words mean enough. Although we know what sentences mean, we do not learn the separate words enough'.

Many children also criticize their French lessons on the grounds that they are not taught enough about France and the French. There is a frequent demand to learn 'more about France', 'more about French children', 'more about how real French people live' and, in particular, 'more about the History and Geography of France'. 'And I don't mean more about the Battle of Hastings and all that', one boy was anxious to explain, 'but more about current affairs in France and French politics'. There are also repeated requests for 'more films about France' and 'more books about the French way of life'. Many children state that they would prefer 'a real French person' to teach them French, simply because they would then have access to a source of first-hand information about France. The majority of children in the sample are strongly oriented towards realism in their studies. They complain that some of the material used in the French lesson is unrealistic and does not equip them with an adequate basis for communication with French-speaking people. 'It does not do you any good learning about children having adventures', wrote one girl, 'because you don't have an adventure every day'. Another wrote: 'Some of the dialogues we learn wouldn't be any use if you wanted to have a conversation with a real French person'. Such comments are indicative of the children's intolerance of fantasy in this context and of their commitment to the view that the sole purpose of learning French is to be able to communicate with other speakers of the language.

French in the Primary School: the Viewpoint of the Primary Head

IN 1967, when the pupils in the first cohort had been learning French for almost three years and were nearing their final term in primary school, the head of each of the primary schools taking part in the experiment was asked to provide a report outlining the effects of the Pilot Scheme on the general life and organization of the school. Very few heads were unable or unwilling to provide such a report: the few who felt unable to do so were, almost without exception, recently-appointed heads who did not feel that their experience of the Pilot Scheme was sufficient to enable them to make a valid assessment of its effects. Throughout the spring and summer of 1967, reports varying greatly in length and style were received from the heads of the Pilot Scheme primary schools. When an analysis was subsequently made of the content of these reports, six major themes were found to recur in almost all of them. The aspects of the Pilot Scheme with which the primary school heads were most concerned were: the impact of the introduction of French on the general life and organization of the school; the integration of French into the school curriculum; problems relating to materials, equipment and accommodation; staffing difficulties; the pupils' response to the introduction of French; the liaison with secondary schools. Each of these topics will be treated separately.

1. The impact of the Pilot Scheme on the general life of the school

The introduction of French appeared to have affected the tone and organization of almost all participating primary schools. In 1967 very few schools had reached the point where French had become 'just another subject'. As the teaching of French was extended to further year-groups, timetables were re-arranged, new teachers were trained, experienced teachers adjusted to new methods and materials, and a stream of visitors observed from the back of classrooms. New school activities deriving from the introduction of French were seen as 'a shot in the arm' for the whole school and a number of heads reported a general enrichment of the life of the school: 'It has opened another window on the children's wonderful world'. In areas where no previous French teaching had existed at the primary level before the introduction of the Pilot Scheme, some heads described the Pilot Scheme as providing 'a stimulus which could not have been obtained in any other way'. The interest aroused by the experiment often extended to the pupils' parents and in several schools a 'French Evening' was held at the beginning of each year, to introduce the parents of eight-year-olds to the methods used in the teaching of French. While the scrutiny of visitors (Her Majesty's Inspectors, research workers, secondary school French teachers) could threaten the balance of the work of the school by inflating the importance of French, it was more often reported as having a stimulating and beneficial effect on the life of the school.

In many schools the introduction of French had promoted the development of extra-curricular activities. In some schools French clubs were formed, meeting regularly after school to provide the interested pupils with an opportunity to delve more deeply into the French language and culture. In other schools French projects were initiated, often with the help of members of staff who were not themselves involved in the teaching of French. In one school, for instance, the Needlework teacher provided the girls who were learning French with an opportunity to make dolls dressed in French regional costumes. French was also used in dramatic or musical productions: 'French carols have been sung at Christmas carol services and the summer concert has included French puppet plays and sketches made up by the children'. As well as giving 'live' performances, children often helped to produce tape-recordings in French which were used to give parents an insight into the work that their children were doing at school. In general, the response of the children's parents to the experiment was reported to be favourable. One head reported that 'many parents attend Adult French classes in order to encourage their children and not to feel "out-done" '. In a minority of cases, parents were reported to be hostile to the scheme. One head wrote: 'We have even heard of one or two instances of parents chiding children and forbidding them to speak French among themselves'. Such reports were rare, however.

Cultural exchanges, often ambitious, were attempted by several schools. Correspondence with 'pen-friends' in France was reported successful and rewarding. As one headmaster wrote: 'Several children are now writing to children in France at Vichy. They have been doing so since last Easter when I was fortunate to make contacts there with a group of children. The children of both countries write in English and French. I help with the French translation at this end and the parents and teachers help at the other'. In a few cases, it had been possible to arrange school visits to France. The head of a primary school in Oxford described how 'a link was established with the town of Poitiers and several schools in Oxford sent a party of children to a 'colonie de vacances' near Poitiers to spend a fortnight with a group of children from French schools in the area'. He added: 'The whole party then returned to England for two weeks at Wytham Camp near Oxford. It is hoped to repeat the venture this year'. A number of primary school heads, at the time of writing their report, were engaged in preparations for a school visit to France. The head of a primary school in Ebbw Vale outlined his plans: 'In order to make this visit more purposeful, I have arranged to contact a school at St. Malo through the travel agency, so that French children can accompany our party on excursions and during the visits to the beach to play games'. He also described his efforts to establish a permanent link with a school in France: 'This will involve a wide variety of activities and a detailed project has been devised involving exchange of tapes, of school work, etc., which should culminate in a visit to France and a return visit to Wales by the French children'. Another headmaster, describing a proposed visit to France, wrote: 'We hope it will give them the opportunity of using their French and seeing a little of the life of a French child from the inside, as they will be staying in a lycée'. One school in the South of England had arranged an annual day trip to Dieppe. 'This seems very limited', wrote the head, 'but in 1965 and 1966 many of the children learning French went on a day trip to Dieppe and it was clear much enthusiasm for the journey had been stimulated by their knowledge of French resulting from the Pilot Scheme'. Some attempts were also made to offer hospitality to visiting teachers from France, with a view to providing the school's French-teaching staff with an opportunity to visit French schools in return. One head reported: 'A teacher from Vichy spent three weeks in our school last July. She talked with the children and entered into our community life so completely that she endeared herself to the children and staff alike. In reciprocation, our two teachers of French will visit Vichy this year.' Successful ventures of this kind, though rare, were reported to have a beneficial influence on the whole life of the school, extending far beyond the confines of the French class.

2. The integration of French into the school curriculum

Integrating the teaching of French into the school curriculum without disturbing the balance of the timetable and creating undesirable specialization was a delicate and often difficult task for those responsible for the organization of the school. Many primary school heads found that, in order to accommodate the daily French lessons, the flexibility of the timetable had to be seriously reduced. As one head explained: 'In most primary schools the head visualizes the timetable in two parts: the "fixed" and "the fluid". The introduction of French has meant a greater portion of the timetable having to be "fixed",—that is, the class teacher cannot alter it, without reference to other teachers and classes'. There were many factors which contributed to the 'rigidity' which it was felt the introduction of French imposed on the timetable. Some schools shared filmed course materials with other schools and therefore had to maintain a strict schedule of lessons. Others were dependent on the availability of visiting teachers. 'As we have visiting teachers, we have had to re-adjust everyone's timetable to fit in with the times these teachers can come: we have to fit in with the other schools to which these teachers go', explained the head of a small rural primary school. It is evident that the small schools dependent on visiting French teachers face particular timetabling difficulties. 'The whole timetable of the small school using the services of a visiting specialist must be related to the period of her visits', wrote the head of one such school. 'For one-fifth of each of four days the timetable is inflexible, and as further year-groups are incorporated, this period is inevitably extended. Not only the small group receiving instruction at any one time is affected, but also members of other subject-groups or partnerships separated for this period who, during this time, are limited to subjects which are studied individually. This is particularly restrictive where children of the same age-group and comparable attainment level are, through force of circumstance, in different French groups, especially when the age-group concerned is too small to allow other appropriate partnerships'. Since many class teachers are responsible for teaching French to classes other than their own, there is a feeling that 'at a certain point, everything has to stop for French'. The frequent interchange of teachers can create the impression that 'the days are split into scrappy short periods' and many heads view with concern the fact that 'if a teacher has to teach French to other classes besides his own, integrated studies become less and less possible'. 'In fact', wrote one headmaster, 'his own class timetable tends to become a succession of subjects which can be most conveniently taught by the other class teachers. Thus the introduction of French has caused indirect specialization'. Class teachers who teach French to several classes may be absent from their own classroom for as much as one and a half hours a day. 'It involves the teacher in an unnecessary strain and French has been given priority over many other subjects', objected one head, adding: 'Other teachers have taken over the spare class for two periods each day and this is not a good aspect of primary education'. A mobile French teacher may find that 'his class is losing considerably from the fact that he is not there with them all day and is not able to throw in the small bits of French just when the opportunity arises'. 'This lack of opportunity for spontaneous French is a very definite loss', reported one head. Similarly, another head felt that children leaving their own classroom to join a French group taught by another teacher stood to lose 'the valuable experience of informal discussion, which can happen at any time in a class'. He added: 'As there are many children involved who have a poor standard of spoken English, this type of classroom experience is essential.' There were also a few reports, however, that 'within limits, this interchange of teachers can be most beneficial and refreshing, even to junior children'.

A significant number of primary school heads considered that too much time was being deducted from other activities in order to provide sufficient time for French. As one head wrote: 'The argument sometimes put forward that, because the primary school timetable is integrated, other subjects will not suffer, ignores the fact that pure French teaching absorbs at least two and a half hours per week. To have a true picture of the time-factor, one must add to the two and a half hours the amount of time consumed by changing classrooms, when audio-visual aids requiring black-out are involved, bearing in mind that both classes changing rooms are wasting time and suffering upheaval—not the least of which is that the displaced class is perpetually functioning outside its own environment. The effect of this secondary time-wasting procedure and unsettling influence should not be minimized.' Although a number of heads complained that the introduction of French had seriously curtailed the time available for other 'more basic' subjects, none reported any evidence of declining standards of attainment in these subjects. Heads often commented that those members of their staff who were not involved in the teaching of French had expressed anxiety about the possibility of a decline in the standard of general attainment, but most agreed that, whether or not the optimum balance of teaching-time had been achieved, such anxiety was without foundation.

There were various ways in which both head and teaching staff had attempted to reduce the effects of teaching French as an isolated subject. In some schools, there were sufficient trained teachers to allow each teacher to take his or her own class for French. As the head of one such school wrote: 'This cuts down specialization and also obviates some of the timetable difficulties. Where this is possible the class teacher, who is also the French teacher, has moved up each year with the class'. In other schools, particularly in the small schools, attempts had been made to reduce the amount of disturbance and classroom change by engaging one group of the whole class in a different activity, such as some form of private study, while the other group was being taught French. The head of a small school described this arrangement: 'During the French lesson I have the full class, one group therefore being engaged in private topic work. This has worked most successfully and no interruptions of the French lesson have been experienced'. Some heads also described attempts to integrate French into the teaching of other subjects. One headmaster wrote: 'We use French occasionally in other subjects, but, as yet, this seems a little artificial. In Maths, however, one group did recently spend some time on the difficulties an English family on holiday in France would experience. This provoked a good deal of discussion about the French way of life and a lot of good Maths, but little spoken French'. Another head, describing his attempts to lessen the isolation of French, wrote: 'Here I mention the purposeful and meaningful aspects of History (Norman conquest) Geography (place names and products), Music (French songs), and Arithmetic (currency and shop products)'. 'French has also entered into Projects and Music: French carols are a pleasant change from our annual bombardment of old favourites', commented another. One head, who felt that his efforts to integrate French into the curriculum had been largely successful, wrote: 'Handiwork, History, Geography, Art and Music have been added to the list of our subjects influenced in some way by the impact of French, and all these subjects have benefited.'

3. Materials, equipment and accommodation

All the schools taking part in the experiment were using audio-visual French courses in which the emphasis fell on the development of the spoken aspects of the language. Several heads commented on the difficulties experienced by their teaching staff in maintaining effective oral teaching methods with large classes. One head wrote: 'The most difficult problem of all, I would feel, is that of taking an oral approach with large classes of 40+. Where the class teacher is also the teacher of French this difficulty does not cause quite the same worry, as she can spend more time with groups of children but,

where classes have to change teachers, it is impossible to devote time
to group-work, except in the very latest stages when the children are
achieving some competence in reading and writing. I realize that
this problem of over-large classes is largely met by the versatile
teacher using many different techniques, but, nevertheless, it is
difficult to find the time to check regularly the shy and the diffident in
this situation'. It was generally agreed that, in classes of more than
40 pupils, 'choral answers must largely be the rule' and one head
made the suggestion that 'if resources are to be limited, a one-year
course in small groups might be better than the three-year arrangement in big classes'.

Many heads also considered that the amount of equipment necessary for the efficient use of the French teaching materials entailed
serious disadvantages. The amount of time needed to prepare lessons
and set up equipment (tape-recorders, screens, projectors, etc.), the
difficulties of transporting such equipment from one classroom to
another, and the problems of maintenance were frequently described.
'The French teachers have to transport the necessary equipment from
room to room. This is far from satisfactory on account of (a) the
weight and quantity of equipment to be carried, (b) the time taken
and (c) the fact that crossings of the playground to temporary
classrooms have to be made in all weathers', wrote one head.
'Movement of apparatus means more maintenance and more repair
problems, because accidents will happen, however well-trained the
monitors may be', wrote another. In schools with a large number of
French classes, the need to duplicate equipment, particularly tape-
recorders, had often been underestimated. 'It has been found
necessary to "set up" tape-recorders before the beginning of a lesson
(i.e. to have the tape on the recorder at the exact place required)', a
head explained. 'This means that at least two tape-recorders are
needed in each room, so that teachers can prepare for the lesson
before each session'. 'The sharing of tape-recorders often causes
harassment to staff, as they sometimes have to be rushed from one
room to another, and tapes changed quickly', another wrote. Since
the tape-recorders are in daily use, repair and maintenance can
present persistent problems. 'The maintenance and repair of equipment has been a nightmare', reported the head of a large primary
school. 'I'm afraid women teachers do not appear to have much
ability with mechanical or electrical equipment', he continued. 'They
appear to prefer to pull a plug out by the wire rather than by the plug
itself. They do not seem to be able to comprehend very clearly the
mechanics of the tape-recorder, with the result that mechanical

failures (mainly shorted wires) are a weekly and very often a daily occurrence.' In small schools, there was often only one tape-recorder available and inadequate facilities for maintenance and repair. As the head of one such school wrote: 'When one considers that there is only one tape-recorder, which is in use every day of the week, breakdowns are inevitable and the French teaching can be held in abeyance for weeks until the fault is rectified'. Most heads, however, reported that they had been able to arrange reasonably adequate provision for the repair and maintenance of equipment. Some had found that 'an extra machine in reserve solves the problem of repairs', while others reported that the Local Education Authority provided an efficient servicing system.

Many heads reported that considerable effort had been expended to provide optimum conditions for the teaching of French by audio-visual methods. The head of a large primary school described the development of a 'French room' as follows: 'We set about reorganizing a "French room" which would allow freedom of movement, space to organize group activities, adequate wall space and space for developing new ideas. The initial requirements were only a table for the tape-recorder and stackable chairs for the children, to provide an open space when it was required. The room was made attractive by the use of posters. As our teaching ideas have developed and reached fruition, the room has passed through many phases: now only the chairs remain from the first stage. Framed wall-display units, to which illustrations and teaching material can be instantly attached, have been made from fibre-wood, and fabric pockets, which hold the group-activity apparatus, line two walls of the room. One corner has become the puppet theatre with its moveable curtains, one complete wall houses the Mini Language Laboratory booths, six in number, each containing head-phones and microphones, and a console to operate the Mini Language Laboratory has been built with all the controls. This system enables the children to listen to the taped exercises through the head-phones and reply through the microphone. At the console, the teacher can listen individually to each child and correct individually when required, by the use of a teacher-microphone coupled up to each booth'. In schools where there was sufficient space available, the majority of heads described similar, if less comprehensive, arrangements for converting spare classrooms into special rooms for the teaching of French, to avoid the necessity of transporting equipment from one classroom to the other. Some heads, however, considered that the creation of a special 'French room', though feasible in their school, was undesirable, since its use would entail the inconvenience of changing classrooms. One head, who had originally provided a separate 'French room', found that his staff preferred to teach French in their own classrooms, because: '(a) They know the children's sitting positions; (b) The children were more at home; (c) Everything necessary was to hand'. He added: 'Acoustically this was not as good as the special room, as there were extraneous noises from the corridor, but all teachers preferred their own rooms'. Other heads reported that their staff found the changing of classrooms for French lessons 'time-consuming and frustrating' and described how they had sought to overcome the acoustic imperfections of the normal classroom. As one head wrote: 'It is completely possible with a little ingenuity to use the normal classroom for all aspects of the course. The problem of acoustics is solved by means of external loudspeakers at the back of the room as well as the recorder at the front'. Other heads were less fortunate in finding a solution to their classroom problems, however. Small schools, with no extra space available, encountered particular difficulties. 'My school consists of two very small rooms, and, during the hour given to the French groups, the rest of the children (aged five to eleven) have to be in the Junior Room doing quiet work, as the rooms are only separated by swing doors. This is difficult for us all, as there is little space for movement and the Infants have to be given appropriate "seat-work"', explained the head of a small rural school. 'The room used by the children taking part in the scheme is 15 feet by 30 feet and contains all the equipment and stock needed for the working of the school, as there are no store-rooms, staff-room, or head teacher's room', reported the head of another small school. 'There is no space for special areas for display devoted to French apparatus', he added. 'The other room in the school is even smaller and is occupied by 22 infants'. In a number of schools, makeshift arrangements were still in force and French lessons were being held in the staff-room, the library, the canteen, or the corridors. Schools with space to spare ('We were able to establish two French rooms where a very Parisian atmosphere was set up') were rare; several heads reported permanently overcrowded conditions. In the majority of schools, however, even in those where accommodation was most limited, attempts had been made to stimulate pupils' interest in learning French by establishing a 'French corner' or providing a library of French books in the pupils' own classroom. Results were often encouraging. 'A "French corner" has proved popular, with competitions on France and the French way of life designed to make the children look up facts and find things out for themselves. They have been encouraged to bring articles for the "French corner" and they have been eager to do so', wrote one head. ' "French corners" do a lot to promote, maintain and encourage an interest in the language and people of France', agreed another. There had also been attempts in many schools to build up a stock of French books, to provide the children with supplementary reading material, but there were frequent complaints regarding the difficulty of obtaining books which were 'both linguistically simple enough and emotionally mature enough' for pupils in the junior age-range. 'Is this a standard difficulty?', inquired one headmaster. Many of his colleagues confirmed that it was.

4. Staffing difficulties

Primary school heads who reported that they had sufficient French-teaching staff to cope with the requirements of the Pilot Scheme were, almost without exception, heads of schools in which the teaching of French had been comparatively well-established before the beginning of the experiment. Almost all heads who reported staffing difficulties were heads of schools in which no French had been taught prior to 1964. The main difficulty encountered in these schools was that of maintaining a sufficient number of trained French teachers to ensure the uninterrupted teaching of French to the Pilot Scheme pupils. Where a shortage of staff existed, the situation was, of course, aggravated after the first year of the experiment, when the teaching of French was extended to succeeding year-groups. Shortage of staff was also often reported to lead to 'over-specialization', regarded as 'contrary to the normal policy of the school' and a source of strain for the teachers concerned. As one head wrote: 'All work now seems to be carried out at a much quicker rate, because of the shorter time available. . . . To prevent standards in the basic subjects from falling off, it has become necessary to put some strain on both children and staff'. In some cases, attempts had been made to ease the staffing situation by the employment of part-time French assistants, but these attempts did not always achieve satisfactory results. 'For a time, a French national came in for conversation classes so that the children had a little contact with a native speaker', one head reported, adding: 'However, these people are not usually qualified and, unless they are familiar with the course material, have difficulty in conversing with the children'. 'We have had five assistants in the course of three years', wrote another head. 'Three of them have been efficient and acceptable as colleagues. Two of them have not contributed much, either to French or to the school: in fact, they have left their mark in the shape of anti-French groups and classes'.

Nearly all heads considered that in-service training was essential for intending or inexperienced French teachers (only two reported that they did not release teachers for training), but it was also recognized that the teachers' absence could have a disruptive effect on the organization of the school. It was not always possible to make satisfactory arrangements for the replacement of absent teachers. 'Quite considerable problems have arisen concerning in-service training. A replacement at one time was 65+ and stone-deaf', wrote one head. 'Continuity has been preserved—on paper!', commented another. 'Supply teachers have been found, and, although classes have had a period of instability, I suppose we have gained in the long run, by acquiring better-trained French teachers', another head reported, pointing out that suitable supply teachers were very 'thin on the ground'. Other heads felt that the hardships were minimal, in relation to the benefits to be derived from in-service training. 'In-service training is most essential', wrote one head. 'The monthly meetings at the local College of Further Education for discussion on method are most valuable and, although the long course in France has a most disrupting influence on the timetable, I think it is immensely valuable and worthwhile, both to the school and the teacher'. 'Releasing teachers for a course in France is something of a problem, both for them domestically and for the class which has to have a different teacher for ten weeks', agreed another, adding: 'but since this release is not likely to happen more often than once every two or three years, I think we shall manage well enough, until more ready-trained teachers are available'. A few heads were disappointed in the effects of in-service training, feeling that the teachers concerned were still not competent to teach French effectively. One head described how, after a year's trial, two of his 'more experienced teachers' who had followed an in-service training programme 'decided that they were not "French" enough to teach the subject as it should be taught. Their accent and French background was not good enough, and they were conscious of their own shortcomings'. Another head reported that, after a period of in-service training, two of his teachers found the teaching of French 'beyond their capabilities'. He added: 'This unfortunate situation has definitely not helped in the reaction of other teaching staff to the introduction of French'. Reports of this kind were rare, however. Most heads were convinced of the value of in-service training and reported a co-operative attitude on the part of members of staff who were not involved in the teaching of French. As one head wrote: 'The attitude is simply that the present French teaching is purely an experiment to discover if such teaching is an educationally viable proposition. Hence, if some useful educational truth emerges, the whole thing will have been worthwhile. Therefore, to this end, we are co-operating willingly and enthusiastically and are anxious to see that the experiment is carried out successfully'. Although enthusiasm was rare among members of staff not involved in the experiment ('There has been no strong opposition to the scheme by the non-French teaching staff, but, on the other hand, there is not great enthusiasm'), a few heads reported reactions such as the following: 'The infant teacher has been so impressed that she has joined the French course for teachers', or 'several teachers comment on the "liveliness" awakened, in otherwise rather "dull" characters'. Other heads reported that some members of staff resented the attention paid to the teaching of French and felt that the school was becoming 'geared' to the subject. As one head wrote: 'Within the staff not concerned at the moment with French, there is a latent feeling of jealousy of the superb conditions provided for French, and not yet available for any other subject'. Another head reported: 'I can see amongst my teachers a firm opinion that the experiment has produced inadequate results and should be abandoned. This school of thought suggests that it is important to use the right yardstick to judge the experiment. The question should not be "Has the introduction of French brought advantages?", but rather "Have these advantages been as great as those that might have been gained if the same amount of time, money, effort and facilities had been devoted to an existing school subject?".'

5. The pupils' response to the introduction of French

Many heads of Pilot Scheme primary schools were confident that considerable cultural and educational benefits had stemmed from the introduction of French. One of them wrote: 'The children's horizons have been greatly broadened and, since we have tended to be an insular nation mainly concerned with our own local problems and with national survival, the teaching of French should lead to a greater understanding of, and co-operation with, other countries —especially France. Even travel abroad can take on a new appearance, and a greater enjoyment can be had with greater linguistic ability.' Another head wrote: 'The children have taken an interest in France as a country which has become real to them. They realize that there are both similarities and differences between their own way of life and that of French children'. The head of a small school, who himself taught French, described his experience in the following terms: 'The learning of a foreign language has been stimulating and exciting for all the children. Success in this subject has encouraged the children who found learning to read and write difficult, to make a sustained effort to improve. The children's powers of concentration and listening have grown, and dramatization has become a daily habit. The children have also grown more self-reliant, as it is necessary for them to work in groups on their own, older and more able children helping those in need'.

The majority of primary school heads had formed equally favourable impressions of the benefits to be derived from teaching French to their more able pupils, but opinion was divided regarding the wisdom of teaching French to the less able. A number of heads considered that the introduction of French had served to increase their less able pupils' confidence, level of attainment, and motivation to learn. They reported how pupils otherwise considered 'dull' had succeeded beyond expectation in oral French. 'There can certainly be no disguising the fact that some low-ability children have a natural ability for the language', one head wrote. 'This type of child has taken more interest in normal classwork because he has been freed from written work in the French room and has made a good response verbally. Many have found obvious pleasure in finding that they can, at long last, shine in some subject', wrote another. 'Many of these have shown quite an aptitude for conversation', agreed a third. There were others who considered that 'the attainment reached by children of limited ability will obviously be limited', but who nevertheless felt that the psychological effect of separating these children from the more able pupils would be extremely damaging. As one head wrote: 'There is some doubt as to the advisability of teaching French to the lower ability-range, but I feel it is important that these children, who in many cases already feel "different", should be allowed the same opportunities as their brighter friends. In many cases, the fact that they have all started as equals has given the lower ability-range a new feeling of being able to keep up with, or occasionally to show a greater aptitude than the others'. 'Would the bottom few really gain by spending this time on English?', asked another head. 'French gives some variety of interest and, in any case, gives some of the less able a new chance. David is a case in point: always very low in class, but one of the top boys in French. This interest may have helped his English by giving him some confidence in succeeding where he had hitherto failed. His reading in English has certainly improved. In a streamlined school, obviously it is easier to have the less able spending the French time on English, but this creates a "snob" A-stream and again penalizes those such as David. This system would also "fix" the streaming more permanently'. 'I would be reluctant to bar the lower-stream children from learning French', stated another head. 'I would have to set one group of children apart from the others, which would be bad psychologically, and it would necessitate sub-dividing the class, as some of the "B" children are obviously capable of learning French'. Another head reported that, in the light of their three years' experience with the Pilot Scheme pupils, 'all members of staff now feel that, if French is to be integrated into the junior school curriculum, then all children, regardless of ability, should take part'.

Others, however, were equally convinced that teaching French to the less able pupils had proved to be 'a waste of time' and that these pupils would derive greater benefit from remedial work in the 'basic' subjects. As one head wrote: 'I am not at all happy about the teaching of French to the less able children. I had felt at the beginning of the course that the purely oral approach would encourage those children who find difficulties in written expression. However, I have noticed that after the initial enthusiasm has worn off, the general atmosphere is one of reluctant acceptance. . . . I feel that the less able children would benefit more by using their time with the general activities in English subjects.' Another head agreed: 'To our minds there are a few children who do not benefit from French in the junior school. These are those whose fluency in spoken language is low, who cannot express themselves easily in English, even to their contemporaries'. Another wrote: 'I feel that it is not desirable to teach a second language to children of low ability. A great deal of time must be spent in the junior school on the teaching of basic skills to these children, and the introduction of a second language limits even more the time available on an already overcrowded timetable. In my opinion, the teaching of the basic subjects must have priority'. After three years' observation of their Pilot Scheme pupils, the conclusion reached by this group of heads was that 'for the less able, the amount of time and energy expended could have been used to more effect in the basic subjects'.

A number of heads also reported that, as the French course advanced, and particularly after the introduction of the written script, the level of performance of the less able children in the class deteriorated sharply relative to that of the abler children. 'The gap between the dull and the bright grows irretrievably wider', wrote one head. 'As the language becomes more difficult, the gap widens between the bright children and those of lesser ability', another head agreed.

'The work is making a greater demand on their ability and the gap in proficiency between the most and the least able is growing wider', observed another. The problems of teaching French effectively to a mixed-ability class in the later stages of the primary course were considered formidable. 'While the really good teacher may be able to devise some form of activity to keep the brighter children really usefully occupied while he gives some attention to the less able, the nature of the subject and the oral approach makes this difficult and demands a degree of skill possessed by few', one head wrote. 'The brighter children become impatient with a too-slow pace and the less able discouraged by their inability to cope', another head confirmed, pointing out that 'in no other subject on the curriculum are children of diverse abilities expected to tackle the same scheme of work at the same speed'.

Another problem with which many heads were concerned was that of absorbing the late entrant into the French class. It was generally agreed that, if late entrants began French during the first year, or during the early part of the second year, integrating them into the French class did not pose too great a problem, although their lack of ability to handle basic sentence-patterns prevented them from taking part in group conversation for a considerable period. 'The teachers have felt for quite a time that these children who came in late to first- and second-year classes have been benefiting very little', wrote one head, adding: 'They are now realizing that on the whole they have been wrong. The children have been understanding quite an amount, but have been slow to utter through uncertainty'. Another head agreed: 'They settle in fairly quickly, provided that they are not expected to play too prominent a part and are left to be "exposed" to French'. However, not all late entrants achieved the process of integration without distress. As one head wrote: 'Late entrants, in spite of being told not to worry, often do, but do not like being left out, and pose a problem of alternative work if they do not take French'. Another head reported: 'In one case, a boy of considerable ability acquired an inferiority complex where French was concerned, because he was not able to reach his usual standard'. In schools with a high mobility rate, such as those serving military establishments, the problem of absorbing late entrants was particularly acute. 'There are many late entrants to the French class, so that it is no longer possible to give them extra tuition in the dinner-hour, which was done at first. The teacher has to be very kind to prevent some of them feeling quite overwhelmed in this difficult situation' reported the head of one such school. In several schools special arrangements had been made, in an attempt to accommodate the late entrant more easily. Individual practice with the tape-recorder, once the pupils had acquired 'some groundwork on which to build', proved effective if the number of late entrants was not too great. One headmaster, who himself taught French, had arranged extra 'remedial sessions' for late entrants, but pointed out that 'this is only possible because I teach French myself'. Another head described how, in his school, 'the teacher does individual work with the child while the rest are writing, illustrating their French books, or working in groups'. In schools where this was not possible to arrange, the pupils themselves were often asked to help the late entrant: 'some friend of the new entrant can be persuaded to teach, for instance, the numbers during playtime'. One headmaster, who had found no effective way of reducing the disadvantage at which late entrants were placed, enquired: 'Would an individual teaching-machine help here?' Others suggested the use of a 'simple programmed text', particularly when the number of late entrants was considerable. One head, drawing on his experience with late entrants, concluded that the extent of the problem depended on the following factors: '1. How far the class has progressed before the late entrant came into the school. For example, one intelligent child missed the first term, but was able to catch up and, by the end of the second year, was one of the best pupils. Children who joined the class during the second or third year of French found much greater difficulty and always needed a lot of help. 2. The type of child and his/her friends in the class. Some groups of children spend playtimes practising short French playlets or the games from the "Activities" section of the lessons. Some groups of children speak French in the dining-room. All these activities are very helpful to the latecomers and given them a base from which to start. 3. The teacher-class relationship. Where the class teacher is also the French teacher, she is able to give more attention to the problem than the teacher who only sees the child as part of a class of 40 for 25 minutes per day'. Another factor emphasized by many heads was that of sheer weight of numbers: a few late entrants could usually be accommodated without undue difficulty; a sudden large influx of new pupils could jeopardize the organization of French teaching throughout the school.

6. Liaison with secondary schools

Almost without exception, the heads of the Pilot Scheme primary schools expressed themselves anxious to establish an effective liaison with the heads and French teaching staff of the secondary schools in their area, in order to ensure that 'all possible will be done there to continue from where the pupils stopped with us'. Efforts towards achieving a smooth transition from the primary to the secondary stage of the experiment included visits by secondary school French teachers to the primary French classes, area meetings involving both primary and secondary heads and teaching staff, courses and conferences sponsored by the Local Education Authority, and personal contact between the heads of the contributing primary schools and the receiving secondary schools. Such efforts often promised to produce satisfactory results. 'The French classes in this school have always been made freely available for observation and the French teachers have given every opportunity to their secondary school colleagues to discuss problems of transfer to secondary schools and the continuation of work begun at the primary level', wrote one primary school head. 'A very satisfactory feature of the Pilot Scheme is the promise that our work in the junior school will be carried on largely in the same way in the secondary school. Liaison between all the schools involved has been good. The Education Authority has held regular conferences at which difficulties have been discussed and, as a result, both grammar school and bilateral school staffs have visited junior schools to meet the teachers and children', wrote another. 'Secondary teachers have visited the pilot primary schools. A panel of primary and secondary teachers, together with the Senior Inspector of Schools and a member of the local College of Education meet monthly with teachers at the in-service training course, to discuss any problems which arise during the course of the experiment', another head reported. 'The liaison with the secondary school is excellent', confirmed another, describing how the secondary school French teacher who was shortly to receive first cohort pupils was 'anxious to come every week and take a group of children, so that he can get to know the primary methods'.

In some areas, however, the heads of the Pilot Scheme primary schools felt that their efforts to promote a smooth transition to the secondary stage had met with small success. 'Liaison with the secondary schools has been very poor', one head wrote. 'Both the secondary modern school next door and the grammar school about half a mile away were offered free access whenever they wished to visit. The secondary modern school teacher has been twice and the head once. The grammar school teachers have not visited at all'. He added: 'Much more, I feel sure, could have been done by the secondary schools themselves'. The head of another primary school reported that 'the barriers have not been broken down sufficiently. Secondary teachers should come and converse more with the children they are to receive. Also, it is important for the children to be given the opportunity of hearing a new voice—so often that of a male—while still feeling comfortable in their junior school classroom environment'. Primary school heads expressed particular apprehension in cases where the secondary school catchment area included both Pilot Scheme schools and primary schools in which there had been little or no French teaching. One primary school head expressed concern for his abler pupils, who would shortly be transferring to grammar schools, 'where there will be some children in next year's intake who have learnt French by one scheme, some by another, and some not at all'. 'How will these be dealt with in schools which do not practice "setting" during the first year?', he inquired. He continued: 'I can foresee a danger of some grammar school teachers, unable to adjust, taking the attitude: "Forget what you have learnt at primary school and do it my way"—probably the way it has been done in the past'. Another primary school head reported that 'grammar school staff are not sympathetic to our work because they feel that we are having the first bite at what they feel is their "cherry"'. He went on: 'As they are receiving only a proportion of children who have had tuition in French, they have made no provision in their first years for these children. Consequently, our children will have to begin at the beginning again'. One head, who felt that the secondary schools in his area were ill-prepared to receive Pilot Scheme pupils, wrote: 'In fairness to secondary teachers, it must be said that they are dealing with an unknown quantity. When they know what stage primary children have reached at the end of the school year, they will be in a better position to formulate a programme. At least we hope so! Otherwise much effort at the primary level will have been expended in vain'. Primary school heads were unanimously of the opinion that, unless a smooth transition between the primary and secondary stages of the Pilot Scheme could be achieved, the experiment was 'doomed to failure'.

The views of the primary school heads have been reported in some detail, not only because of their intrinsic interest, but also because of the critical importance of this body of opinion in the context of a national experiment designed to study the effects of curricular innovation at the primary level. There can be little doubt that the attitudes and opinions of the head of a school exert a powerful influence on both staff and pupils. A case in point is the association reported earlier[1] between the attitude of the head and the level of achievement

[1] BURSTALL, C. op cit.

TABLE 14. *Battery 1 French Tests. Mean scores by head's attitude towards French and pupil's parental occupation category*

BATTERY 1 FRENCH TEST ATTITUDE OF HEAD		Professional and Clerical	Skilled	Semi-skilled	Unskilled	TOTAL
		PARENTAL OCCUPATION				
Speaking Test	N	158	180	134	67	539
Unfavourable Head	x̄	29·60	26·71	21·38	16·92	25·02
	SD	10·02	8·98	9·20	9·62	9·72
Speaking Test	N	143	174	80	52	449
Favourable Head	x̄	39·21	30·96	23·75	20·71	31·12
	SD	10·39	9·57	7·67	8·21	9·88
Listening Test	N	745	971	699	383	2798
Unfavourable Head	x̄	24·01	21·67	19·36	16·85	21·06
	SD	7·76	7·71	6·88	6·31	7·72
Listening Test	N	690	816	529	279	2314
Favourable Head	x̄	24·80	22·76	20·31	19·39	22·40
	SD	7·97	7·67	7·50	7·34	7·93
Reading Test	N	740	962	704	373	2779
Unfavourable Head	x̄	31·01	27·43	24·42	20·71	26·72
	SD	11·76	11·17	9·63	8·51	11·15
Reading Test	N	689	804	507	277	2277
Favourable Head	x̄	32·81	28·06	24·86	22·72	28·14
	SD	11·53	10·46	10·23	8·84	11·15
Writing Test	N	507	648	378	153	1686
Unfavourable Head	x̄	20·68	18·34	16·54	14·94	18·33
	SD	9·50	9·81	9·15	9·27	9·70
Writing Test	N	616	692	419	183	1910
Favourable Head	x̄	24·23	19·26	15·80	13·44	19·55
	SD	11·33	10·06	9·76	8·86	10·96

in French reached by the less able pupils in the school. These early findings have recently been confirmed and extended: analysis of the Battery 1 French test results has shown that the mean scores of second cohort pupils in schools where the head has a predominantly favourable attitude towards the teaching of French to the whole ability-range are significantly higher than those of pupils in schools where the head has a correspondingly unfavourable attitude. These results are shown in summary form in Table 14 and presented in greater detail in Tables 4.1 to 4.4 in Appendix 4. These tables show mean scores for each Battery 1 French test, distributed by attitude of head, sex of pupil, and parental occupation category.

These findings are not confined to low-achieving pupils, but apply to the whole of the second cohort sample. They also appear to be specific to French: no association has been found, for instance, between the attitude of the head towards the teaching of French and pupils' performance on the general attainment battery. Evidence of this kind suggests that the viewpoint of the head is an important factor to be taken into consideration in an educational experiment such as the Pilot Scheme for the introduction of French at the primary level.

The HMI Evaluation of the Primary Stage of the Pilot Scheme

SINCE its inception in 1964, members of HM Inspectorate have been assisting in the evaluation of the Pilot Scheme for the teaching of French in primary schools by visiting each of the French classes taking part in the experiment and providing the research team with detailed reports on the teaching situation. These reports, written after each visit to a Pilot Scheme class, have been completed in questionnaire form. The questionnaire used on the occasion of an Inspector's first visit to a French class includes the following areas of inquiry: the qualifications, initial and in-service training, previous teaching experience and linguistic competence of the French teacher; the nature and scope of the French lesson; general classroom conditions; the teaching materials and audio-visual equipment used during the French lesson; the quality of the pupils' spoken French and the nature of the pupils' response to the teaching of French. On second and subsequent visits to a particular French class, a shorter version of the questionnaire is used to obtain an evaluation of the progress made by the class since the Inspector's previous visit. The shortened version of the questionnaire requires an assessment of any changes in the French-teaching situation which might have taken place during the period under study. The areas of inquiry covered by this questionnaire include the development of the teacher's own command of French, the pupils' fluency in French (the latter with specific reference to pronunciation, intonation, accuracy, audibility and confidence in speaking French), the enthusiasm for French of both teacher and pupils, the opportunities provided for the whole class and for the individual pupil to practise French, and the extent to which slower pupils participate actively in the French lesson. Developments in each of these areas are rated on a four-point scale, with judgement intervals ranging from 'marked improvement' to 'regression'. In addition, HM Inspectors are asked to identify the major factors in the French-teaching situation which they believe to be contributing to the facilitation or inhibition of the pupils' progress in learning French.

The data arising from both the original and the shortened version of the questionnaire are processed whenever a sufficient number of completed questionnaires have been received and are analysed at the end of each school year. The results of earlier analyses have already been reported:[1] the present account refers to data collected during the school year 1967-68, when the pupils in the second cohort were in their final year of primary school. The data obtained from an Inspector's initial visit to a French class were analysed first by reference to the rated fluency in French of the class. Classes whose spoken French had been rated as 'very fluent' or 'fluent' ('highly fluent' classes) were identified and compared with classes rated 'fairly fluent', 'hesitant' or 'very hesitant' ('less fluent' classes). Chi-square tests were carried out to determine whether 'highly fluent' and 'less fluent' classes differed significantly from one another on any of the other rated variables. The results of the chi-square tests are shown in Table 5.1 in Appendix 5. All variables which proved to be non-significant have been omitted from Table 5.1. As might be expected, the pupils in the 'highly fluent' and 'less fluent' classes were shown to differ significantly from one another with respect to specific aspects of their command of French. Pupils in 'highly fluent' classes tended to have 'very good' or 'good' pronunciation and intonation, to make only occasional mistakes when speaking French and to speak in a clearly audible manner, frequently imitating their teacher's efforts to convey 'French-ness' through movement, gesture and facial expression. Pupils in 'less fluent' classes, on the other hand, tended to have 'reasonable' or 'poor' pronunciation and intonation, to make frequent mistakes when speaking French, to be 'audible' or 'barely audible' in their speech, and to make little attempt to convey 'French-ness' of manner. 'Highly fluent' classes tended also to be those in which the pupils were given greater opportunities for individual practice in speaking French and in which all members of the class took an active part in the French lesson. 'Less fluent' classes tended to be those in which the individual pupil was given little opportunity to practise speaking French, except in the group or whole-class situation. 'Less fluent' classes were also those in which active participation in the French lesson was confined to selected members of the class. In 'highly fluent' classes, pupils were considered to be highly responsive to the French lesson and to give evidence of ability to use their language skills creatively, whereas, in 'less fluent' classes, pupils were regarded as considerably less responsive to the French lesson and unable to make use of their language skills outside the confines of familiar teaching situations.

[1] BURSTALL, C. op. cit.

Those who taught French to 'highly fluent' and 'less fluent' classes also differed significantly from one another in certain respects. Teachers of 'highly fluent' classes tended themselves to be rated 'very fluent' or 'fluent' in their command of French, with 'very good' or 'good' pronunciation and intonation and an ability to convey 'a feeling of French-ness', through the use of movement, gesture and facial expression, either 'completely' or 'to a considerable extent'. They also tended to be 'very competent' in their handling of audio-visual materials and equipment. Teachers of 'less fluent' classes tended to be 'fairly fluent' or 'hesitant' in their command of French, to have 'reasonable' or 'poor' pronunciation and intonation and to be relatively unsuccessful in conveying 'French-ness' of manner. They also tended to be less than competent in their use of audio-visual equipment. Teachers of 'highly fluent' and 'less fluent' classes also differed significantly from one another in the extent to which they conducted their lessons in French, used an entirely oral approach to language teaching, and made use of other activities to reinforce and develop the children's oral skills. In 'highly fluent' classes, teachers tended to adopt an entirely oral approach to teaching French and to use no English at all during the French lesson, making 'imaginative and effective' use of activities to develop the children's use of spoken French. In 'less fluent' classes, greater use was made of the written script and English was 'occasionally' or 'frequently' spoken by both teacher and pupils. Little attempt was made to develop the children's creative use of language through other activities. In 'highly fluent' classes, the aims of the French lesson were frequently described by visiting Inspectors as being 'completely' achieved, whereas, in 'less fluent' classes, the aims of the French lesson were usually reported to be only 'partially' achieved. Teachers of 'highly fluent' and 'less fluent' classes did not differ significantly from one another, however, with regard to their age, training and qualifications, nor with regard to the accuracy of their spoken French. Neither was any positive association apparent between the fluency of the class and the organizational policy of the school: 'highly fluent' classes were not found to differ significantly from 'less fluent' classes with respect to the size and composition of the class, nor with respect to general classroom conditions.

The data relating to first visits to a French class were also analysed with reference to the rated responsiveness of the class to the French lesson. Classes considered 'very responsive' to the French lesson ('highly responsive' classes) were identified and compared with those considered 'quite responsive', 'not very responsive', or 'unresponsive' to the French lesson ('less responsive 'classes). Chi-square tests were again carried out to determine whether 'highly responsive' classes differed significantly from 'less responsive' classes in regard to any of the other rated variables. The results of the chi-square tests are shown in Table 5.2 in Appendix 5. All variables which proved to be non-significant have been omitted from Table 5.2. The responsiveness of the class to the French lesson appears to be closely associated with the fluency of the class: in most respects, significant differences between 'highly responsive' and 'less responsive' classes parallel those between 'highly fluent' and 'less fluent' classes. 'Highly responsive' and 'less responsive' classes do not, however, differ significantly from one another with regard to the accuracy of the pupils' spoken French, nor with regard to the opportunities provided for the class to practise speaking French. Unlike fluency, the responsiveness of the class to the French lesson does not appear to be significantly associated with the extent to which the lesson is presented orally, nor with the extent to which English is used during the French lesson.

Classes in which there was reported to be no English used by teacher or pupils during the French lesson ('non-English' classes) were identified and compared with those in which English was reported to be used 'occasionally' or 'frequently' by both teacher and pupils during the course of the French lesson ('English' classes). Chi-square tests were carried out to determine whether 'non-English' and 'English' classes differed significantly from one another with regard to any other of the rated variables. The results of the chi-square tests are shown in Table 5.3 in Appendix 5. All variables which proved to be non-significant have been omitted from Table 5.3. The results of the comparison between 'non-English' and 'English' classes suggest that those teachers who do not use English at all during the French lesson are not only more fluent in French than those who make 'occasional' or 'frequent' use of English but also more successful in their efforts to achieve the active participation of all members of the French class. This confirms an earlier finding[1] that the more fluent teacher does not dominate classroom conversation, but rather uses his fluency to encourage all pupils to play an active part in the French lesson. Pupils in 'non-English' classes tend to be rated as more fluent and more accurate in their spoken French than pupils in classes where French is taught partly through the medium of English. Pupils in 'non-English' classes are also considered

---

[1] BURSTALL, C. op cit.

to have significantly better intonation and a more authentic 'French manner' than those in 'English' classes, although the two groups do not differ significantly with regard to their pronunciation of French. Pupils in 'non-English' classes also tend to give more evidence of their ability to use language creatively than do those in 'English' classes. In addition, the aims of the French lesson are more often seen to be 'completely' achieved in 'non-English' classes and only 'partially' achieved in 'English' classes.

The questionnaire data relating to second and subsequent visits to French classes during 1967-68 were analysed first by reference to the rated improvement in fluency of the French class. Classes reported to be showing marked improvement in fluency ('high-progress' classes) were identified and compared, on the one hand, with those reported to be showing some improvement in fluency ('moderate-progress' classes) and, on the other, with those reported to be showing no improvement in fluency or actual regression from a previously higher standard of performance ('low-progress' classes). Chi-square tests were carried out to determine whether these classes differed significantly from one another with regard to any of their other characteristics. The results of the chi-square tests are shown in Table 5.4 in Appendix 5. All variables which proved to be non-significant have been omitted from Table 5.4. Improvement in the overall fluency of the class is associated with improvement in specific aspects of the development of language skills and also with increasing confidence and enthusiasm. Pupils in 'high-progress' classes showed 'marked' improvement in their pronunciation, intonation, accuracy and audibility in speaking French, and a correspondingly marked increase in their confidence and enthusiasm for French. Pupils in 'moderate-progress' classes gave evidence of similar but less marked improvement in their attitudes and achievement. Pupils in 'low-progress' classes, however, gave no evidence of improvement in any aspect of spoken French and, in some cases, were reported to have regressed from a previously higher level of achievement, with a corresponding decline in confidence and enthusiasm.

Teachers of 'high-progress' classes were reported to show marked improvement in their own command of French during the period under study and to give evidence of increased enthusiasm for the teaching of French. Teachers of 'moderate-progress' classes were also reported to have achieved some improvement in their command of French and to show increased enthusiasm for French, but teachers of 'low-progress' classes were considered to have given no evidence of improvement in either respect. In 'high-progress' and 'moderate-progress' classes, opportunities for both the class and the individual pupil to practise French had increased during the period under study, as had the extent to which the slower pupils were able to participate in the French lesson. In 'low-progress' classes, opportunities for the class and the individual pupil to practise French had remained static or had actually decreased, as had opportunities for the slower pupils to play an active part in the French lesson. In 'high-progress' and 'moderate-progress' classes, the written script, if introduced, was considered to have exerted a beneficial effect on the pupils' achievement in French and on their attitudes towards learning French. In 'low-progress' classes, however, the introduction of written French was seen either to have had an adverse effect on attitudes and achievement, or else to have produced no effect at all. There were no significant differences between the three groups of classes with regard to the stage at which reading and writing had been introduced into the French lesson.

The French classes were also compared on the basis of their rated enthusiasm for learning French. Classes reported to be showing a marked increase in their enthusiasm for French ('highly enthusiastic' classes) were identified and compared with classes reported to be showing some increase in enthusiasm for French ('moderately enthusiastic' classes) and also with those reported to be showing no increase in enthusiasm for French or less enthusiasm than hitherto ('unenthusiastic' classes). Chi-square tests were carried out to determine whether classes showing differing degrees of enthusiasm for French also differed significantly from one another in other respects. The results of the chi-square tests are shown in Table 5.5 in Appendix 5. All variables which proved to be non-significant have been omitted from Table 5.5. Classes with varying degrees of enthusiasm for French show corresponding variations in their level of achievement in French: 'highly enthusiastic' and 'moderately enthusiastic' classes tend to be those in which both overall fluency and specific aspects of the pupils' command of spoken French are reported to have shown marked or moderate improvement during the period under study; 'unenthusiastic' classes tend to be those in which little or no evidence of improvement has been reported. The pattern of significant differences between 'highly enthusiastic', 'moderately enthusiastic' and 'unenthusiastic' classes closely parallels that which exists between 'high-progress', 'moderate-progress' and 'low-progress' classes. Almost the only point of difference is that pupils in 'highly enthusiastic' and 'moderately enthusiastic' classes differ significantly from those in 'unenthusiastic' classes in the extent to which their pronunciation is considered to have improved, whereas pupils in 'high-progress', 'moderate-progress' and 'low-progress' classes do not differ significantly from one another in this respect. Neither improved fluency nor increased enthusiasm for French appear to be significantly related to the size or composition of the French class, although there is a tendency for classes containing fewer than 20 pupils to show less improvement in fluency than classes containing more than 20 pupils.

On second and subsequent visits to a French class, HM Inspectors were asked to indicate the major factors in the teaching situation to which the improvement of the class, or failure to show improvement, might be attributed. They were also invited to amplify their answers to the pre-coded sections of the questionnaire if they considered that any aspect of a particular teaching situation had received inadequate coverage. Additional material contributed in this manner proved extremely valuable in helping to identify and illuminate the factors leading to success or failure in learning French. In classes where pupils were reported to be making little or no progress in their command of French, or were failing to maintain a previously higher standard of performance, the teaching situation was rarely felt to be deficient from a single point of view, but rather to suffer from a combination of unfavourable circumstances. Factors considered most inimical to the progress of the class in French included: an inexperienced teacher, unfamiliar with the demands of the oral approach to language teaching; a teacher who was linguistically competent, but who had received no specific training for primary teaching; a teacher whose linguistic competence was inadequate to meet the demands of teaching French at the primary level; an over-active teacher, who allowed the pupils no scope for initiative; prolonged absence of the French teacher or frequent changes of teaching staff; lack of provision for systematic revision of familiar material; a class containing a disproportionate number of low-achieving pupils; a class of abnormal size; a class with a high mobility rate; poor classroom conditions. In classes where pupils were reported to be making good progress, it was generally agreed that the pupils' achievement in French was mainly attributable to the teacher's skill in establishing good teacher-pupil relationships, maintaining the pupils' enthusiasm for French, and making the most effective use of the French teaching materials. Other factors which were thought to contribute towards a high level of achievement in French included: a marked increase over the period of the experiment in the fluency, confidence and enthusiasm of the French teacher; the successful involvement of all members of the class in the activities of the French lesson; continuity of teaching; appropriate and stimulating French teaching materials; systematic revision of familiar material; a stable class of reasonable size; good classroom conditions.

It was evident from the reports received, however, that no feature of the teaching situation was considered as important a factor in the development of proficiency in French as the teacher's skill in the use of primary teaching methods. Such skill was felt to outweigh even linguistic competence as a determinant of successful French teaching at the primary level. Classes reported to be making little or no progress were felt to be receiving 'inadequate' teaching, but such inadequacy was rarely felt to result solely or primarily from the teacher's poor command of French. Some teachers were felt to be hampered by lack of confidence in their linguistic ability, and a few were considered to have only a 'shaky' grasp of French, but, on the whole, standards of proficiency in French were thought to be adequate to meet the demands of the situation, provided that the teachers concerned could make effective use of primary teaching methods. 'Inadequate' teaching was generally held to derive, not from the French teacher's lack of linguistic ability, but rather from lack of experience as a primary teacher or lack of specific training for primary teaching. 'Poor' teachers were described as having 'much to learn about technique' and 'little idea of oral methods', showing 'lack of appreciation of the children's difficulties' and allowing their pupils 'little scope for using their initiative'. They were frequently reported to monopolize classroom conversation, prompting the children's replies to such an extent that the children themselves rarely formulated complete sentences and came to accept a passive role as observers of the teacher's dramatic performance. The successful French teacher, on the other hand, was characteristically described as one who did not dominate classroom conversation, but instead worked to develop a high level of class participation.

The pupils' response to learning French was generally considered to be directly related to the teacher's skill, confidence and enthusiasm. In classes where the pupils were seen to be making good progress, the pace of the French lesson was reported to be brisk, the presentation of material lively and confident; in classes where there was little evidence of progress, the pace of the lesson was reported to be slow, the presentation dull. A brisk pace, lively presentation of material, the involvement of all pupils in a variety of well-directed activities—these were considered essential to ensure a good response from the class. Examples of good practice were frequently given, but it was also reported that the successful use of group work was rarely observed. Group work was more often reported as tending to become noisy and over-active, with 'the action outstripping the command of French'. It was generally felt that there was a need for greater emphasis on the development of group work, particularly in mixed-ability classes, where the less able pupils were frequently observed to be insufficiently involved in the activities of the French lesson. It was recognized, however, that, in a number of schools, unfavourable classroom conditions (lack of space, fixed seating arrangements, an abnormally large or small class) hindered the successful development of group work.

The classes under observation varied considerably in size and composition. In 58 per cent of the classes, the pupils were being taught French in mixed-ability groups; in the remainder, they were streamed according to ability. The French classes ranged in size from three to 49 pupils: 15 per cent of the classes contained 10 pupils or less, 13 per cent contained 11-20 pupils, 16 per cent contained 21-30 pupils, 45 per cent contained 31-40 pupils and the remaining 11 per cent contained 41 pupils or more. The difficulties of teaching French by audio-visual methods in classes of abnormal size were frequently described. In very small classes, a stimulating atmosphere proved difficult to sustain. The tendency for classes containing fewer than 20 pupils to show less improvement in fluency than those containing 20 pupils or more, noted above, was illustrated by comments such as: 'The group is too small and so lacks vitality'; 'The children seek safety in chorus answers'; 'The group is so small that it tended to be a little shy and withdrawn'; 'The group has become too small to be really stimulating'. In large mixed-ability classes, on the other hand, the main problem encountered was that of organizing group work which would actively involve the less able members of the class. In some mixed-ability classes, the progress of the less able pupils had exceeded expectation and reports were received of 'the confidence and success with which less able children use the language', their 'impressive performance' and 'enthusiastic, efficient response'. In some cases, progress was less marked, but the children's response to learning French was nevertheless enthusiastic: 'Although the headmaster and teacher find that progress is slow, the pupils' obvious enjoyment of the lesson and their keen effort in the activities suggest that the course is worthwhile for them'. In other classes of similar size and composition, however, it was reported that the less able pupils were making very little progress and had 'lost heart'. Pupils were reported to have 'only the most limited ability to manipulate the language' or to be capable merely of 'limited Pavlovian responses'. Teachers were seen to be 'losing patience with the slowest ones' or to have 'given up the attempt to ensure understanding'. A corresponding 'sense of failure on the part of the children' was observed. There was general agreement that the 'least able need the stimulus of being more individually involved' and that their active participation in the French lesson could only be achieved by means of effective and imaginative group work. This point of view is supported by the finding that classes whose fluency had markedly improved during the period under study tended to be those in which the teacher had been able to increase the opportunities for less able pupils to take an active part in the French lesson.

Another factor considered to have an important effect on pupils' attitudes and achievement was the maintenance of continuity in the teaching of French. In schools which had suffered from 'a considerable number of changes of French teacher' during the period under study, adverse effects on the pupils' response to French were discerned. Even when stability had ultimately been achieved, 'the ravages of previous staff instability' were often still evident in the form of 'anti-French feeling' as well as in lack of fluency. In a few cases, however, a change of French teacher had produced a beneficial effect on class attitudes and achievement. There were several reports of how 'effective salvage' could 'transform' a class which had previously received 'slipshod' teaching, producing an 'amazing improvement in attitude and attainment'.

The systematic revision of familiar material and the timely provision of supplementary materials were also mentioned as factors contributing to achievement in French. A common criticism of the French teaching materials in use in the classes under observation was that there was a lack of revision material and an insufficient provision of reading matter. Pupils were reported to be 'insecure' in classes where the teacher had failed to 'consolidate' the pupils' earlier learning and had attempted to force too rapid a pace. Teachers who had devised their own revision materials were often considered to have 'saved' the class. The pupils' enthusiasm for French was also reported to have increased in classes where the French teacher had been able to provide supplementary reading materials of an appropriate level of difficulty, but it was generally agreed that suitable material was in scarce supply. There were several reports that the BBC television film series 'La Chasse au Trésor', intended for primary school pupils in their third year of learning French, had stimulated the pupils' interest in French and had increased their confidence in their ability to understand spoken French.

The evaluation of the French-teaching situation in the Pilot Scheme primary schools by members of HM Inspectorate will continue until the end of the primary stage fieldwork in the summer of 1971. It is anticipated that the analysis of all reports relating to the primary stage will be completed early in 1972.

SECTION SIX

Achievement in French in the Secondary School

IN September 1967 the pupils forming the first experimental cohort transferred to their secondary schools. Efforts were made to trace all pupils who had been included in the original experimental sample in 1964 and who were known to be in Pilot Scheme primary schools at the time of the final administration of the general attainment battery. Approximately 4,400 of the 5,700 first cohort pupils initially tested for general attainment in 1964 were subsequently re-tested for general attainment before leaving their primary schools. Most of these pupils were traced fairly rapidly, but it soon became apparent that, in some areas, the parents of the most able pupils in the sample had exercised their right to send their children to independent or direct grant schools, which were not among the secondary schools specifically prepared to receive pupils from the primary schools taking part in the experiment. In order to preserve the wide range of ability present in the original sample, it was therefore necessary to locate each secondary school whose intake included pupils from the Pilot Scheme primary schools, even though these pupils might be few in number. This proved to be a lengthy process, since some of these schools were outside the original Pilot Scheme areas. Eventually, however, all secondary schools whose first-year intake included six or more pupils from the original first cohort sample were traced: by the spring of 1968, 4,300 first cohort pupils had been traced to 85 secondary schools. This group of schools was composed of 37 secondary modern schools, 28 grammar schools (maintained, direct grant and independent), eight comprehensive schools, six bilateral schools, five county secondary schools and one senior high school. It was found that 55 per cent of the first cohort pupils had transferred to the secondary modern schools, 25 per cent to the grammar schools, 11 per cent to the comprehensive schools, five per cent to the bilateral schools and the remaining four per cent to the county secondary schools. Pupils in the different parental occupation categories were not found to be evenly distributed among the different types of secondary school. The secondary modern and bilateral schools in the sample had received proportionately fewer pupils in the 'professional' and 'clerical' parental occupation categories and proportionately more pupils in the 'semi-skilled' and 'unskilled' categories than had the grammar schools or the comprehensive schools. The grammar schools had also received proportionately more pupils in the 'clerical' parental occupation category and proportionately fewer pupils in the 'skilled' and 'semi-skilled' categories than had the comprehensive schools. The social composition of the different types of secondary school whose intake included first cohort pupils is shown in Table 15 and presented in greater detail in Table 6.1 in Appendix 6. Table 6.1 shows the distribution of the sample by type of school, sex of pupil, and parental occupation. Since they are so few in number, first cohort pupils attending secondary schools other than secondary modern, grammar, or comprehensive schools have been grouped together for purposes of analysis.

TABLE 15: *Cohort 1. Distribution of sample by type of school and parental occupation*

TYPE OF SCHOOL		PARENTAL OCCUPATION					
		Profess-ional	*Clerical*	*Skilled*	*Semi-skilled*	*Un-skilled*	TOTAL
Secondary Modern	N	161	301	956	591	376	2385
	%	6·75	12·62	40·08	24·78	15·77	100
Grammar	N	234	276	369	131	67	1077
	%	21·73	25·63	34·26	12·16	6·22	100
Comprehensive	N	81	79	176	81	35	452
	%	17·92	17·48	38·94	17·92	7·74	100
All Other Types	N	21	49	92	155	69	386
	%	5·44	12·69	23·83	40·16	17·88	100
All Types Combined	N	497	705	1593	958	547	4300
	%	11·55	16·40	37·05	22·28	12·72	100

The final stage of the evaluation of the Pilot Scheme includes an assessment of the level of achievement in French reached by the pupils in the experimental sample at the end of their second year in secondary school. Arrangements were accordingly made to administer an advanced battery of French tests (Battery 2) in the summer of 1969 to all first cohort pupils who had been successfully traced to their secondary schools. Battery 2 contains three group tests, designed to measure listening comprehension, reading comprehension, and ability to write in French, and one individually-administered test designed to measure ability to speak in French. The construction of Battery 2 will only be described in outline at the present time, since the tests which make up the battery are still subject to the security requirements of the experiment. The detailed specifications of the tests will be made available in a later report, when all the pupils taking part in the experiment have completed their second year in secondary school.

The Battery 2 Listening test is in three parts and carries a maximum score of 40. The first part of the test contains 20 multiple-choice picture-items. Each item consists of a tape-recorded sentence or sentences in French, describing one of a series of four pictures printed in the pupil's test booklet. The pupil is required to identify the picture which he hears described and to indicate his choice by marking his test booklet appropriately. The second part of the test consists of 14 remarks or questions, tape-recorded in French. The pupil's task is to select the most appropriate rejoinder or reply to each remark or question from among four alternative responses. The final part of the test contains six short passages of spoken French, in the form of tape-recorded broadcasts or announcements. The passages are followed by multiple-choice questions in French, to test the pupil's understanding of the material. All instructions for the test are given in English and each part of the test is preceded by appropriate practice examples. The test is paced by the master-tape and takes less than 20 minutes to administer.

The Battery 2 Reading test is in two parts and carries a maximum score of 44. The first part of the test contains 20 multiple-choice sentence-completion items. Each sentence has one word omitted. The pupil is required to select the missing word from among the four alternatives printed in his test booklet. He is not required to write the word in question, but simply to identify it. The second part of the test contains eight short prose passages in French, followed by multiple-choice questions in French, designed to test the pupil's understanding of what he has read. As for the Listening test, all instructions for the Reading test are given in English and appropriate practice examples precede each part of the test. The maximum time allowance for the test is 35 minutes.

The Battery 2 Writing test is in three parts and carries a maximum score of 80. The first part of the test contains 24 sentence-completion items. Each item consists of a sentence in French from which one word has been omitted. The pupil is required to supply the missing word. The second part of the test contains a short prose passage in French from which certain words have been omitted. The pupil is expected to supply the missing words and to write them in the appropriate spaces in his test-booklet. The final part of the test contains 10 sentences in French, of which only the first few words have been provided. The pupil is required to complete each sentence in free style. All instructions for the Writing test are given in English and suitable practice examples are provided. The maximum time allowance for the test is 35 minutes.

The Battery 2 Speaking test is in four parts and carries a maximum score of 99. The first part of the test consists of 20 short sentences in French, which the pupil is required to listen to and then repeat. In the second part of the test, the pupil is expected to respond in French to 10 simple questions, each of which refers to a black and white illustration in the pupil's test booklet. In the third part of the test, the pupil is provided with a large and fairly complex picture and is asked to describe it in French. In the final part of the Speaking test, the pupil is required to read aloud a short passage of French prose. Throughout the test, the pupil's responses are recorded on magnetic tape. All instructions for the test are given in English and practice examples are provided where appropriate. There is no time limit for the Speaking test, since each pupil is allowed to work at his own speed, but, in practice, pupils rarely require more than six minutes in which to complete the test.

Battery 2 was administered to the first cohort in the summer of 1969. All pupils took the three group tests. The Speaking test was administered to a sub-sample of one in ten, from which had been excluded all pupils with a known speech defect, all pupils considered by their teachers to be psychologically unsuited for individual testing, and any pupil who had been absent during the administration of the three group tests. The results obtained from the administration of the Battery 2 French tests are summarized below.

Administration of Battery 2: summary of results.

A detailed breakdown of the Battery 2 test scores is presented in Tables 6.2 to 5.5 in Appendix 6. These tables show mean scores for each French test, distributed by type of school, sex of pupil, and parental occupation. As before, the 'professional' and 'clerical' parental occupation categories have been combined to form a single category. Secondary schools other than secondary modern, grammar or comprehensive schools have likewise been considered as a single group for purposes of analysis. The results obtained from the administration of Battery 2 may be summarized as follows:

1. *Sex Differences*

Taking the sample as a whole, mean scores for girls are significantly higher than those for boys. Significant differences between mean scores in favour of the girls occur to a greater extent on the Reading test and the Writing test than on the Speaking test and the Listening test. Significant differences between the sexes with regard to test performance tend to occur more frequently in the secondary modern schools than in the comprehensive schools or the grammar schools. The results for each of the Battery 2 French tests will be considered separately:

(i) *Speaking test*. With all school groups and parental occupation categories combined, there is a significant difference between mean scores in favour of the girls: this difference is significant at the one per cent level. Within the different types of school, however, significant differences between mean scores in favour of the girls only occur in the secondary modern schools and in the 'all other types' group of schools. Mean scores for boys and girls in the grammar schools and in the comprehensive schools do not differ significantly.

(ii) *Listening test*. With all school groups and parental occupation categories combined, there is a significant difference between mean scores in favour of the girls: this difference is significant at the 0·1 per cent level. Within the different types of school, but with all parental occupation categories combined, significant differences in favour of the girls occur only in the secondary modern schools and in the 'all other types' group of schools: these differences are significant at the 0·1 per cent level. In the comprehensive schools, significant differences between mean scores in favour of the girls occur in the 'professional and clerical' and 'semi-skilled' parental occupation categories, but the differences between the sexes are not significant when all parental occupation categories are combined. In the grammar schools, there are no significant differences between boys' and girls' mean scores.

(iii) *Reading test*. When all school groups are combined, there are significant differences between mean scores in favour of the girls within each parental occupation category: these differences are all significant at the 0·1 per cent level. Within the different types of school, but with all parental occupation categories combined, significant differences between mean scores in favour of the girls reach the 0·1 per cent level in the secondary modern schools and in the schools of the ' all other types' group, but reach the one per cent level in the grammar schools and the comprehensive schools. Significant differences in favour of the girls are concentrated in the 'professional and clerical' and 'semi-skilled' parental occupation categories in both the grammar and the comprehensive schools.

(iv) *Writing test.* When all school groups are combined, there are significant differences between mean scores in favour of the girls within each parental occupation: these differences are all significant at the 0·1 per cent level. Within the different types of school, but with all parental occupation categories combined, significant differences between mean scores in favour of the girls reach the 0·1 per cent level in the grammar schools, the secondary modern schools and the schools of the 'all other types' group. In the comprehensive schools, however, boys' and girls' mean scores do not differ significantly.

These results are shown in summary form in Table 16 and are presented in greater detail in Tables 6.2 to 6.5 in Appendix 6.

TABLE 16: *Battery 2 French Tests. Mean scores by sex of pupil*

SEX OF PUPIL		BATTERY 2 SPEAKING TEST	BATTERY 2 LISTENING TEST	BATTERY 2 READING TEST	BATTERY 2 WRITING TEST
Boys	N	217	1986	2006	2002
	x̄	56·33	18·29	19·86	19·05
	SD	23·61	6·78	9·44	17·45
Girls	N	231	2184	2204	2173
	x̄	63·21	19·78	23·24	24·93
	SD	23·79	6·86	9·80	18·22

2. Parental Occupation

Taking the sample as a whole, the Battery 2 results point to a linear relationship between test score and parental occupation. High mean scores on each Battery 2 French test coincide with high-status parental occupation and low mean scores with low-status parental occupation: mean scores for pupils in the different parental occupation categories differ significantly at the 0·1 per cent level. When the results for pupils in the various groups of schools are considered separately, however, the relationship between test score and parental occupation does not obtain with equal consistency within each type of secondary school. The results for each of the Battery 2 French tests will be considered separately:

(i) *Speaking test.* When scores for pupils of both sexes and in each type of secondary school are combined, high mean scores coincide with high-status parental occupation and low mean scores with low-status parental occupation. When each type of school is considered separately, however, differences between mean scores for pupils in the various parental occupation categories reach the one per cent level of significance in the grammar schools, but fail to reach a significant level in any other type of school.

(ii) *Listening test.* When scores for pupils of both sexes and in each type of secondary school are combined, high mean scores coincide with high-status parental occupation and low mean scores with low-status parental occupation. When each type of school is considered separately, mean scores for pupils in the various parental occupation categories differ significantly at the 0·1 per cent level in the secondary modern, comprehensive, and grammar schools, but do not differ significantly in the 'all other types' group of schools. Within the grammar and comprehensive schools, mean scores for pupils in the 'unskilled' category do not differ significantly from those for pupils in the 'semi-skilled' category.

(iii) *Reading test.* When scores for pupils of both sexes and in each type of secondary school are combined, high mean scores coincide with high-status parental occupation and low mean scores with low-status parental occupation. When each type of school is considered separately, mean scores for pupils in the various parental occupation categories differ significantly at the 0·1 per cent level in the secondary modern, grammar, and comprehensive schools and at the five per cent level in the 'all other types' group of schools. In this latter group of schools and in the secondary modern schools, mean scores for pupils in the 'unskilled' category do not differ significantly from those for pupils in the 'semi-skilled' category.

(iv) *Writing test.* When scores for pupils of both sexes and in each type of secondary school are combined, high mean scores coincide with high-status parental occupation and low mean scores with low-status parental occupation. When each type of school is considered separately, mean scores for pupils in the various parental occupation categories differ significantly at the 0·1 per cent level in the secondary modern, grammar, and comprehensive schools and at the one per cent level in the 'all other types' group of schools. Mean scores for pupils in the 'unskilled' category in each of these types of school do not, however, differ significantly from those for pupils in the 'semi-skilled' category.

These results are shown in summary form in Table 17 and are presented in greater detail in Tables 6.2 to 6.5 in Appendix 6. The association between test score and parental occupation is also illustrated in Figures 6.1 to 6.3 in Appendix 6. These figures show the distribution of scores for each of the Battery 2 group tests for pupils within each parental occupation category, but with scores for pupils of both sexes and within each school group combined.

TABLE 17: *Battery 2 French Tests. Mean scores by parental occupation*

| FRENCH TEST | | PARENTAL OCCUPATION | | | | TOTAL |
		Professional and Clerical	*Skilled*	*Semi-skilled*	*Unskilled*	
Battery 2	N	129	179	91	49	448
Speaking Test	x̄	70·09	57·64	55·23	49·81	59·88
	SD	24·13	22·30	24·12	19·53	23·95
Battery 2	N	1173	1543	925	529	4170
Listening Test	x̄	22·06	18·96	17·05	16·27	19·07
	SD	7·32	6·47	5·91	5·88	6·86
Battery 2	N	1183	1553	936	538	4210
Reading Test	x̄	26·82	21·09	18·28	17·59	21·63
	SD	9·97	9·36	8·03	8·26	9·77
Battery 2	N	1177	1546	922	530	4175
Writing Test	x̄	32·10	21·02	15·39	14·79	22·11
	SD	19·51	16·87	14·21	13·98	18·09

3. *School Type*

There are obvious differences in the test performance of pupils in the different types of secondary school. Mean scores obtained by the grammar school pupils on each of the Battery 2 French tests are significantly higher than those obtained by the comprehensive school pupils. Both sets of scores are significantly higher than those obtained by the secondary modern school pupils or by the pupils in the 'all other types' group of schools. Mean scores obtained by secondary modern pupils do not differ significantly from those obtained by pupils in the 'all other types' group of schools.

These results are shown in summary form in Table 18 and presented in greater detail in Tables 6.2 to 6.5 in Appendix 6. The results for each of the Battery 2 groups test are also illustrated in Figures 6.4 to 6.6 in Appendix 6. These figures show the distribution of scores within each school group, with scores for pupils of both sexes and within the different parental occupation categories combined.

TABLE 18: *Battery 2 French Tests. Mean scores by type of secondary school*

TYPE OF SCHOOL		BATTERY 2 SPEAKING TEST	BATTERY 2 LISTENING TEST	BATTERY 2 READING TEST	BATTERY 2 WRITING TEST
	N	249	2306	2342	2307
Secondary	x̄	50·83	16·19	16·93	13·11
Modern	SD	21·66	5·25	6·84	11·18
	N	107	1046	1044	1054
Grammar	x̄	78·22	25·56	32·23	42·62
	SD	18·64	5·83	6·90	14·47
	N	53	444	448	442
Comprehensive	x̄	69·47	20·76	24·88	26·89
	SD	21·90	6·99	9·98	17·92
	N	39	374	376	372
All Other Types	x̄	54·33	16·67	17·59	14·11
	SD	19·70	4·93	6·96	11·84

4. *Correlations Between the Battery 2 French Test Scores*

The French tests which make up Battery 2 correlate highly with one another. The extent to which the scores on the four tests correlate with one another is shown in Table 19. The highest correlation is that of 0·89, between the Reading and Writing test scores, and the lowest correlation is that of 0·74, between the Speaking and Listening test scores. It was anticipated that the Reading and Writing test scores would correlate highly with one another, since both tests are designed to measure ability to understand and use the written forms of the language, but the high correlation between the Speaking and Writing test scores was unexpected. Further analysis of the Speaking test sub-scores will therefore be undertaken, to determine the extent to which the different sections of the test contribute towards this correlation.

It must be emphasized, of course, that the results reported above represent no more than the first phase of the evaluation of the

TABLE 19: *Cohort 1. Correlations between the Battery 2 French test scores*

BATTERY 2 TEST	SPEAKING	LISTENING	READING	WRITING
Speaking	1·00	—	—	—
Listening	0·74	1·00	—	—
Reading	0·81	0·81	1·00	—
Writing	0·82	0·79	0·89	1·00

Note: The correlations shown in Table 19 between the Listening, Reading and Writing test scores are based on 3,979 cases. The correlations between the Speaking test scores and the Listening, Reading and Writing test scores are based on 440 cases.

secondary stage of the experiment. The Battery 2 French tests will be administered to the pupils in the second cohort in 1970 and to the pupils in the third cohort in 1973. The same tests will also be administered in 1970 to control groups of secondary school pupils, who did not learn French during their primary school career but were introduced to the language in their first term of secondary school. Some control groups will consist of pupils who are the same age as the pupils in the experimental groups at the time of testing, but who will have been taught French for a shorter period than the latter. Other control groups will consist of pupils who will have received as much instruction in French as the pupils in the experimental groups at the time of testing, but who will be older than the latter. The final analysis of the Battery 2 French test results, to be carried out during 1973-1974, will conclude this phase of the evaluation.

Pupils' Attitudes Towards Learning French in the Secondary School

THE pupils in the first experimental cohort completed their second year of secondary education in the summer of 1969. This point in time also marked the end of their fifth year of learning French and the final opportunity to assess their attitudes towards learning French. Towards the end of the summer term, therefore, all pupils involved in the longitudinal study were asked to indicate their attitudes towards learning French by completing a 28-item attitude questionnaire. This questionnaire also contained a sentence-completion section, in which pupils were asked to complete sentences such as: 'What I like about learning French is . . .' In addition, pupils were encouraged to comment on any aspect of learning French which had not been specifically covered by the questionnaire items. Most of these items had previously been used in the attitude questionnaire administered to the first cohort at the end of the primary stage in 1967, but some new items had been introduced which invited comparison of the primary and secondary stages of learning French, such as: I like learning French more now than I did in the primary school', or 'I think everyone should start learning French in the primary school'. The purpose of repeating items originally used in the primary stage questionnaire was to provide a basis for the assessment of any shift in opinion which might have taken place during the intervening two-year period of secondary education.

As on previous occasions, the questionnaires were completed in class. Pupils were encouraged to express their opinions freely and were given the assurance that neither their teacher nor their classmates would read what they had written. All pupils were instructed to write their name on the questionnaire before responding to the items and to indicate in general terms whether they liked learning French or not. This was to enable a subsequent comparison of pupils' attitudes towards learning French with their performance on the Battery 2 French tests.

Approximately 4,300 completed questionnaires were returned to the NFER during the summer of 1969. Since the initial analysis of the Battery 2 French test results had revealed marked differences in pupils' level of achievement in the different types of secondary school, the questionnaire data were analysed with reference to school type as well as to pupils' sex and general attitudes towards learning French. For reasons of economy, the analysis of the questionnaire data was confined to the three main types of secondary school—secondary modern, grammar, and comprehensive—which between them accounted for more than 90 per cent of the first cohort pupils. The responses made by these pupils to the questionnaire items are shown in full in Tables 7.1-7.28 in Appendix 7. These tables show the percentage of pupils who agree with each item statement, distributed by type of school, sex of pupil, and general attitude towards learning French.

When they were in their final primary term, more than half the pupils in the first cohort had unfavourable attitudes towards learning French: 53 per cent stated that they disliked learning French, whereas 47 per cent stated that they liked it. After two years in the secondary school, a more favourable trend is apparent: 56 per cent of the first cohort now like learning French, compared with 44 per cent who do not. Girls are still more favourably inclined towards learning French than boys are: 63 per cent of the girls in the first cohort enjoy learning French, but only 49 per cent of the boys do so. Table 20 shows the percentage of first cohort pupils who like or dislike learning French, distributed within the three main types of secondary school.

It is immediately apparent that the secondary modern schools contain a disproportionately large number of pupils with unfavourable attitudes towards learning French. This group of schools contains the highest percentage of both boys and girls who dislike French and, correspondingly, the lowest percentage of those who like French. The converse is true of the grammar schools. In the comprehensive schools, the percentage of pupils who like or dislike French falls approximately midway between that found in the other two types of secondary school. In this instance, only pupils' general attitudes towards learning French are in question, but, when pupils' responses to specific questionnaire items are examined, a similar pattern emerges: whatever the point at issue, unfavourable attitudes towards learning French are most frequently found among secondary modern school pupils, favourable attitudes are most frequently found among grammar school pupils, while pupils in comprehensive schools tend to occupy an intermediate position. For example, a significantly higher percentage of pupils in grammar schools than in secondary modern or comprehensive schools agree that they would like to speak several languages, that they would like to go to France and

Pupils' Attitudes Towards Learning French in the Secondary School

TABLE 20: *Percentage of pupils who like/dislike French within the different types of secondary school*

TYPE OF SCHOOL SEX OF PUPIL	PUPILS WHO LIKE FRENCH (%)	PUPILS WHO DISLIKE FRENCH (%)
Secondary Modern Boys	40	60
Secondary Modern Girls	58	42
Secondary Modern Total	49	51
Grammar Boys	67	33
Grammar Girls	72	28
Grammar Total	70	30
Comprehensive Boys	54	46
Comprehensive Girls	67	33
Comprehensive Total	61	39

meet French people, that they find French easier than other subjects and want to continue learning French in their third year, that French will be useful to them in future life, that their parents are pleased that they are learning French, and that all children should start to learn French in the primary school. Grammar school pupils also tend to to support the view that learning French facilitates the subsequent learning of other modern languages. They frequently claim that their knowledge of French has helped them to speak and understand languages such as Russian or German. Secondary modern pupils tend to take a considerably less favourable view of learning French. A significantly higher percentage of pupils in secondary modern schools than in grammar or comprehensive schools agree that they are not interested in learning foreign languages, that it is a waste of

99

time to learn French, since they are unlikely ever to speak French once they leave school, that French is becoming increasingly difficult and is harder for them than other subjects, that there are many more important subjects than French to learn in school, and that the French should learn English rather than the reverse. On each of these issues, pupils in comprehensive schools respond more favourably than secondary modern school pupils, but less favourably than grammar school pupils.

Unfavourable attitudes towards learning French, whatever the specific point at issue, are more characteristic of the boys in the sample than the girls. This is particularly true of the pupils in the secondary modern schools, where there is a high concentration of boys who dislike learning French. Fifty-eight per cent of these boys regard learning French as a waste of time; 67 per cent believe that a knowledge of French will be of no use to them, once they leave school. As one of them wrote: 'What use is this French to me? I would like to be involved with electricity, so where will French come in?' 'I would rather learn electronics than French', wrote another. Boys in the secondary modern schools tend to regard French as 'a ladies' language' or as a language for 'high society', of little relevance to their own future. Favourable attitudes towards learning French are more typically held by the girls in the sample, particularly those attending grammar schools. Eighty-five per cent of the grammar school girls who like learning French consider that their knowledge of French will be useful to them when they leave school; 94 per cent of this group are eager to continue learning French. The corresponding percentages for the sample as a whole on these two issues are respectively 61 per cent and 55 per cent. Significantly more girls than boys also consider that all children should start to learn French in the primary school. The only reservation that girls tend to express regarding the introduction of French at the primary stage is that the French course materials do not include enough 'written work'. The view more typically taken by boys is that 'young children have more important things to learn', or that French is 'too hard to understand' and 'too confusing' for primary school children.

Significant differences between the attitudes held by boys and girls are found much more frequently among secondary modern and grammar school pupils than among comprehensive school pupils. In the comprehensive schools, boys and girls tend to share the same attitudes towards learning French, in the same way that they tend to reach similar levels of achievement. Within each type of secondary school, however, the pupils' level of achievement in French appears to be closely associated with their attitudes towards learning French. After two years in the secondary school, the pattern of achievement is very similar to that reported at the end of the primary stage: boys and girls with favourable attitudes towards learning French tend to obtain significantly higher scores on each of the French tests than do those with unfavourable attitudes towards learning French. Significant differences between mean scores are particularly evident in the higher parental occupation categories. On the Speaking test, for example, girls in the 'professional and clerical' parental occupation category who like French obtain a mean score of 74·92, whereas those who dislike French obtain a mean score of 46·45. Within the same parental occupation category, boys who like French obtain a mean score of 75·37, while those who dislike French obtain a mean score of 57·23. The results of the three group tests follow a similar pattern: for pupils of both sexes, high scores are associated with favourable attitudes towards French and low scores with unfavourable attitudes. On the Writing test, for example, boys in the 'professional and clerical' category who like French obtain a mean score of 35·78, whereas boys who dislike French obtain a mean score of 20. Girls in the same parental occupation category who like French obtain a mean score of 40·29, whereas those who dislike French obtain a mean score of 26·09. This pattern of results is repeated within each parental occupation category. The results for each of the Battery 2 French tests, distributed by pupils' sex, attitude towards French, and parental occupation category, are shown in summary form in Tables 21 to 24.

The Battery 2 French test results, summarized in Tables 21 to 24, are shown in greater detail in Tables 7.29 - 7.32 in Appendix 7. These tables show mean scores for each of the Battery 2 French tests, distributed by type of school, sex of pupil, attitude towards French, and parental occupation category.

The association between attitude and achievement, outlined above, is extremely similar to that reported at the end of the primary stage. Similarly, after two years in the secondary school, pupils' attitudes towards the different aspects of learning French show only minor variations from the attitudes which they held at the end of their fourth year in the primary school. The majority of pupils, particularly those with favourable attitudes towards learning French, still consider that the main reason for learning French is to be able to communicate with French-speaking people. As one grammar school pupil wrote: 'I like French, because it is a sort of passport to other people's countries.' Another wrote: 'It brings us closer to people if we speak their language and this is important to stop wars'. Most of

TABLE 21: *Battery 2 Speaking Test. Mean scores by sex of pupil, attitude towards French, and parental occupation*

SEX OF PUPIL ATTITUDE TO FRENCH		Professional and Clerical	Skilled	Semi-skilled	Unskilled	TOTAL
		PARENTAL OCCUPATION				
Boys who like French	N	45	49	17	10	121
	x̄	75·37	62·97	52·05	54·60	65·36
	SD	23·43	22·61	21·32	19·79	24·11
Boys who dislike French	N	13	35	16	12	76
	x̄	57·23	43·20	37·31	42·66	44·27
	SD	26·41	14·73	12·47	11·18	17·65
Girls who like French	N	55	65	25	11	156
	x̄	74·92	66·63	69·36	63·81	69·79
	SD	22·56	20·52	24·25	19·87	22·20
Girls who dislike French	N	11	18	15	10	54
	x̄	46·45	44·61	53·13	40·20	46·53
	SD	13·43	17·58	25·71	17·78	20·07

TABLE 22: *Battery 2 Listening Test. Mean scores by sex of pupil, attitude towards French, and parental occupation*

SEX OF PUPIL ATTITUDE TO FRENCH		Professional and Clerical	Skilled	Semi-skilled	Unskilled	TOTAL
		PARENTAL OCCUPATION				
Boys who like French	N	313	324	151	88	876
	x̄	23·60	21·30	18·27	17·23	21·19
	SD	7·25	6·87	5·98	6·03	7·15
Boys who dislike French	N	200	379	193	138	910
	x̄	18·51	16·26	14·73	14·44	16·15
	SD	6·09	5·41	4·87	5·78	5·70
Girls who like French	N	423	480	230	129	1262
	x̄	24·38	20·90	19·36	17·58	21·45
	SD	7·04	6·50	6·65	6·30	7·08
Girls who dislike French	N	177	264	196	108	745
	x̄	19·90	17·53	15·93	16·01	17·45
	SD	6·88	5·65	5·25	5·23	6·01

TABLE 23: *Battery 2 Reading Test. Mean scores by sex of pupil, attitude towards French, and parental occupation*

SEX OF PUPIL ATTITUDE TO FRENCH		Professional and Clerical	Skilled	Semi-skilled	Unskilled	TOTAL
Boys who like	N	313	321	154	90	878
French	x̄	28·59	23·90	19·35	18·21	24·19
	SD	9·42	9·70	8·24	8·69	10·02
Boys who dislike	N	200	384	203	137	924
French	x̄	20·24	16·44	14·97	14·78	16·69
	SD	8·79	7·72	5·91	6·94	7·76
Girls who like	N	428	484	229	132	1273
French	x̄	31·09	24·76	22·44	21·10	26·09
	SD	9·12	9·28	8·91	9·34	9·90
Girls who dislike	N	177	268	198	112	755
French	x̄	23·89	19·01	17·35	17·02	19·42
	SD	8·69	7·97	7·39	7·26	8·31

TABLE 24: *Battery 2 Writing Test. Mean scores by sex of pupil, attitude towards French, and parental occupation*

SEX OF PUPIL ATTITUDE TO FRENCH		Professional and Clerical	Skilled	Semi-skilled	Unskilled	TOTAL
Boys who like	N	318	326	150	88	882
French	x̄	35·78	25·65	16·55	16·70	26·86
	SD	19·41	18·41	14·41	14·63	19·37
Boys who dislike	N	201	377	206	136	920
French	x̄	20·00	13·15	10·10	9·66	13·45
	SD	16·70	13·05	9·73	10·41	13·49
Girls who like	N	418	483	226	130	1257
French	x̄	40·29	27·34	23·05	21·34	30·25
	SD	18·55	16·65	17·12	16·86	18·90
Girls who dislike	N	175	264	191	110	740
French	x̄	26·09	17·84	13·38	13·27	17·96
	SD	16·22	15·07	12·18	11·53	15·02

the pupils in the first cohort (84 per cent of the sample) expressed eagerness to visit France and establish contact with French people. This is particularly true of the girls in the sample. As a girl in one of the comprehensive schools explained: 'I'd like to see the French people's faces when they're trying to speak to me in English and I just answer them in fluent French'. Relatively few pupils (only 17 per cent of the sample) had actually been to France, however. At the time of completing the attitude questionnaire, 31 per cent of the comprehensive school pupils, 23 per cent of the grammar school pupils and 12 per cent of the secondary modern school pupils had been to France. Boys and girls were equally represented in the number of pupils visiting France, but, in each type of secondary school, the proportion of pupils visiting France increased with the social status of the pupils' parents. Of those pupils who had visited France, 44 per cent had parents whose occupation fell within the 'professional and clerical' category, 34 per cent had parents whose occupation fell within the 'skilled' category, 16 per cent fell within the 'semi-skilled' category and the remaining six per cent within the 'unskilled' category. Viewed in relation to the social composition of the total sample, the pupils who had visited France represent 25 per cent of all pupils in the 'professional and clerical' parental occupation category, 15 per cent of all pupils in the 'skilled' category, 12 per cent of all those in the 'semi-skilled' category and eight per cent of those in the 'unskilled' category. The level of achievement in French of the pupils who had been to France proves to be significantly higher than that of the pupils who had not been to France, but the differing social structure of the two groups must be emphasized when their test performance is compared. Taking the sample as a whole, pupils who have been to France score significantly higher on each of the Battery 2 French tests than do those who have not been to France: differences between mean scores on each test are significant at the 0·1 per cent level. Within the different types of secondary school, significant differences between mean scores in favour of pupils who have visited France occur more frequently in the comprehensive and secondary modern schools than in the grammar schools. Mean scores for each of the Battery 2 French tests, distributed by pupils' contact with France and parental occupation category, but with scores for pupils of both sexes and in all school groups combined, are shown in summary form in Table 25. These results are presented in greater detail in Tables 7.33 to 7.36 in Appendix 7.

Pupils who have been to France also differ significantly from the rest of the sample in certain of their attitudes towards learning French.

Pupils' Attitudes Towards Learning French in the Secondary School

TABLE 25: *Battery 2 French Tests. Mean scores by pupils' contact with France and parental occupation*

BATTERY 2 FRENCH TEST CONTACT WITH FRANCE		Professional and Clerical	Skilled	Semi-skilled	Unskilled	TOTAL
Speaking Test:	N	38	27	11	5	81
Pupils who have	x̄	71·47	61·59	70·72	67·40	67·82
visited France	SD	20·55	25·01	25·38	10·96	22·49
Speaking Test:	N	89	152	81	41	363
Pupils who have not	x̄	69·66	56·94	52·70	48·41	58·15
visited France	SD	25·95	21·88	23·59	19·93	24·10
Listening Test:	N	306	238	115	46	705
Pupils who have	x̄	23·62	20·32	18·39	17·73	21·27
visited France	SD	7·45	6·97	6·08	6·22	7·33
Listening Test:	N	853	1280	800	469	3402
Pupils who have not	x̄	21·64	18·77	16·84	16·17	18·68
visited France	SD	7·21	6·33	5·86	5·85	6·69
Reading Test:	N	309	244	119	47	719
Pupils who have	x̄	29·05	23·76	20·30	18·68	25·13
visited France	SD	9·29	9·70	8·52	8·60	9·97
Reading Test:	N	859	1282	806	477	3424
Pupils who have not	x̄	26·22	20·68	18·07	17·56	21·02
visited France	SD	10·08	9·22	7·94	8·26	9·60
Writing Test:	N	305	236	112	44	697
Pupils who have	x̄	37·06	25·94	18·71	16·72	29·06
visited France	SD	18·39	18·53	16·16	13·79	19·37
Writing Test:	N	858	1283	803	472	3416
Pupils who have not	x̄	30·79	20·34	14·96	14·75	20·93
visited France	SD	19·78	16·45	13·96	14·10	17·64

For instance, a significantly higher proportion of the pupils who have been to France than of those who have not agree that they would like to speak many languages. A significantly higher proportion of those who have been to France also agree that all children should start to learn French in the primary school and state that they are looking forward to continuing their study of French in the third year of secondary school. Similarly, significantly more pupils who have been

105

to France consider that French will be useful to them in their future life and are confident that their parents approve their efforts to learn French. Pupils who have been to France also differ significantly from the rest of the sample in the extent to which they prefer speaking French to reading or writing it. They frequently comment on the satisfaction which they derive from their ability to communicate in another language. As one girl wrote: 'French gives me a chance to put my ideas into a language other than English'. Those who dislike learning French and who have had no contact with France, on the other hand, comment with equal frequency on their inability to master spoken French and describe their sense of inadequacy when confronted with the necessity to speak in French. 'I feel ashamed if I make a mistake in front of the class', wrote a girl in one of the secondary modern schools. 'I hate it when I have to speak in French. The class laughs at me if I say something wrong', wrote another. Twenty-one per cent of the sample (29 per cent of those who dislike French and 15 per cent of those who like French) admit to being afraid of speaking in French. This fear is more often expressed by girls than by boys and is more frequently reported by pupils in secondary modern schools than by those in any other type of secondary school.

At the end of the primary stage, 75 per cent of those who disliked French reported that they did not always understand what they were saying when they spoke in French, but simply repeated sounds which held no meaning for them. After two years in the secondary school, 74 per cent of those who dislike French report that they are still experiencing difficulties of a similar nature. Pupils in secondary modern schools, and especially the boys in these schools, seem particularly handicapped by their inability to understand spoken French. One such boy described his difficulties in the following terms: 'It is like teaching a parrot to speak. It can talk, but it doesn't know what it's talking about. After five years' training, I hardly understand a word of French'. Another secondary modern pupil wrote: 'I can speak in French, but I don't know what I am saying. I can even answer questions in French and still not understand'. A third concluded: 'French depends a lot on your teacher. Some are gentle in making you understand it, others just drill it into you until you repeat it to their liking, even though you don't understand it'. Most pupils agree that they find it more difficult to understand spoken French when they are listening to the tape-recorder than when they are listening to their French teacher. Whatever their attitude towards learning French, the majority of pupils in each type of secondary school (86 per cent of the total sample) report that they find the tape-recorder difficult to understand. In addition, pupils who dislike French frequently instance the difficulty of understanding the tape-recorded sections of the French lesson as the main reason for their dislike of French, while those who like French tend to describe the tape-recorded material as dull, repetitive and boring. The majority of pupils express a strong preference for realistic communication situations, 'not just listening to a tape'. One grammar school pupil wrote: 'Our teacher does not use the tape-recorder—she teaches us out of her own mind. I think this is much better because she teaches us how to ask for the toilets and how to buy something in a shop. It is much better than sitting back listening to the tape-recorder'. Few pupils appear to enjoy the predominantly passive role which listening to tape-recorded material entails, and the majority state a definite preference for visually-presented material. The tendency to prefer a visual rather than an auditory presentation of material was apparent among primary school pupils and is even more pronounced among secondary school pupils. The majority of pupils (77 per cent of the total sample) agree that it is easier to remember French words if they are presented visually rather than aurally, and express a marked preference for the visual components of their French course materials.

The pupils' preference for realistic teaching materials, noted in the primary school, is also more in evidence after two years in the secondary school. The pupils' most common criticism of their French course materials is that they are too 'babyish' in content. One grammar school pupil wrote: 'We should read French newspapers, etc., and have more active work, not listen to stories of little children'. A comprehensive school pupil agreed: 'There should be different projects in French which you could learn from and follow up—not just listening to a tape and watching a film'. Other pupils wanted to learn 'more about the French people', 'more about the French countryside and animal life', 'more about current affairs in France', or 'more about historical things'. On this last point, most pupils were careful to explain that they were interested in recent, rather than remote, historical events: 'Not the Battle of Hastings, but things like the first aeroplane or the life of Dr. Livingstone'. Pupils rarely lose sight of the fact that their main motive for learning French is to be able to communicate with French-speaking people and they criticise their course materials if the content does not appear to further the aim of communication. They are impatient with 'stories which hardly ever happen, or which go on forever about silly children messing around and getting mixed up with contraband men'. They complain that the dialogues which they learn in the French lesson are unlikely to be of use in a normal conversational setting. As one grammar school pupil wrote: 'I dislike the lack of probability. You wouldn't go up to a Frenchman and say "Le chat est noir".' Another wrote: 'I don't think the sort of things we learn in French will be of any use in conversations with French people. They do not give us enough scope to pick out words to use in conversations.' A third explained: 'We don't know how to make up our own sentences. It is not much help if all you know are sentences about kids going on picnics and drinking lemonade. It would be better if we could have French children visiting us, so that we could practise speaking French with them'.

Many pupils also complain that they are not given enough opportunity to practise spoken French in class, and therefore press for more group work, where 'everyone gets a chance to speak', or for smaller classes, where French could be taught 'more individually'. 'If there were just a few in the class, we would be able to get on with our French better and enjoy it more', explained a grammar school pupil. A number of pupils are in favour of 'setting' for French, on the grounds that 'some people find French harder than others and need more attention'. It emerges clearly from the pupils' comments that a considerable number, particularly in the secondary modern schools, find the pace of the French lesson still too fast and the greater emphasis on written work an increasing burden. 'In French we always have to do our best handwriting, all the time, and so little time to do it in', wrote a boy in one of the secondary modern schools, adding: 'And when I write my best, I cannot write fast, so I have many unfinished pieces of work'. Another wrote: 'I think French should be taught at different speeds. People who are good at French should be taught fast. People who do not understand should be taught at a much slower pace and should be given a fair chance to pick up the language'. He added: 'I myself am a slow learner'. Boys tend to favour 'setting' more than girls do: girls are more inclined to the view that French should be taught in mixed-ability classes, where 'the more backward in French could be asked to take part and be given a chance', and are aware that 'setting' might entail disadvantages for the low-achievers. As a girl in one of the grammar schools wrote: 'I don't like the idea of sets, because the lower set might feel inferior and think they were no good, and therefore not bother. Teachers sometimes get fed up with the hopeless and then make enemies of them'.

Although the majority of pupils in the first cohort agree that their enjoyment of French has increased during the secondary stage, this attitude is not equally characteristic of pupils in the different types of secondary school. The highest percentage of pupils whose liking for French has increased since the primary stage is found in the grammar schools and the lowest in the secondary modern schools. Secondary modern school pupils seem particularly to regret the loss of the activity methods of the primary school and to be deterred by the increasing emphasis on written work. 'We are learning verbs all the time now and we have no time to play games or have any fun', wrote one secondary modern pupil. 'In French all we do is write, write and write. We are behind in our schedule and we never get a chance to play games', wrote another. 'There is too much learning now and no songs and plays for us', wrote a third, concluding: 'I think that for the first four years we should only do French orally'. For grammar school pupils, on the other hand, interest in French often dates from the introduction of the written script and increases with the development of more advanced written work. To judge from the pupils' own comments, there is a strong case for redefining the objectives of teaching French, to meet the pupils' differing needs.

SECTION EIGHT

French in the Secondary School: the Viewpoint of the Secondary Head

IN the spring of 1969, when the first cohort pupils were in their second year of secondary school, a questionnaire was sent to the head of each of the 85 secondary schools whose intake included Pilot Scheme pupils. The purpose of the questionnaire was to elicit the head's impression of the effects of the Pilot Scheme at the secondary level, as observed in his own school, and to obtain details of any staffing and organizational problems which the need to provide French teaching to the Pilot Scheme intake might have caused. The secondary schools in the sample varied considerably in their experience of modern language teaching. The grammar schools, for example, tended to have a long-established tradition of language teaching and to offer, in addition to French, at least one other modern language (usually German, Spanish or Russian) and one classical language. The secondary modern schools, on the other hand, tended to offer French only and to have initiated their French programme in 1967, to cater for the first intake of pupils taught French under the Pilot Scheme.

The head of each school was asked to give his personal impression of the impact of the Pilot Scheme on the teaching of French at the secondary level and to indicate whether he was, on the whole, in favour of the introduction of French at the primary stage or not. When the completed questionnaires had been returned to the NFER, analysis of the heads' responses revealed a wide variety of opinions regarding the effects of the Pilot Scheme: heads' assessments were couched in terms which ranged from enthusiasm to hostility. The most enthusiastic advocates of the introduction of French at the primary stage are undoubtedly to be found in the secondary modern schools and in the comprehensive schools. The secondary modern and comprehensive school heads recognize that, as a result of the Pilot Scheme, more of their pupils than ever before are being given the opportunity to learn a second language and are successfully reaching a high level of achievement in the oral, if not the written, aspects of the language. As the head of a comprehensive school wrote: 'If it were not for the Pilot Scheme, most of these pupils

110

would not be studying French'. A secondary modern school head, anticipating that a greater proportion of his pupils would in future reach a higher level of achievement in public examinations, wrote: 'The considerable oral knowledge acquired by the children in the primary schools should form the basis for a greater competence than has usually been possible in former years at O- and A-level, and this competence should be attained by a larger proportion of pupils'. A few secondary modern school heads have nothing but praise for the results of the experiment. 'The scheme is wholly advantageous and will prove more so as experience grows', wrote one such head. 'French has served to widen the outlook of many of the pupils, whose background is often limited', wrote another, adding: 'It is difficult to believe that there has not been a transfer of benefit to other subjects from the pupils' increased confidence and interest'.

Heads of grammar schools, on the other hand, tend to view the experiment somewhat less favourably. The heads of no less than half of the grammar schools in the sample take either an unfavourable or a noncommittal view of the effects of the Pilot Scheme at the secondary level. Those who view the experiment unfavourably report that their intake now includes pupils 'whose inertia is not easy to overcome', or whose attitude towards learning French is one of open hostility. As one grammar school head wrote: 'The majority of children on entering this school are indifferent to French, if not openly hostile, and in their case the scheme appears to have done little good. We are able to restore some enthusiasm gradually, but in many cases the three years' French has been of little value'. Another wrote: 'Only a handful of the more intelligent pupils show any interest at all in any aspect of the subject'. Other grammar school heads complain of discipline problems, which they ascribe to the 'free play-way methods' used in the teaching of primary French, and of a decline in general attainment, which they feel must be linked with the introduction of French at the primary stage. One grammar school head asked: 'Is the decline in the standard of English of the less able 11 + entrants and the marked deterioration in English spelling to be attributed to the introduction of primary French, as well as the lack of general knowledge which is becoming more marked in History and Mathematics?' Another commented: 'Whether primary French is the cause or no, we do not know, but these children write less easily than former groups'. In a quarter of the grammar schools in the sample, the head adopts a noncommittal attitude towards the introduction of French at the primary stage, reserving his judgment until the results of O- or A-level examinations are to hand. 'I do not think we can be too sure of their attainments until we see the standard at fifth form stage', wrote a grammar school head of his Pilot Scheme pupils. 'Clearly they have certain skills in French, notably in speaking, which their contemporaries have not, but it is too early to say whether their general competence in French will be markedly better after, say, five years in the secondary school', commented another. 'As one might have expected', wrote a third, 'the Pilot Scheme pupils are a long way ahead of their contemporaries orally—whether they continue to hold this advantage remains to be seen. It is too early to make a proper comparison. I shall be interested to see how they perform at O-level in two years' time'. He added: 'Twice in the last four years the whole of our "B" stream passed at O-level in their fourth year and with good grades. We therefore have standards against which to assess the Pilot Scheme.'

The heads' assessments of the effects of the Pilot Scheme at the secondary level have been classified as 'highly favourable', 'mainly favourable', 'favourable, but for able pupils only', 'unfavourable', and 'noncommittal'. The distribution of favourable, unfavourable, and noncommittal assessments within the different types of secondary school is shown in Table 26.

The majority of secondary school heads, even those who are not entirely in favour of introducing French at the primary stage, nevertheless agree that the standard of oral French achieved by their Pilot

TABLE 26: *Secondary school heads' assessments of the effects of the Pilot Scheme*

TYPE OF SCHOOL	'HIGHLY FAVOUR-ABLE'	'MAINLY FAVOUR-ABLE'	'FAVOURABLE, FOR ABLE PUPILS'	'UNFAVOUR-ABLE'	'NON-COMMITTAL'	TOTAL
Secondary Modern	4	13	11	6	3	37
Grammar	1	12	1	7	7	28
Comprehensive	2	3	2	0	1	8
Bilateral	0	0	2	3	1	6
Others	2	2	0	1	1	6
Total	9	30	16	17	13	85

Scheme pupils is high. There is general agreement that the Pilot Scheme pupils' fluency, their readiness to converse in French and their ability to understand spoken French, compare most favourably with the level of achievement in oral French of pupils taught by more traditional methods. 'There is no doubt that much greater fluency has been achieved in comparison with pupils of similar age who have not taken part in the scheme', wrote a grammar school head. 'They show a pleasing readiness to speak in French. They understand well and are good at guessing what they don't know. Their pronunciation is far better than in the days of "free-lance" French teaching in the primary schools', commented another grammar school head. 'Pupils' understanding of spoken French is much more advanced than that of their predecessors', agreed another. One grammar school head observed that his Pilot Scheme pupils' ability to understand spoken French enabled their teacher to 'speak French without concession'. Similar reports were received from heads of other types of secondary school. The head of a comprehensive school, who had described his impression of the effects of the Pilot Scheme at the secondary level as 'very favourable', commented: 'Pupils have developed good listening comprehension and oral fluency. The most noticeable thing is their readiness to speak in French'. 'Most encouraging', agreed the head of a county secondary school: 'As long as the sentences are short and uncomplicated, the children are able and willing to converse rapidly and with comprehension and to act simple sketches in French, while the best can often think in simple French to a pleasing degree'. The achievement of a high standard of oral expression in French by their Pilot Scheme pupils is reported with particular frequency by the heads of the secondary modern schools in the sample. 'There is an obvious oral advantage', wrote one such head: 'The children are fluent, they comprehend fairly rapid French and can read aloud very well, making few mistakes even in texts at first sight'. 'Without doubt, the scheme proves the value of introducing the spoken word at eight', wrote another: 'Orally, the children have much more confidence in the use of the second language than under what we might call "conventional" approaches'. 'From the point of view of oral work, the scheme is a great improvement on the traditional methods, especially for the less able pupils', reported the head of another secondary modern school. 'Their standard of comprehension is extremely high and their interest is well maintained', agreed another. There are a few reports that fluency tends to falter outside the familiar context of the French teaching materials, and that pupils show little ability to use their oral skills in unfamiliar situations, but these are rare. Most heads take the view that the level of achievement in oral French of the Pilot Scheme pupils represents a considerable advance on past performance.

There is also general agreement that pupils' reading comprehension in French is extremely good. Their level of achievement in written work, on the other hand, is almost universally regarded as unsatisfactory. Even those who comment most favourably on their pupils' level of achievement in oral French express considerable dissatisfaction with their ability to write in French. Grammar school heads, in particular, consider that the written work produced by pupils taught French under the Pilot Scheme compares unfavourably with that of pupils who started to learn French in their first term of secondary school. 'The group as a whole make far more mistakes in written French than those taught by a conventional text-book method', wrote the head of a grammar school. 'There is difficulty in reaching the usual second-year standard in written French', agreed another, adding: 'If pupils were to write spontaneously for 30 minutes, the number of mistakes made would defy correction'. The most frequent criticism of pupils' written work in French is that it is persistently inaccurate and of too low a standard to permit the development of free composition. The general consensus of opinion is that the emphasis placed on oral fluency during the primary stage has allowed habits of 'imprecision and inaccuracy' to develop. 'The majority are too easily satisfied with an approximate answer, if they can get away with it', wrote one grammar school head. 'They are quick to grasp the meaning of a sentence as a whole, but they are not "word-conscious",' wrote another, adding: 'Unfortunately, those who have been allowed or encouraged to express themselves too freely in inaccurate spoken or written French are severely handicapped, as bad habits appear almost ingrained'. A similar view was put forward by the head of a secondary modern school, who wrote: 'It would appear that there was not enough attention to mistakes in pronunciation at the primary stage, so that certain errors (e.g. confusion of le/la, un/une, grand/grande) did persist. Also, the fact that the children did understand the gist of sentences may have led to inattention to component words, so that a rough estimate was too easily accepted in written work. The children are still easily satisfied with superficial understanding: they do not ask many questions about words'. Most secondary school heads are of the opinion that the written aspects of the language received insufficient emphasis during the primary stage. 'The introduction of written matter in the Pilot Scheme came too late and led to confusion', wrote the head of a grammar school. 'There

114

is not sufficient written work in the early stages', agreed another. Some heads fear that the late introduction of written work during the primary stage will permanently hamper the development of written skills. As the head of a bilateral school wrote: 'Children who intend to take the normal GCE course may well be handicapped in their ability to pass this examination by the small quantity of formal written work done in the early stages of the Pilot Scheme'. Grammar school heads, in particular, would welcome the explicit teaching of 'formal grammatical rules'. As one of them wrote, expressing the general view: 'There is little real progress unless there is systematic teaching of grammar from the first year of the secondary stage'. They report that their abler pupils are anxious to receive grammatical explanations and to be given 'rules to explain errors made'. They criticize the teaching methods used during the primary stage for their over-optimistic assumption that pupils would 'automatically adopt grammatically correct forms without their being taught'.

Although they express dissatisfaction with the standard of written work achieved, the majority of secondary school heads nevertheless consider that their pupils' increased oral fluency justifies the intro-duction of French at the primary stage,—at least insofar as the abler pupils are concerned. Many have serious reservations, however, regarding the wisdom of attempting to teach French to pupils of all levels of ability. As the head of a comprehensive school wrote: 'We take in the whole ability range of every year-group. I am convinced, however, that not more than 60 per cent of each year-group can profit from the teaching of French. The teachers who teach the lower sets are becoming very frustrated, as the power of retention of these children is very small indeed'. The head of a grammar school agreed: 'The weaker pupils have difficulty in remembering sentence patterns for very long, however often they are repeated and revised. I would say that the results of teaching primary French are clearly beneficial to the teaching in secondary schools, in 60 to 70 per cent of pupils.' The problems of teaching French to the whole ability range are seen in their most acute form in the secondary modern schools, whose intake includes a high proportion of low-achieving pupils. The head of one of the secondary modern schools in the sample wrote: 'The "B" forms (which, in our case is really a "C" stream) seen to be learning practically nothing and I feel that their time could be more profitably devoted to basic subjects, in which they are very weak. The difficulty of teaching French to the less able pupils is even more pronounced when these are taught as one class, but, nevertheless, the problem still exists in a mixed-ability class'.

115

The head of another secondary modern school wrote: 'It is, I feel, a failure with "C" stream pupils. These seem to get more and more lost and consequently lose confidence and interest'. Another agreed: 'We feel that towards the end of the second year our poorer children have reached the limit of their ability to absorb French lessons, and that, in the case of the very poor children, one year's French in the secondary school is enough for both pupil and teacher'. The head of another secondary modern school, asked to give his impression of the effects of the Pilot Scheme at the secondary level, summed up as follows: 'I am sceptical of its benefit to our lowest streams from the junior schools. It might even be best to start or restart the course with these streams when they reach the secondary school, if it is worth doing at all'. Heads of other secondary modern schools describe the pupils in their lower streams as 'able to contribute very little', sometimes 'completely lost'. They regard the attempt to teach French to these pupils as 'not educationally worthwhile', 'of little benefit', even 'a complete waste of time and money'. Occasionally, heads of secondary modern schools advocate the continuation of purely oral work in French for pupils in the lowest streams, but the majority opinion is that expressed by the secondary modern school head who wrote : 'As headmaster, I am very doubtful whether the least able children should be allowed to continue beyond the primary stage. Their powers of retention are so weak that they cannot recall from one day to the next. They begin to sense failure and this adds to their emotional instability'. The general view is that the pupils concerned would derive greater benefit if the time set aside for French lessons were devoted instead to extra tuition in the basic subjects, particularly English, a view frequently expressed by the pupils themselves. One secondary modern school head wrote: 'We are satisfied that the great majority of our children involved in the scheme are deriving much more educational benefit from the subject than by other more established methods. Our one reservation concerns our very poor "D-streamers". In their cases, we feel that time devoted to French could perhaps be better employed helping them with basic English'. Another agreed: 'The effect of the course on the able children is undoubtedly good. I am doubtful if there is any gain for the less able children and suspect there is a loss, compared with the gains which would have been made by the use of the time for work in English and Mathematics, particularly in the primary school'. Although many heads are careful to point out that the pupils who do not appear to benefit at all from the teaching of French represent a small proportion of their total intake, the numbers involved are

116

sufficiently large to create serious organizational problems, particularly in the secondary modern schools.

Further organizational problems are caused at the secondary stage by the experimental nature of the Pilot Scheme. Most of the secondary schools in the sample have several Pilot Scheme primary schools in their catchment area. The pupils in these primary schools may follow different French courses and, even in areas where all the Pilot Scheme primary schools use the same teaching materials, the pupils concerned may not all proceed at the same pace. Pupils from several different primary schools tend, therefore, to enter a given secondary school with disparate levels of attainment in French. The situation is aggravated by the fact that, in the majority of secondary schools, the first-year intake includes not only Pilot Scheme pupils, but also pupils who have received variable amounts of French teaching in primary schools which are not included in the experimental sample, together with pupils who have been taught no French at all. The head of a secondary modern school described a situation typical of many other schools when he wrote: 'The primary schools which provide our intake vary in their attitude to French, in the time they allot to it, in the courses they use, and in the thoroughness and efficiency with which they use them. Since our intake is not set in any way at the moment, a great variety of ability, experience of French and length of its study exists in each form.' In many secondary schools, but particularly in secondary modern and bilateral schools, the creation of a timetable capable of accommodating so variable an intake presented formidable difficulties and was hampered by lack of qualified staff and shortage of classroom and storage space. Nevertheless, no matter how difficult the circumstances, most secondary heads succeeded in making separate provision for their Pilot Scheme intake: in the majority of schools, separate French classes were formed for the Pilot Scheme pupils and they continued their study of French at a level appropriate to their primary school experience. In some schools, continuity of French teaching was achieved, but the Pilot Scheme pupils had to be taught in classes which also contained pupils with a more limited knowledge of French. In others, the Pilot Scheme intake proved too small to permit the formation of a separate French class or any continuity of teaching: the pupils concerned joined beginners' French classes. In a few schools, the low-achieving pupils were separated from the rest of the intake and were either placed in beginners' classes for French or else discontinued their study of the language. In one secondary modern school, the whole of the Pilot Scheme intake started to learn French again 'from scratch', because

117

their level of achievement in French was judged inadequate for more advanced study.

The organizational problems caused by the need to accommodate a mixed intake varied in severity according to the type of secondary school: they were apparently less severe in the grammar schools than in the other types of school represented in the sample. In all but two of the grammar schools, continuity of teaching was maintained and separate French classes were formed to accommodate all pupils who had been learning French under the Pilot Scheme for three years. In three of these schools, a small number of pupils who had joined a Pilot Scheme primary school in the recent past and had, in consequence, only a limited knowledge of French, were separated from the rest of the intake and placed in beginners' classes. Two of the grammar schools in the sample had too small an intake of Pilot Scheme pupils (fewer than 15 pupils in each school) to permit the formation of a separate French class, so the pupils concerned joined beginners' classes. In 21 of the 37 secondary modern schools, all Pilot Scheme pupils were able to continue their study of French at a level appropriate to their primary school experience. In these schools, the Pilot Scheme pupils were usually taught French in separate classes, but were sometimes joined by pupils who had been learning French for less than three years in schools outside the experimental areas. In eight of the secondary modern schools, most Pilot Scheme pupils were accommodated in separate French classes, but a small number of pupils (3-18) who had been placed in remedial classes discontinued their study of French. In five of the secondary modern schools, all Pilot Scheme pupils except those in the lowest sets or streams continued to learn French at an appropriate level, but were taught in classes containing pupils who had been learning French for a considerably shorter period. Pupils allocated to the lowest sets or streams were placed in beginners' French classes. In two secondary modern schools, the number of Pilot Scheme pupils received was too small (fewer than 10 pupils in each school) to form a separate French class: these pupils were placed in beginners' classes, as were all the Pilot Scheme pupils of the secondary modern school mentioned above, judged to have made little progress during the primary stage of the experiment. In five of the eight comprehensive schools, all Pilot Scheme pupils, with the exception of a small number placed in remedial classes and no longer taught French, continued to learn French at an appropriate level in classes containing a few pupils whose experience of French was more limited than that of the Pilot Scheme intake. The remaining three comprehensive schools had too small an intake of Pilot Scheme pupils (fewer than 18 pupils in each school) to form separate French classes: in these schools, the pupils concerned were placed in beginners' classes. A similar organizational pattern was observed in the other types of secondary school represented in the sample (bilateral, county secondary, senior high): continuity of teaching was preserved for most Pilot Scheme pupils, but pupils in the lowest sets or streams tended to be placed in beginners' classes for French or to discontinue their study of the language; where the Pilot Scheme intake was too small to make up a separate class, the pupils concerned joined a beginners' class for French.

There is general agreement among secondary school heads that the problems of organizing French classes for their Pilot Scheme pupils are seriously aggravated by the lack of uniformity at the primary stage. 'I would have thought it essential that children in Pilot Scheme primary schools should have used the same course throughout the three years', wrote the head of a secondary modern school. 'There are difficulties in keeping pace with the Scheme and meeting its requirements. Children enter the school having reached different stages and have to be taught together', pointed out the head of a bilateral school. 'The most desperate need is that they should all have covered a fairly similar amount', agreed the head of a grammar school. Most secondary heads consider that some form of 'setting' is needed to cope with the variable level of achievement in French of the Pilot Scheme intake, but shortage of staff and lack of space often prevent the realization of this policy. 'Setting' for French within the Pilot Scheme group proved feasible in approximately 50 per cent of the schools in the sample and was more frequently encountered in the grammar schools than in any other type of school. The most common criterion for the formation of sets was the pupil's level of achievement in French, as indicated by his primary school report. In some schools, sets were formed on the basis of the different French courses followed in the contributory primary schools; in others, sets were based on the pupil's performance on general attainment tests; in one school, sets were formed with reference to the pupils' friendship groups. Even when it is possible to create sets for French, some heads feel that the difficulties of coping with the wide range of achievement in French are so great that it would be preferable to restrict the teaching of French at the primary stage. As the head of a grammar school wrote: 'The problems created by attempting to have a course which begins at eight years in the primary school and continues for at least two years in the secondary school are very great. Most secondary schools

119

have many intake schools and pupils have reached varied stages with varying comprehension. In my opinion, we would do better to concentrate on improving the teaching of language in the secondary schools and be satisfied with introducing the subject and encouraging participation in the primary schools. In other words, what the pupil starts with in the secondary school should not depend upon the material dealt with in the primary school but on the general approach. This will enable those who have "got lost" in the primary school to make a fresh start.' A further problem arising from the variable pace of French teaching at the primary stage concerns the teaching materials themselves. In the case of course materials designed to span both the primary and secondary stages, pupils who had proceeded at a slower pace than that envisaged by the authors of the materials reached their secondary schools with a considerable amount of the primary stage material as yet unexplored. This was particularly true of the pupils in the first cohort: in the first year of secondary school, many of these pupils were still using course materials designed for the junior age-range. 'The speed of the Pilot course, as planned, was unrealistic, leaving secondary schools with a year of primary work not covered, so that some material was unsuitable for secondary school use', wrote the head of a grammar school whose pupils had complained of the 'babyish' nature of the French course materials. 'Since a number of grammar and other secondary schools are starting with material designed for the last year of primary school, the reading and writing component should be given earlier and greater prominence', agreed another grammar school head, who had expressed disappointment in the written work produced by his Pilot Scheme pupils. None of the secondary schools in the sample was reported to be entirely free from the organizational problems caused by a first-year intake with variable experience of French. The majority view is undoubtedly that expressed by the grammar school head who wrote: 'More uniformity at the primary stage can only lead to greater efficiency at the secondary stage'.

In many secondary schools, organizational problems are further aggravated by serious staffing difficulties. Secondary modern and bilateral schools, with only a recent history of modern language teaching, suffer most from the shortage of qualified staff. 'The scheme would have been more effective if steps (at national level) had been taken to ensure an adequate supply of trained teachers', wrote the head of a bilateral school. In two-thirds of the secondary modern schools and in all but one of the bilateral schools, heads reported unresolved staffing problems. In some schools, these problems were

120

caused by the departure of the only French teacher and inability to recruit a replacement; in others, they stemmed from the employment of untrained or non-specialist teachers; in most cases, the number of trained language teachers available was simply inadequate to cope with the whole of the Pilot Scheme intake. Many secondary modern heads, faced with a shortage of qualified staff and a large intake of Pilot Scheme pupils, were forced to discontinue the teaching of French to certain pupils or classes at the end of the first or second year. In these instances, the higher-achieving pupils were selected to continue the study of French, while the lower-achieving pupils were usually given remedial teaching in English or Mathematics. One secondary modern head wrote: 'With reference to the staffing situation, we could possibly continue for another year under the present scheme, but, after that, it will become almost impossible'. Severe staffing problems appear to be encountered less often in the comprehensive schools in the sample and rarely in the grammar schools.

The members of staff responsible for teaching French to the Pilot Scheme intake are reported to be coping with the demands of the situation with varying degrees of enthusiasm and success. At one extreme, the head of a secondary modern school reports that 'the Head of the French Department cannot wait to finish the experiment'; at the other, the head of a comprehensive school reports that 'the Pilot Scheme has given tremendous zest to the French Department by demonstrating the considerable rewards of lively mobile lessons'. Most heads take the view that the teaching of French by predominantly audio-visual methods produces extremely good results 'in the hands of a gifted teacher', but demands far more of the teacher than do traditional methods of language-teaching. Heads report a considerable strain on those teachers responsible for teaching French to a large number of classes, and comment on the amount of time and energy which the preparation of the French lessons absorbs. A number of heads report that 'teachers accustomed to more formal methods find difficulty in adjusting', but, for those in sympathy with the increased emphasis on the spoken aspects of the language, 'aiming for greater oral efficiency is more demanding on the teacher, but worth the effort'. The head of a secondary modern school for girls summed up her impression of the French teaching in her school as follows: 'In spite of intermittent difficulties, staffing problems, etc., the staff and girls have enjoyed the work and found it worthwhile. To me as an onlooker, and a listener from time to time, the lessons have been a delight, and I feel sure that the work of excellent teachers has been given an added impetus by the Pilot Scheme work'. The general opinion is that the greater emphasis on the development of oral skills entails 'hard, but in the main, very rewarding work'.

Although staffing and organizational problems are prominent at the secondary level, the heads of most of the secondary schools in the sample consider that the majority of their Pilot Scheme pupils are deriving benefit from their early introduction to French, especially with regard to the development of oral skills. Most of them also consider that the standard of written work achieved is unsatisfactory and, furthermore, seriously question the wisdom of teaching French to the least able pupils. Some heads prefer to defer judgement until they are in a position to assess the performance of their Pilot Scheme pupils in O- and A-level examinations, but, on the whole, the attitude of the secondary school heads towards their first intake of pupils taught French under the Pilot Scheme has been more favourable than otherwise. The final comment is made by the headmistress of a grammar school, who wrote: 'I think that our acquaintance with this scheme has been stimulating and that teaching in the school will certainly benefit from it. Perhaps in this, as in so many educational experiments, familiarity encourages flexibility and discourages dogmatism'.

SECTION NINE

The HMI Evaluation of the Secondary Stage of the Pilot Scheme

THE HMI evaluation of the secondary stage of the Pilot Scheme began in September 1967, when the pupils in the first cohort transferred to secondary school. As before, HM Inspectors completed a detailed report in questionnaire form after each visit to a class, set, or group in which Pilot Scheme pupils were being taught French. The questionnaire used during the secondary stage of the evaluation contained both pre-coded and open-ended sections, since it was considered essential for HM Inspectors to be given the opportunity to express their views freely, but equally important to respect the requirements of efficient data-processing. The areas of inquiry covered by the pre-coded sections of the questionnaire included the following: the overall competence of the French teacher, with specific reference to his linguistic competence and his skill in the use of audio-visual equipment; the attitudes of the head, the French teacher and the head of his department towards the teaching of French to Pilot Scheme pupils; the nature, scope, length and distribution of the French lessons; the composition of the French class; the course materials used in the teaching of French; the availability and maintenance of audio-visual equipment; the quality of the pupils' spoken and written French and the nature of their attitudes towards learning French.

The questionnaire data were processed whenever a sufficient number of completed questionnaires had been returned and were analysed at the end of each school year. During 1968-69, HM Inspectors were also contributing reports on visits made to classes containing second cohort pupils in their first year of secondary school, but the analysis of the data contained in these reports will not be presented until the data for 1969-70 are available. The present account refers to data arising from visits made to 135 first cohort classes during 1967-68 ('Year 1') and to 129 such classes during 1968-69 ('Year 2'). These data were first analysed by reference to the rated fluency in French of the class. Classes whose general fluency had been rated 'good' ('highly fluent' classes) were identified and compared with classes whose general fluency had been rated 'fair'

123

('moderately fluent' classes) or 'poor' ('less fluent' classes). Chi-square tests were carried out to determine whether 'highly fluent', 'moderately fluent' and 'less fluent' classes differed significantly from one another during Year 1 or Year 2 on any other variable. The results of the chi-square tests are shown in Table 9.1 in Appendix 9. All variables which proved to be non-significant in both Year 1 and Year 2 have been omitted from Table 9.1. Classes which differed significantly from one another with respect to the pupils' general fluency in French were also shown to differ significantly with respect to the pupils' responsiveness and enthusiasm, and the extent to which specific language skills were being developed in the French class. In 'highly fluent' classes, the pupils' response to the French lesson tended to be rated 'good' and their attitude towards learning French 'highly enthusiastic', whereas, in 'moderately fluent' and 'less fluent' classes, the pupils' response tended to be 'fair' or 'poor' and their attitude towards learning French less enthusiastic. 'Highly fluent' classes also differed significantly from 'moderately fluent' and 'less fluent' classes in the extent to which the pupils' spoken and written skills in French and their knowledge of cultural background were being developed in the context of the French lesson: in 'highly fluent' classes, such skills were being 'fully' developed; in 'moderately fluent' and 'less fluent' classes, they were being developed 'to some extent' or 'not at all'. In 'highly fluent' classes, the French lesson as a whole tended to leave the visiting Inspector with a favourable impression; in 'moderately fluent' and 'less fluent' classes, a generally unfavourable impression was more frequently recorded. Teachers of 'highly fluent' classes also differed significantly in certain respects from teachers of 'moderately fluent' or 'less fluent' classes: those teaching 'highly fluent' classes tended to be rated 'excellent' or 'good' in their command of French, their skill in the handling of audio-visual equipment and their general competence; those teaching 'moderately fluent' and 'less fluent' classes tended to be rated 'average', 'fair' or 'poor' in each of these respects. In Year 1, significantly more teachers of 'highly fluent' classes had a favourable attitude towards teaching French to Pilot Scheme pupils and significantly more teachers of 'moderately fluent' and 'less fluent' classes a noncommittal or un-favourable attitude, but, by Year 2, classes differing in fluency no longer differed significantly from one another according to the attitude of the French teacher. In Year 1, classes differing in fluency did not differ significantly according to school type, but, by Year 2, significantly more 'highly fluent' classes were to be found in grammar schools, significantly more 'moderately fluent' classes in comprehensive schools and significantly more 'less fluent' classes in secondary modern schools. In 'highly fluent' classes, pupils were considered to have benefited 'a great deal' from their primary French course, whereas, in 'moderately fluent' and 'less fluent' classes, pupils were thought to have benefited from their introduction to French at the primary level 'to some extent' or even, in a few cases, 'not at all'.

The questionnaire data were also analysed with reference to the rated responsiveness of the class to the French lesson. Classes considered to be making a 'good' response to the lesson ('highly responsive' classes) were identified and compared with those making a 'fair' response ('moderately responsive' classes) or a 'poor' response ('less responsive' classes). Chi-square tests were carried out to determine whether classes differing in their responsiveness to the French lesson also differed significantly from one another in other respects. The results of the chi-square tests are shown in Table 9.2 in Appendix 9. All variables which proved to be non-significant in both Year 1 and Year 2 have been omitted from Table 9.2. In most respects, significant differences between classes varying in responsiveness to the French lesson paralleled those between classes differing in fluency: the pupils in 'highly responsive' classes tended to receive higher ratings for fluency and enthusiasm than did those in 'moderately responsive' and 'less responsive' classes; pupils' spoken and written skills and knowledge of cultural background were being developed to a greater extent in 'highly responsive' classes than in 'moderately responsive' or 'less responsive' classes; the teachers of 'highly responsive' classes tended to receive higher ratings for linguistic and overall competence and for skill in handling audio-visual equipment than did teachers of 'moderately responsive' or 'less responsive' classes; and the pupils in 'highly responsive' classes were considered to have derived the most benefit from their primary French course. In Year 1, there were no significant differences between 'highly responsive', 'moderately responsive' and 'less responsive' classes with regard to the development of reading comprehension but, by Year 2, reading comprehension was being developed 'fully' or 'to some extent' in significantly more 'highly responsive' classes and 'not at all' in significantly more 'moderately responsive' and 'less responsive' classes. In both Year 1 and Year 2, significantly more teachers of 'highly responsive' classes had a favourable attitude towards teaching French to Pilot Scheme pupils and significantly more teachers of 'moderately responsive' and 'less responsive' classes a noncommittal or unfavourable attitude. Classes differing in their responsiveness to the French lesson did not, however, differ significantly from one another with respect to school type.

The French classes were also compared on the basis of the pupils' attitudes towards learning the language, as indicated by the enthusiasm displayed during the French lesson. 'Highly enthusiastic' classes were identified and compared with 'moderately enthusiastic' and 'unenthusiastic' classes. Chi-square tests were carried out to determine whether classes varying in the extent of their enthusiasm for learning French also differed significantly from one another in other respects. The results of the chi-square tests are shown in Table 9.3 in Appendix 9. All variables which proved to be non-significant in both Year 1 and Year 2 have been omitted from Table 9.3. As might be expected, classes varying in the degree of their enthusiasm for learning French differed also in their responsiveness and fluency and in the characteristics and competence of their French teacher. During Year 1 there were no significant differences between 'highly enthusiastic', 'moderately enthusiastic' and 'unenthusiastic' classes with regard to the development of written skills. By year 2, however, written skills were being developed 'fully' or 'to some extent' in significantly more 'highly enthusiastic' and 'moderately enthusiastic' classes, but were not being developed at all in significantly more 'unenthusiastic' classes. The classes did not differ significantly in either year with regard to the development of reading comprehension.

In the open-ended sections of the questionnaire, the topic which attracted the most comment was undoubtedly that of the extent to which the different aspects of language acquisition were being developed in the context of the French lesson. There was general agreement that, over the sample as a whole, the main teaching emphasis continued to fall on the development of the pupils' oral skills; reading comprehension, written skills and knowledge of cultural background were being developed to a much lesser extent. The continuing development of the pupils' oral skills was welcomed, but it was frequently observed that their spoken French, although confident and indicative of a high standard of comprehension, was marred by persistent inaccuracy. Comments such as the following were widespread and frequent: 'Children responded well, but usually inaccurately'; 'They were competent in being able to answer questions, but their oral work was riddled with mistakes'; 'Their comprehension and attack are good, but they are singularly cavalier with gender and person, particularly in pronouns'; 'Pupils' oral fluency is seriously handicapped by their inability to distinguish between the pronouns they want to use'; 'There are some good

accents and pleasing intonations here, but strangely little sense of
elementary structure or power of analogy'; 'They were confident but
not always comprehensible. Their sense of structure was shaky';
'Understanding is well ahead of ability to use vocabulary and
structures'. Failure to enunciate clearly was also noted in a number of
classes: 'Inaudibility, and especially weak enunciation, detracted
from even the most able pupils' responses'. In some cases, the pupils'
growing self-awareness was felt to be hindering the development of
fluency: 'Already self-consciousness is proving inhibiting and speech
lacks confidence and is indistinct.'

Pupils' lack of flexibility in the use of well-known sentence-
patterns was also frequently observed: pupils were often hesitant if
they deviated from 'well-drilled responses' and showed little ability
to use the language creatively, to express their own ideas, even though
they were eager to do so. The following comments are typical of many
others on this point: 'Within the limits of the material the pupils are
quite fluent. What they do not seem to have acquired is flexibility in
applying their knowledge to their everyday life. It remains closely
tied to the text and they are at sea when asked questions about
themselves'; 'The pupils find it difficult to answer questions not
directly related to the course material'; 'There is much achieved, but
it falls below what the pupils feel they want to express. There was no
conversation, just minimal but correct answers to questions'; 'This
is an eager class capable of some sustained French outside the question
and answer, but at this moment frustrated because the means of
expression at their disposal are so limited and do not meet their
needs'. In a few classes, however, pupils were reported to have an
excellent and flexible command of oral French, showing themselves
to be adaptable and creative in their use of the language. At best, it
was possible for a visiting Inspector to talk 'naturally and casually'
with the pupils, who were able to 'converse in French, not just
respond to questions' and who showed themselves 'ready to search
for ways of expressing their own ideas'.

Classes in which a uniformly high standard of fluency prevailed
were rare, however. In most French classes the pupils' level of
achievement was uneven: 'Some are very good indeed, most seem to
understand, but quite a few do not contribute anything'; 'Some tend
to be too silent, others tend to monopolize the opportunities for
talking French'. In some classes, low-achieving pupils were reported
to have adopted a passive or hostile attitude towards learning French
and were considered to have reached the limits of their achievement:
'These pupils have probably reached their top performance already.

... Only an outstanding teacher could take them further.' Occasionally, 'outstanding' teachers were available and were reported to be achieving considerable success in developing the fluency in French of pupils of 'very limited ability', as the following comments indicate: 'Although this class is so limited, they are producing phrases with tremendous enthusiasm; these are realistic statements concerned about their everyday lives and interests and, though limited and simple, they produce them'; 'A convincing demonstration of success with pupils of very limited ability, in the hands of a sensitive teacher who understands their difficulties'; 'The notable effectiveness of lively oral practice sustains keenness even in the least able'; 'Well-planned and effective lesson. The teacher expects the children to work hard and the response is encouraging, even from the less able'; 'Very satisfactory progress, even by the least able linguists'; 'This is an interesting example of less able pupils getting more satisfaction and achieving more success than some of the abler divisions in the school'. In classes where effective teaching was lacking, however, there seemed little hope of further progress for the less able pupils. The extent to which the progress of the less able depends upon the quality of the teaching received is indicated by comments such as the following: 'Poor teaching has made recovery virtually impossible for these pupils'; 'The weaker pupils need more effective help'; 'It may be that many of them would, in any event, have made little further progress, but this cannot be proved on data available from this school, where poor teaching has obscured the outcome of the experiment'; 'Great difficulties of staffing at this secondary stage have practically obliterated any gains at the primary stage . . . circumstances were against their making any real progress'.

The extent to which both oral and silent reading were being developed during the first two years of the secondary stage varied greatly from one French class to another. In general, oral reading predominated during the first year; the development of silent reading received greater emphasis during the second year, particularly in the grammar schools. Standards of performance in oral reading were reported to vary from 'very good' to 'very halting and inaccurate'—often within a single French class. At best, pupils were 'individually much involved in reading aloud' and were reported to read 'confidently and with good accents', giving every evidence of comprehension and maintaining 'pronunciation and intonation of a very high standard'. At worst, pupils were reported to be 'hardly able to read a short, simple sentence': their attempts to read aloud in French were 'very poor, lifeless and inaccurate', giving no evidence of comprehension. It was generally agreed that, for pupils who were making little headway with oral reading, more frequent and varied opportunities for individual practice, greater emphasis on the attainment of acceptable standards of pronunciation, intonation and audibility, and, above all, a livelier pace and a more dynamic teaching approach were essential, if progress was to be achieved: 'More repetition, to consolidate basic pronunciation and intonation, is desirable and more demands for improved audibility are suggested'; 'A livelier pace by the teacher is required for optimum progress in this respect as in others, in order to involve more pupils and provide more repetitive practice'; 'Performance could be improved with more dynamic teaching'. The emphasis placed on the development of silent reading in French varied considerably from one class to another. During the first year of the secondary stage, very little silent reading was observed. In a number of classes, and particularly in those with a high proportion of able pupils, visiting Inspectors felt that the development of silent reading had already been too long delayed: 'The pupils are interested and keen to go on and the opportune moment to develop the reading habit may be lost'; 'There is no feeling of progress. Reading, which might add interest and lighten the load of completely oral work on both staff and pupils, has not yet been introduced'; 'This is a class very keen to co-operate. Perhaps a few more opportunities of reading and seeing the written word might help to relieve the effort of teacher and class to continue oral work all lesson'. In other classes, the pupils' ability was not considered 'equal to' the further development of silent reading: 'These children should not be seeing the printed word—it does them no good'. During the second year of the secondary stage, an increasing emphasis on the development of silent reading was noted, particularly in the grammar schools, and frequent reports were received of pupils whose ability to read in French had outstripped the reading material available: 'It has proved impossible to satisfy their needs: they mop up the small booklets provided so quickly'; 'They are keen enough to do some reading on their own if more were available'; 'The material available seriously underestimates what they are capable of doing'. Many Inspectors commented on the need for suitable 'genuine French books', to stimulate the development of 'more ambitious' silent reading.

As with the development of silent reading, the development of the pupils' ability to write in French received very little emphasis during the first year of the secondary stage but gained prominence during the second year, particularly in the grammar schools. At first, writing

E

was limited to copy-writing, supplying written answers to questions in work-books and simple dictation: 'Copying and dictation are producing accuracy, but no sign of the beginnings of guided composition'; 'Work in exercise books contained mainly copying, but there was some good answering of questions'; 'Writing still limited to dictation, copy-writing and memory writing'; 'Writing is very limited as yet. Even when many of these children merely copy, their work contains mistakes'. Some pupils proceeded to 'guided' composition during the second year, but many others were reported to be having 'great difficulty' with even the simplest forms of writing: 'An attempt showed that some can cope, but in other cases the writing was almost double-Dutch. The grammatical accuracy, even of the simple present tense, was surprisingly weak'; 'These pupils are very insecure in spelling even the simplest words. They have not seen the printed word enough'; 'They are still at the stage of very simple dictation. Grammatical spellings in such sentences as "Elles sont jaunes" still elude them'; 'Inaccuracy reveals the need to consolidate the knowledge of simple basic structures'; 'The range of ability needs to be borne in mind when written work is set: one or two can hardly write'. Several Inspectors thought that earlier and greater emphasis should have been placed on the development of accurate written work, particularly with regard to the abler pupils, whose potential for 'far more exacting written work' was felt to be seriously underestimated: 'Not enough is being done to develop written skills, especially as these children have considerable ability'; 'Writing is mainly restricted to answering questions and dictation. These able pupils need more opportunity for creative writing'; 'Too little attention is being paid to written work'; 'This is purely copying: they are capable of more'; 'Written work is infantile, thin, and of doubtful value'; 'The pupils need more scope for using their own initiative and should be stretched more fully'. In some classes, abler pupils were reported to be making good progress with 'guided' composition in French: 'Some guided composition: very well done by many children'; 'Some good accurate written work, including a little "controlled" composition'; 'One of the few classes known to me where composition is done on a considerable scale—carefully guided, of course'. Such reports were rare, however, and tended to be confined to grammar school classes.

The obvious variations in the pupils' level of achievement in French at the secondary stage were mainly attributed to the quality and continuity of the teaching received, the wide range of ability present in the experimental sample, differences in the length of time during which French had been studied in the primary school, and the extent to which the primary French course material had been covered before the pupils transferred to secondary school. The fact that a number of classes contained pupils who had followed different French courses during the primary stage caused few problems and was not considered an important source of variation in achievement: 'Despite different courses in primary school, they have progressed evenly in their present class'; 'The class includes pupils coming from a number of primary schools and, although most have used the Nuffield course, the others have had no difficulty in adjusting'; 'No difficulty appears to arise from the different experience of the minority'; 'The difference in courses has caused no problem'. A wide range of achievement was far more frequently noted in classes containing pupils who had all followed the same French course in primary school, but whose rate of progress had differed markedly: 'What differences there are arise, not from the nature of the primary course followed, but from the varying points in the course reached in the contributory primary schools'. Where marked differences in attainment existed within a single French class, most French teachers attempted to redress the balance by increasing opportunities for individual practice and by giving more time to group work. Reports of successful group work were rare, however, and the majority of Inspectors recommended strongly that this aspect of language teaching should receive greater emphasis at the secondary stage.

The evaluation of the progress made during the secondary stage by pupils taught French under the Pilot Scheme is still continuing: the present account is an interim statement only. During 1969-70, members of HM Inspectorate visited the secondary schools taking part in the experiment and provided detailed reports on the second cohort classes. These reports will be analysed during 1971 and the results presented in 1972, together with further analysis of the data relating to the first cohort.

APPENDIX ONE

General Attainment in the Primary School

(Tables 1.1 - 1.10)

Appendix One

TABLE 1.1: *Comparison of experimental and control groups. Primary Verbal Test: mean scores by school group and parental occupation.*

SCHOOL GROUP		Professional and Clerical	Skilled	Semi-skilled	Unskilled	TOTAL
		PARENTAL OCCUPATION				
Group 1 (Cohort 1)	N	216	360	368	185	1129
	$\bar{x}$	74·91	69·57	64·76	56·56	66·89
	SD	9·74	13·35	15·05	18·98	15·53
Group 1 (Cohort 2)	N	258	448	357	163	1226
	$\bar{x}$	72·28	68·61	62·83	53·45	65·69
	SD	12·36	13·30	16·39	17·05	15·76
Group 1 Controls	N	703	956	837	426	2922
	$\bar{x}$	74·33	67·93	60·50	56·55	65·68
	SD	11·14	14·79	18·79	19·56	17·26
Group 2 (Cohort 1)	N	646	860	819	399	2724
	$\bar{x}$	75·06	69·52	62·56	54·79	66·59
	SD	9·89	13·60	16·45	20·68	16·45
Group 2 (Cohort 2)	N	688	999	816	387	2890
	$\bar{x}$	73·99	68·58	62·65	57·72	66·74
	SD	11·51	13·57	16·93	18·75	15·89
Group 2 Controls	N	312	606	507	284	1709
	$\bar{x}$	71·35	65·67	59·22	54·45	62·93
	SD	12·67	16·54	19·26	20·03	18·29
Group 3	N	74	165	164	94	497
	$\bar{x}$	70·07	65·49	62·22	53·37	62·61
	SD	13·58	15·48	17·05	20·11	17·62
Group 3 Controls	N	86	189	184	95	554
	$\bar{x}$	70·80	66·29	62·79	57·33	64·29
	SD	13·44	16·11	16·66	19·50	17·06

Notes

1. *Group 1 schools.* Taking the sample as a whole, mean scores for Cohort 1 pupils in Group 1 schools are slightly higher than mean scores for pupils in the internal control groups. Differences between mean scores are significant at the five per cent level. Within separate parental occupation categories, but with the scores for pupils of both sexes combined, there is a significant difference ($p < 0.001$) between mean scores in favour of the Cohort 1 pupils in the 'semi-skilled' category: this is the only instance of a significant difference between mean scores

for the pupils in the experimental and control groups. Mean scores for Cohort 2 pupils in Group 1 schools do not differ significantly from those obtained by the pupils in the internal control groups.

2. *Group 2 schools.* Mean scores for Cohort 1 and Cohort 2 pupils in Group 2 schools are significantly higher than those for pupils in the external control groups. Taking the sample as a whole, differences between mean scores are significant at the 0·1 per cent level. Differences between means in favour of the experimental groups tend to reach higher levels of significance in the higher-status parental occupation categories than in the lower-status categories.

3. *Group 3 schools.* There is a tendency for the pupils in the matched control schools to obtain slightly higher mean scores than those obtained by the pupils in the experimental schools, but differences between mean scores do not reach a significant level.

TABLE 1.2: *Comparison of experimental and control groups. Mechanical Arithmetic Test: mean scores by school group and parental occupation.*

SCHOOL GROUP		PARENTAL OCCUPATION				TOTAL
		Professional and Clerical	Skilled	Semi-skilled	Unskilled	
Group 1 (Cohort 1)	N	215	363	368	187	1133
	x̄	31·06	26·73	24·15	21·07	25·78
	SD	8·33	9·46	9·73	9·24	9·84
Group 1 (Cohort 2)	N	259	452	357	165	1233
	x̄	28·30	25·25	23·29	18·03	24·36
	SD	9·82	9·21	9·17	8·54	9·73
Group 1 Controls	N	347	488	382	225	1442
	x̄	31·84	26·10	22·37	19·94	25·53
	SD	6·06	7·17	8·03	8·50	7·80
Group 2 (Cohort 1)	N	646	857	819	399	2721
	x̄	30·88	26·77	21·78	18·85	25·08
	SD	9·11	9·62	9·56	9·58	10·38
Group 2 (Cohort 2)	N	691	1002	810	387	2890
	x̄	29·36	25·13	21·41	19·29	24·32
	SD	9·27	9·77	9·64	9·07	10·14
Group 2 Controls	N	310	604	509	278	1701
	x̄	26·56	24·47	22·54	20·85	23·68
	SD	7·08	7·79	8·08	7·92	7·99
Group 3	N	74	164	162	93	493
	x̄	25·64	23·62	21·18	17·33	21·94
	SD	9·54	9·62	10·23	8·90	10·01
Group 3 Controls	N	86	189	184	95	554
	x̄	26·51	23·58	21·21	19·94	22·62
	SD	8·85	9·79	9·63	9·83	9·84

Notes

1. *Group 1 schools.* Taking the sample as a whole, mean scores for Cohort 1 pupils in Group 1 schools do not differ significantly from those for pupils in the internal control groups. Within separate parental occupation categories, but with the scores for pupils of both sexes combined, there is a significant difference ($p < 0.05$) between mean scores in favour of the Cohort 1 pupils in the 'semi-skilled' category: this is the only instance of a significant difference between mean scores for the pupils in the experimental and control groups. Mean scores

for Cohort 2 pupils in Group 1 schools tend to be slightly lower than those obtained by the pupils in the internal control groups, but differences between mean scores only reach the five per cent level of significance when the scores for pupils of both sexes and in each parental occupation category are combined.

2. *Group 2 schools.* There is a tendency for the pupils in the experimental groups to obtain slightly higher mean scores than those obtained by the pupils in the external control groups, but significant differences between mean scores in favour of the experimental groups are confined to the pupils in the 'professional and clerical' parental occupation category.

3. *Group 3 schools.* Taking the sample as a whole, there is a tendency for the pupils in the matched control schools to obtain slightly higher mean scores than those obtained by the pupils in the experimental schools, but differences between mean scores do not reach a significant level.

Appendix One

TABLE 1.3. *Comparison of experimental and control groups. Reading Test: mean scores by school group and parental occupation.*

SCHOOL GROUP		Professional and Clerical	Skilled	Semi-skilled	Unskilled	TOTAL
		PARENTAL OCCUPATION				
Group 1 (Cohort 1)	N	217	372	382	192	1163
	x̄	37·34	33·97	31·54	28·19	32·85
	SD	5·35	7·50	7·42	8·96	7·93
Group 1 (Cohort 2)	N	257	443	359	160	1219
	x̄	36·20	34·05	30·27	26·59	32·41
	SD	7·00	7·16	8·37	8·14	8·25
Group 1 Controls	N	707	957	839	430	2933
	x̄	37·57	33·26	29·28	27·27	32·28
	SD	6·28	7·80	9·25	9·51	8·97
Group 2 (Cohort 1)	N	651	868	813	399	2731
	x̄	37·32	33·64	30·13	26·62	32·44
	SD	6·24	7·36	8·37	9·66	8·59
Group 2 (Cohort 2)	N	678	990	816	390	2874
	x̄	36·53	33·22	30·07	27·85	32·38
	SD	6·57	7·19	8·37	9·06	8·22
Group 2 Controls	N	310	604	509	276	1699
	x̄	35·78	32·87	29·72	26·99	31·50
	SD	6·88	8·17	9·43	10·08	9·15
Group 3	N	72	166	160	93	491
	x̄	33·07	31·28	29·70	24·48	29·74
	SD	9·42	8·24	7·59	10·06	9·03
Group 3 Controls	N	84	189	185	93	551
	x̄	34·45	30·88	28·56	27·11	30·01
	SD	7·67	8·45	8·65	8·51	8·75

Notes

1. *Group 1 schools.* Taking the sample as a whole, mean scores for Cohort 1 pupils in Group 1 schools are slightly higher than those for pupils in the internal control groups. Differences between mean scores are significant at the five per cent level. Within separate parental occupation categories, however, mean scores do not differ significantly except in the 'semi-skilled' category, where there is a significant difference ($p < 0.001$) between mean scores in favour of the Cohort 1 pupils. Over the sample as a whole, mean scores for Cohort 2 pupils in Group 1

137

schools do not differ significantly from those for pupils in the internal control groups, but, within separate parental occupation categories, mean scores for pupils in the 'professional and clerical' category differ significantly ($p < 0.001$) in favour of the control groups.

2. *Group 2 schools.* Taking the sample as a whole, mean scores for pupils in the experimental groups are significantly higher than those for pupils in the external control groups. Mean scores differ in favour of the Cohort 1 pupils at the 0·1 per cent level and in favour of the Cohort 2 pupils at the one per cent level. Within separate parental occupation categories, however, there is only one instance of a significant difference between mean scores: mean scores for pupils in the 'professional and clerical' category differ significantly in favour of the Cohort 1 pupils at the 0·1 per cent level.

3. *Group 3 schools.* There are no significant differences between the mean scores obtained by the pupils in the experimental schools and those obtained by the pupils in the matched control schools.

TABLE 1.4. *Comparison of experimental and control groups. Problem Arithmetic Test: mean scores by school group and parental occupation.*

SCHOOL GROUP		Professional and Clerical	Skilled	Semi-skilled	Unskilled	TOTAL
		PARENTAL OCCUPATION				
Group 1 (Cohort 1)	N	216	367	377	192	1152
	x̄	22·82	20·07	18·60	16·34	19·48
	SD	5·05	5·55	5·78	6·14	5·99
Group 1 (Cohort 2)	N	260	446	361	161	1228
	x̄	21·39	19·87	18·18	15·34	19·10
	SD	5·64	5·63	5·79	5·70	5·98
Group 1 Controls	N	709	956	839	431	2935
	x̄	23·36	20·39	17·77	16·03	19·72
	SD	5·09	5·88	6·55	6·56	6·52
Group 2 (Cohort 1)	N	652	867	812	395	2726
	x̄	22·90	20·26	17·67	15·62	19·45
	SD	5·13	5·70	5·93	6·47	6·27
Group 2 (Cohort 2)	N	674	994	815	391	2874
	x̄	22·30	19·83	17·43	15·95	19·20
	SD	5·15	5·67	6·13	6·35	6·18
Group 2 Controls	N	308	596	474	258	1636
	x̄	22·00	19·66	17·82	15·76	18·95
	SD	5·65	6·44	6·43	6·71	6·64
Group 3	N	74	166	158	93	491
	x̄	19·69	18·64	16·72	13·80	17·27
	SD	5·35	6·12	6·46	6·62	6·51
Group 3 Controls	N	84	189	185	91	549
	x̄	20·79	18·46	16·87	15·74	17·83
	SD	5·37	6·56	6·64	6·81	6·64

Notes

1. *Group 1 schools.* Taking the sample as a whole, mean scores for Cohort 1 pupils in Group 1 schools do not differ significantly from those for pupils in the internal control groups. Within the 'semi-skilled' parental occupation category, however, there is a significant difference ($p < 0.05$) between mean scores in favour of the Cohort 1 pupils. Mean scores for Cohort 2 pupils in Group 1 schools are slightly lower than those for pupils in the internal control groups. Over the sample as a whole, mean scores differ significantly at the one per cent level in favour of

139

the control groups. Within separate parental occupation categories, mean scores for pupils in the 'professional and clerical' category differ significantly at the 0·1 per cent level in favour of the control groups: there are no other instances of significant differences between the mean scores of the pupils in the experimental and control groups.

2. *Group 2 schools.* The test performance of the pupils in the experimental groups differs little from that of the pupils in the external control groups. Mean scores for Cohort 1 pupils in the 'professional and clerical' category are slightly higher than those for control pupils in the same category and differ significantly at the five per cent level, but there are no other significant differences between mean scores.

3. *Group 3 schools.* Taking the sample as a whole, the test performance of the pupils in the experimental schools does not differ significantly from that of pupils in the matched control schools. Mean scores for pupils in the 'unskilled' category differ significantly in favour of the control schools at the five per cent level, but there are no other significant differences between mean scores.

Appendix One

TABLE 1.5. *Comparison of experimental and control groups. English Test: mean scores by school group and parental occupation.*

SCHOOL GROUP		Professional and Clerical	Skilled	Semi-skilled	Unskilled	TOTAL
		PARENTAL OCCUPATION				
Group 1 (Cohort 1)	N	220	376	371	186	1153
	x̄	50·74	44·40	39·88	33·04	42·32
	SD	10·53	13·33	13·61	16·40	14·59
Group 1 (Cohort 2)	N	258	443	357	158	1216
	x̄	47·43	43·88	38·26	30·27	41·21
	SD	12·90	13·38	14·80	14·80	14·91
Group 1 Controls	N	707	947	837	423	2914
	x̄	51·91	44·27	37·81	33·26	42·67
	SD	11·06	14·60	16·58	16·71	16·11
Group 2 (Cohort 1)	N	657	868	817	396	2738
	x̄	50·51	43·35	36·46	30·83	41·20
	SD	11·45	13·81	14·97	16·58	15·59
Group 2 (Cohort 2)	N	684	977	804	385	2850
	x̄	49·40	42·74	36·99	32·99	41·40
	SD	11·50	13·60	15·19	15·74	14·99
Group 2 Controls	N	312	601	510	283	1706
	x̄	48·19	42·60	37·34	32·81	40·43
	SD	13·03	14·49	16·65	17·10	16·17
Group 3	N	70	165	159	93	487
	x̄	45·44	40·52	36·81	29·05	37·82
	SD	13·74	15·30	15·74	17·46	16·48
Group 3 Controls	N	84	187	182	94	547
	x̄	45·87	40·13	36·77	34·18	38·86
	SD	14·94	15·77	15·22	16·62	16·04

Notes

1. *Group 1 schools.* Taking the sample as a whole, mean scores for Cohort 1 pupils in Group 1 schools do not differ significantly from those for pupils in the internal control groups. Within separate parental occupation categories, mean scores for Cohort 1 pupils in the 'semi-skilled' category are just significantly higher ($p < 0.05$) than those for control pupils in the same category, but no other instances of significant differences between mean scores occur. Over the sample as a whole, mean scores for Cohort 2 pupils in Group 1 schools are significantly

lower ($p < 0.01$) than those for pupils in the internal control groups. Within separate parental occupation categories, there are significant differences between mean scores in favour of the control pupils in the 'professional and clerical' category at the 0·1 per cent level and in favour of the control pupils in the 'unskilled' category at the five per cent level.

2. *Group 2 schools.* The test performance of the pupils in the experimental groups differs little from that of the pupils in the external control groups. Cohort 1 pupils in the 'professional and clerical' category obtain significantly higher ($p < 0.01$) mean scores than those obtained by the control pupils in the same category, but there are no other instances of significant differences between mean scores.

3. *Group 3 schools.* Taking the sample as a whole, the mean scores obtained by the pupils in the experimental schools do not differ significantly from those obtained by the pupils in the matched control schools. Mean scores for pupils in the 'unskilled' parental occupation category differ significantly in favour of the control schools at the five per cent level, but there are no other instances of significant differences between mean scores.

Appendix One

TABLE 1.6. *Primary Verbal Test. Mean scores by cohort, school group, sex of pupil, and parental occupation.*

COHORT SCHOOL GROUP SEX OF PUPIL		PARENTAL OCCUPATION				TOTAL
		Professional and Clerical	*Skilled*	*Semi-skilled*	*Unskilled*	
Cohort 1	N	103	200	181	93	577
Group 1	x̄	73·22	67·69	64·65	54·89	65·66
Boys	SD	11·60	14·74	15·45	20·12	16·44
Cohort 1	N	113	160	187	92	552
Group 1	x̄	76·45	71·91	64·86	58·24	68·17
Girls	SD	7·32	10·92	14·65	17·58	14·42
Cohort 1	N	216	360	368	185	1129
Group 1	x̄	74·91	69·57	64·76	56·56	66·89
Total	SD	9·74	13·35	15·05	18·98	15·53
Cohort 2	N	124	225	171	79	599
Group 1	x̄	71·58	66·62	61·84	51·11	64·24
Boys	SD	12·78	14·44	17·23	17·42	16·57
Cohort 2	N	134	223	186	84	627
Group 1	x̄	72·93	70·62	63·75	55·64	67·07
Girls	SD	11·92	11·71	15·53	16·40	14·81
Cohort 2	N	258	448	357	163	1226
Group 1	x̄	72·28	68·61	62·83	53·45	65·69
Total	SD	12·36	13·30	16·39	17·05	15·76
Cohort 1	N	313	428	411	210	1362
Group 2	x̄	74·15	67·89	61·80	50·48	64·81
Boys	SD	10·89	15·23	17·17	22·18	17·96
Cohort 1	N	333	432	408	189	1362
Group 2	x̄	75·91	71·14	63·33	59·59	68·37
Girls	SD	8·76	11·53	15·66	17·67	14·57
Cohort 1	N	646	860	819	399	2724
Group 2	x̄	75·06	69·52	62·56	54·79	66·59
Total	SD	9·89	13·60	16·45	20·68	16·45
Cohort 2	N	350	517	380	200	1447
Group 2	x̄	73·33	67·75	60·45	55·61	65·61
Boys	SD	12·25	14·22	18·93	19·91	17·16
Cohort 2	N	338	482	436	187	1443
Group 2	x̄	74·66	69·46	64·56	59·97	67·97
Girls	SD	10·64	12·78	14·71	17·15	14·41
Cohort 2	N	688	999	816	387	2890
Group 2	x̄	73·99	68·58	62·65	57·72	66·74
Total	SD	11·51	13·57	16·93	18·75	15·89

143

Notes

1. *Sex differences.* Taking the sample as a whole, there is a tendency for the girls in each cohort to obtain higher mean scores than the boys. In Group 1 schools, mean scores for Cohort 1 pupils in the 'professional and clerical' parental occupation category differ significantly in favour of the girls at the five per cent level, but mean scores for Cohort 2 pupils in the same category do not differ significantly. In the 'skilled' parental occupation category, mean scores for pupils in both cohorts differ significantly in favour of the girls at the five per cent level, but there are no significant differences between mean scores for boys and girls in the 'semi-skilled' and 'unskilled' categories. In Group 2 schools, mean scores for Cohort 1 pupils in the 'professional and clerical' parental occupation category differ significantly in favour of the girls at the five per cent level, but mean scores for Cohort 2 pupils in the same category do not differ significantly. Mean scores for Cohort 1 pupils in the 'skilled' and 'unskilled' parental occupation categories differ significantly in favour of the girls at the 0·1 per cent level; those for Cohort2 pupils in the same parental occupation categories differ significantly in favour of the girls at the five per cent level. In the 'semi-skilled' category, mean scores for Cohort 1 pupils do not differ significantly, but those for Cohort 2 pupils differ significantly in favour of the girls at the 0·1 per cent level.

2. *Parental occupation.* There is a linear relationship between test score and parental occupation: for both boys and girls in each school group and cohort, high scores coincide with high-status parental occupation and low scores with low-status parental occupation.

3. *School group.* With all parental occupation categories combined, the test performance of pupils in Group 1 schools differs little from that of pupils in Group 2 schools, whether scores for girls and boys are considered separately or together. Within separate parental occupation categories, but with the scores for pupils of both sexes combined, there is a significant difference ($p < 0.05$) between mean scores in favour of Group 1 schools for Cohort 1 pupils in the 'semi-skilled' category, but there is also a significant difference ($p < 0.01$) between mean scores in favour of Group 2 schools for Cohort 2 pupils in the 'unskilled' category. There are no other significant differences between mean scores.

4. *Cohort.* With all parental occupation categories combined, there are no significant differences between mean scores for Cohort 1 and Cohort 2 pupils, whether scores for pupils of both sexes and in both school groups are considered separately or together. Within separate parental occupation categories, but with the scores for pupils of both sexes and in both school groups combined, there is a significant difference ($p < 0.01$) between mean scores in favour of Cohort 1 for pupils in the 'professional and clerical' category: this is the only instance of a significant difference between mean scores for pupils in Cohorts 1 and 2.

TABLE 1.7. *Mechanical Arithmetic Test. Mean scores by cohort, school group, sex of pupil, and parental occupation.*

COHORT SCHOOL GROUP SEX OF PUPIL		*Professional and Clerical*	*Skilled*	*Semi-skilled*	*Unskilled*	TOTAL
				PARENTAL OCCUPATION		
Cohort 1	N	102	200	182	93	577
Group 1	x̄	30·07	25·80	23·44	19·77	24·84
Boys	SD	9·09	9·58	9·47	8·89	9·87
Cohort 1	N	113	163	186	94	556
Group 1	x̄	31·96	27·88	24·85	22·36	26·76
Girls	SD	7·46	9·17	9·94	9·41	9·71
Cohort 1	N	215	363	368	187	1133
Group 1	x̄	31·06	26·73	24·15	21·07	25·78
Total	SD	8·33	9·46	9·73	9·24	9·84
Cohort 2	N	125	228	174	79	606
Group 1	x̄	28·07	23·99	23·18	17·44	23·75
Boys	SD	9·97	9·15	9·35	8·40	9·77
Cohort 2	N	134	224	183	86	627
Group 1	x̄	28·51	26·52	23·40	18·57	24·95
Girls	SD	9·68	9·09	8·99	8·64	9·66
Cohort 2	N	259	452	357	165	1233
Group 1	x̄	28·30	25·25	23·29	18·03	24·36
Total	SD	9·82	9·21	9·17	8·54	9·73
Cohort 1	N	313	426	411	210	1360
Group 2	x̄	30·20	26·62	21·76	17·23	24·52
Boys	SD	9·35	9·72	9·70	9·35	10·53
Cohort 1	N	333	431	408	189	1361
Group 2	x̄	31·52	26·92	21·79	20·64	25·64
Girls	SD	8·83	9·52	9·42	9·51	10·19
Cohort 1	N	646	857	819	399	2721
Group 2	x̄	30·88	26·77	21·78	18·85	25·08
Total	SD	9·11	9·62	9·56	9·58	10·38
Cohort 2	N	349	519	378	201	1447
Group 2	x̄	29·45	24·66	20·08	18·84	23·81
Boys	SD	9·48	9·96	9·84	9·13	10·45
Cohort 2	N	342	483	432	186	1443
Group 2	x̄	29·28	25·63	22·57	19·77	24·82
Girls	SD	9·05	9·53	9·31	8·97	9·79
Cohort 2	N	691	1002	810	387	2890
Group 2	x̄	29·36	25·13	21·41	19·29	24·32
Total	SD	9·27	9·77	9·64	9·07	10·14

Notes

1. *Sex differences.* Taking the sample as a whole, there is a tendency for the girls in each cohort to obtain higher mean scores than the boys, but differences between mean scores rarely reach a significant level. In Group 1 schools, the only significant differences between mean scores in favour of the girls are for pupils in the 'skilled' parental occupation category: these differences are significant at the five per cent level for Cohort 1 pupils and at the one per cent level for Cohort 2 pupils. In Group 2 schools, mean scores for Cohort 1 pupils in the 'unskilled' parental occupation category and for Cohort 2 pupils in the 'semi-skilled' category differ significantly in favour of the girls at the 0·1 per cent level.

2. *Parental occupation.* There is a linear relationship between test score and parental occupation: for both boys and girls in each school group and cohort, high scores coincide with high-status parental occupation and low scores with low-status parental occupation.

3. *School group.* With all parental occupation categories combined, Cohort 1 pupils in Group 1 schools obtain somewhat higher mean scores than do those in Group 2 schools. However, differences between the two groups of scores only reach the five per cent level of significance when the girls' scores are considered alone or when the boys' and girls' scores are combined. When the parental occupation categories are considered separately, significant differences in favour of Group 1 school pupils occur only within the 'semi-skilled' (p < 0·001) and 'unskilled' (p < 0·01) categories. With all parental occupation categories combined, there are no significant differences between the mean scores of Cohort 2 pupils in Group 1 or Group 2 schools, whether scores for boys and girls are considered separately or together. Within separate parental occupation categories, the only significant difference between mean scores occurs in the 'semi-skilled' category: this difference favours pupils in Group 1 schools and is significant at the one per cent level.

4. *Cohort.* Taking the sample as a whole, mean scores for Cohort 1 pupils are significantly higher (p < 0·001) than those for Cohort 2 pupils. Within separate parental occupation categories, but with scores for both sexes and school groups combined, significant differences between mean scores in favour of Cohort 1 are concentrated in the higher parental occupation categories: differences reach the 0·1 per cent level of significance in the 'professional and clerical' and 'skilled' categories, but are insignificant in the 'semi-skilled' and 'unskilled' categories. With school groups combined, differences between mean scores in favour of Cohort 1 reach a higher level of significance for girls (p < 0·001) than for boys (p < 0·05). With scores for both sexes combined, differences in favour of Cohort 1 are more significant for pupils in Group 1 schools (p < 0·001) than for those in Group 2 schools (p < 0·01).

Appendix One

TABLE 1.8: *Reading Test. Mean scores by cohort, school group, sex of pupil, and parental occupation.*

COHORT SCHOOL GROUP SEX OF PUPIL		PARENTAL OCCUPATION				TOTAL
		Professional and Clerical	*Skilled*	*Semi-skilled*	*Unskilled*	
Cohort 1	N	103	204	187	98	592
Group 1	x̄	37·45	33·25	31·73	27·50	32·55
Boys	SD	5·82	7·97	7·39	9·64	8·32
Cohort 1	N	114	168	195	94	571
Group 1	x̄	37·24	34·84	31·36	28·90	33·15
Girls	SD	4·89	6·78	7·44	8·13	7·51
Cohort 1	N	217	372	382	192	1163
Group 1	x̄	37·34	33·97	31·54	28·19	32·85
Total	SD	5·35	7·50	7·42	8·96	7·93
Cohort 2	N	127	222	175	76	600
Group 1	x̄	36·11	33·47	30·19	25·03	32·00
Boys	SD	7·59	7·87	8·50	9·03	8·83
Cohort 2	N	130	221	184	84	619
Group 1	x̄	36·21	34·64	30·35	28·00	32·81
Girls	SD	6·37	6·32	8·24	6·96	7·63
Cohort 2	N	257	443	359	160	1219
Group 1	x̄	36·20	34·05	30·27	26·59	32·41
Total	SD	7·00	7·16	8·37	8·14	8·25
Cohort 1	N	319	429	413	217	1378
Group 2	x̄	37·29	33·45	30·11	24·80	31·98
Boys	SD	6·41	8·09	8·88	10·46	9·33
Cohort 1	N	332	439	400	182	1353
Group 2	x̄	37·35	33·82	30·15	28·79	32·92
Girls	SD	6·07	6·58	7·80	8·09	7·71
Cohort 1	N	651	868	813	399	2731
Group 2	x̄	37·32	33·64	30·13	26·62	32·44
Total	SD	6·24	7·36	8·37	9·66	8·58
Cohort 2	N	340	517	375	200	1432
Group 2	x̄	36·36	33·35	29·63	27·11	32·22
Boys	SD	6·97	7·37	9·36	9·82	8·80
Cohort 2	N	338	473	441	190	1442
Group 2	x̄	36·70	33·07	30·45	28·62	32·53
Girls	SD	6·15	6·99	7·40	8·12	7·60
Cohort 2	N	678	990	816	390	2874
Group 2	x̄	36·53	33·22	30·07	27·85	32·38
Total	SD	6·57	7·19	8·37	9·06	8·22

Notes

1. *Sex differences.* The test performance of the boys in the sample differs little from that of the girls. There are only a few significant differences between mean scores, but each of these differences favours the girls. In Group 1 schools, girls' mean scores are slightly higher than boys' when all parental occupation categories are combined, but significant differences in favour of the girls occur only in the 'skilled' category for Cohort 1 pupils and in the 'unskilled' category for Cohort 2 pupils: both of these differences are significant at the five per cent level. In Group 2 schools, there is a significant difference in favour of the girls at the 0·1 per cent level for Cohort 1 pupils in the 'unskilled' parental occupation category: there are no other significant differences between mean scores.

2. *Parental occupation.* There is a linear relationship between test score and parental occupation: for both boys and girls in each school group and cohort, high scores coincide with high-status parental occupation and low scores with low-status parental occupation.

3. *School group.* The test performance of pupils in Group 1 schools does not differ significantly from that of pupils in Group 2 schools: this finding applies equally to the pupils in each cohort.

4. *Cohort.* The test performance of the pupils in Cohort 1 does not differ significantly from that of the pupils in Cohort 2.

Appendix One

TABLE 1.9. *Problem Arithmetic Test. Mean scores by cohort, school group, sex of pupil, and parental occupation.*

COHORT SCHOOL GROUP SEX OF PUPIL		Professional and Clerical	Skilled	Semi-skilled	Unskilled	TOTAL
				PARENTAL OCCUPATION		
Cohort 1	N	104	201	187	97	589
Group 1	x̄	22·85	19·84	18·99	16·52	19·55
Boys	SD	5·58	5·93	5·65	6·16	6·12
Cohort 1	N	112	166	190	95	563
Group 1	x̄	22·80	20·36	18·21	16·16	19·41
Girls	SD	4·51	5·04	5·88	6·12	5·86
Cohort 1	N	216	367	377	192	1152
Group 1	x̄	22·82	20·07	18·60	16·34	19·48
Total	SD	5·05	5·55	5·78	6·14	5·99
Cohort 2	N	127	224	174	77	602
Group 1	x̄	21·61	19·66	18·29	14·92	19·07
Boys	SD	5·58	5·74	6·04	6·02	6·16
Cohort 2	N	133	222	187	84	626
Group 1	x̄	21·18	20·07	18·07	15·71	19·12
Girls	SD	5·69	5·51	5·54	5·36	5·81
Cohort 2	N	260	446	361	161	1228
Group 1	x̄	21·39	19·87	18·18	15·34	19·10
Total	SD	5·64	5·63	5·79	5·70	5·98
Cohort 1	N	318	428	412	214	1372
Group 2	x̄	22·73	20·73	17·99	15·24	19·51
Boys	SD	5·38	5·71	6·12	6·66	6·44
Cohort 1	N	334	439	400	181	1354
Group 2	x̄	23·06	19·81	17·34	16·06	19·38
Girls	SD	4·88	5·66	5·71	6·21	6·10
Cohort 1	N	652	867	812	395	2726
Group 2	x̄	22·90	20·26	17·67	15·62	19·45
Total	SD	5·13	5·70	5·93	6·47	6·27
Cohort 2	N	337	519	374	202	1432
Group 2	x̄	22·53	19·90	17·13	15·95	19·24
Boys	SD	5·18	5·72	6·36	6·47	6·33
Cohort 2	N	337	475	441	189	1442
Group 2	x̄	22·07	19·75	17·68	15·95	19·16
Girls	SD	5·10	5·61	5·92	6·22	6·03
Cohort 2	N	674	994	815	391	2874
Group 2	x̄	22·30	19·83	17·43	15·95	19·20
Total	SD	5·15	5·67	6·13	6·35	6·18

Notes

1. *Sex differences.* The test performance of the boys in the sample differs little from that of the girls. There is only one instance of a significant difference between mean scores: this occurs in Group 2 schools where mean scores of Cohort 1 pupils in the 'skilled' parental occupation category differ significantly in favour of the boys at the five per cent level.

2. *Parental occupation.* There is a linear relationship between test score and parental occupation: for both boys and girls in each school group and cohort, high scores coincide with high-status parental occupation and low scores with low-status parental occupation.

3. *School group.* The test performance of pupils in Group 1 schools does not differ significantly from that of pupils in Group 2 schools: this finding applies equally to the pupils in each cohort.

4. *Cohort.* There is little difference between the test performance of the pupils in Cohort 1 and those in Cohort 2. When the scores for all pupils are combined, there is a significant difference ($p < 0.05$) between mean scores in favour of Cohort 1, but this difference is confined to pupils in the 'professional and clerical' parental occupation category.

TABLE 1.10: *English Test. Mean scores by cohort, school group, sex of pupil, and parental occupation.*

COHORT SCHOOL GROUP SEX OF PUPIL		Professional and Clerical	Skilled	Semi-skilled	Unskilled	TOTAL
		PARENTAL OCCUPATION				
Cohort 1 Group 1 Boys	N	107	208	188	96	599
	x̄	48·84	41·76	38·65	30·99	40·32
	SD	11·50	13·80	13·48	16·19	14·74
Cohort 1 Group 1 Girls	N	113	168	183	90	554
	x̄	52·53	47·68	41·15	35·23	44·49
	SD	9·17	11·95	13·64	16·34	14·11
Cohort 1 Group 1 Total	N	220	376	371	186	1153
	x̄	50·74	44·40	39·88	33·04	42·32
	SD	10·53	13·33	13·61	16·40	14·59
Cohort 2 Group 1 Boys	N	123	225	175	76	599
	x̄	45·54	40·70	35·92	26·91	38·55
	SD	13·42	14·18	15·02	15·55	15·49
Cohort 2 Group 1 Girls	N	135	218	182	82	617
	x̄	49·15	47·16	40·51	33·38	43·80
	SD	12·16	11·61	14·22	13·34	13·83
Cohort 2 Group 1 Total	N	258	443	357	158	1216
	x̄	47·43	43·88	38·26	30·27	41·21
	SD	12·90	13·38	14·80	14·80	14·91
Cohort 1 Group 2 Boys	N	324	433	417	212	1386
	x̄	48·59	40·58	34·48	26·65	38·49
	SD	12·09	14·70	15·10	16·29	16·20
Cohort 1 Group 2 Girls	N	333	435	400	184	1352
	x̄	52·37	46·10	38·53	35·65	43·98
	SD	10·46	12·25	14·55	15·58	14·42
Cohort 1 Group 2 Total	N	657	868	817	396	2738
	x̄	50·51	43·35	36·46	30·83	41·20
	SD	11·45	13·81	14·97	16·58	15·59
Cohort 2 Group 2 Boys	N	345	512	368	199	1424
	x̄	47·71	40·63	33·07	29·95	38·90
	SD	12·33	13·90	15·89	16·18	15·75
Cohort 2 Group 2 Girls	N	339	465	436	186	1426
	x̄	51·12	45·08	40·30	36·24	43·90
	SD	10·31	12·87	13·73	14·57	13·75
Cohort 2 Group 2 Total	N	684	977	804	385	2850
	x̄	49·40	42·74	36·99	32·99	41·40
	SD	11·50	13·60	15·19	15·74	14·99

French in the Primary School

Notes

1. *Sex differences.* Taking the sample as a whole, mean scores for girls are higher than those for boys. In Group 1 schools, mean scores for boys and girls in the 'professional and clerical' parental occupation category differ significantly in favour of the girls at the one per cent level for Cohort 1 pupils and at the five per cent level for Cohort 2 pupils. In the 'skilled' parental occupation category, differences between mean scores in favour of the girls reach the 0·1 per cent level of significance for pupils in both cohorts. In the 'semi-skilled' and 'unskilled' categories, differences in favour of the girls are significant at the five per cent level for Cohort 2 pupils, but do not reach a significant level for Cohort 1 pupils, although the mean scores for girls are in each instance higher than those for boys. In Group 2 schools, pupils' mean scores differ significantly in favour of the girls at the 0·1 per cent level: this finding applies equally to the pupils in each cohort and within each parental occupation category.

2. *Parental occupation.* There is a linear relationship between test score and parental occupation: for both boys and girls in each school group and cohort, high scores coincide with high-status parental occupation and low scores with low-status parental occupation.

3. *School group.* There are few significant differences between the test performance of pupils in Group 1 schools and those in Group 2 schools. Mean scores for Cohort 1 pupils differ significantly in favour of Group 1 schools at the five per cent level, when boys' and girls' scores are combined or when boys' scores are considered separately, but this significant difference is confined to pupils in the 'semi-skilled' parental occupation category. The test performance of Cohort 2 pupils in Group 1 schools does not differ significantly from that of Cohort 2 pupils in Group 2 schools.

4. *Cohort.* The test performance of pupils in Cohort 1 does not differ significantly from that of pupils in Cohort 2.

152

APPENDIX TWO

Achievement in French in the Primary School

(Tables 2.1 - 2.7; Figures 2.1 - 2.9)

French in the Primary School

TABLE 2.1: *Test RCA. Mean scores by school group, sex of pupil, and parental occupation.*

SCHOOL GROUP SEX OF PUPIL		Professional and Clerical	Skilled	Semi-skilled	Unskilled	TOTAL
		PARENTAL OCCUPATION				
Group 1 Boys	N	103	190	185	92	570
	x̄	31·34	26·82	24·49	21·41	26·01
	SD	8·98	8·77	8·65	9·14	9·36
Group 1 Girls	N	111	163	183	91	548
	x̄	35·25	31·80	28·43	23·10	29·93
	SD	8·49	9·56	8·93	8·52	9·78
Group 1 Total	N	214	353	368	183	1118
	x̄	33·37	29·12	26·45	22·25	27·93
	SD	8·95	9·48	9·01	8·88	9·77
Group 2 Boys	N	317	421	403	210	1351
	x̄	30·23	26·34	22·99	19·37	25·17
	SD	9·14	8·99	9·08	9·18	9·78
Group 2 Girls	N	327	428	393	173	1321
	x̄	34·31	30·88	26·65	25·12	29·72
	SD	8·34	9·69	9·82	10·12	10·05
Group 2 Total	N	644	849	796	383	2672
	x̄	32·31	28·63	24·80	21·97	27·42
	SD	8·98	9·62	9·63	10·03	10·17
Groups 1 & 2 Boys	N	420	611	588	302	1921
	x̄	30·50	26·49	23·46	19·99	25·42
	SD	9·12	8·93	8·98	9·22	9·66
Groups 1 & 2 Girls	N	438	591	576	264	1869
	x̄	34·55	31·13	27·22	24·42	29·78
	SD	8·39	9·66	9·58	9·64	9·97
Groups 1 & 2 Total	N	858	1202	1164	566	3790
	x̄	32·57	28·77	25·32	22·06	27·57
	SD	8·98	9·58	9·47	9·67	10·06

Notes

1. *Sex differences.* In both school groups and within each parental occupation category, girls obtain significantly higher mean scores than boys. Differences between mean scores in favour of the girls are significant at the 0·1 per cent level.

154

2. *Parental occupation.* There is a linear relationship between test score and parental occupation: for both boys and girls in each school group, high mean scores coincide with high-status parental occupation and low mean scores with low-status parental occupation. Differences between mean scores are significant at the 0·1 per cent level.

3. *School group.* Pupils in the two groups of schools differ little in their test performance. In Group 1 schools, girls in the 'semi-skilled' parental occupation category obtain mean scores which are significantly higher ($p < 0.05$) than those obtained by girls in the same category in Group 2 schools, but this is the only instance of a significant difference between the mean scores obtained by the pupils in the two groups of schools.

French in the Primary School

TABLE 2.2: *Battery 1 Speaking Test. Mean scores by type of school, sex of pupil, and parental occupation.*

PARENTAL OCCUPATION

TYPE OF SCHOOL SEX OF PUPIL		Professional and Clerical	Skilled	Semi-skilled	Unskilled	TOTAL
Large Primary Boys	N	150	152	113	62	477
	x̄	31·29	28·55	20·95	16·71	26·07
	SD	20·46	18·66	16·37	14·55	19·02
Large Primary Girls	N	151	202	101	57	511
	x̄	37·04	29·00	23·73	20·61	29·40
	SD	19·80	17·85	16·13	15·32	18·75
Large Primary Total	N	301	354	214	119	988
	x̄	34·17	28·80	22·27	18·58	27·79
	SD	20·34	18·20	16·32	15·05	18·95
Small Primary Boys	N	6	10	19	6	41
	x̄	48·33	36·30	36·52	36·50	38·19
	SD	16·51	12·14	14·10	9·48	14·10
Small Primary Girls	N	7	20	10	6	43
	x̄	48·42	38·45	27·80	29·16	36·30
	SD	17·37	11·98	12·77	14·21	15·23
Small Primary Total	N	13	30	29	12	84
	x̄	48·38	37·73	33·51	32·83	37·22
	SD	16·98	12·07	14·27	12·62	14·72
Comprehensive Boys	N	42	72	37	15	166
	x̄	29·95	20·44	18·67	20·27	22·44
	SD	19·08	14·50	18·46	19·80	17·73
Comprehensive Girls	N	53	81	36	27	197
	x̄	31·96	30·11	26·69	22·15	28·89
	SD	17·57	18·57	18·47	18·26	18·52
Comprehensive Total	N	95	153	73	42	363
	x̄	31·07	25·56	22·63	21·48	25·94
	SD	18·28	17·46	18·89	18·85	18·45

Notes

1. *Sex differences.* In the large primary schools, girls tend to obtain higher mean scores than boys, but the differences between mean scores only reach significance in the 'professional and clerical' parental occupation category and

156

when all parental occupation categories are combined. In the small primary schools, there are no significant differences between the mean scores of boys and girls in the 'professional and clerical' and 'skilled' parental occupation categories. In the 'semi-skilled' and 'unskilled' categories, and when all parental occupation categories are combined, boys tend to obtain higher mean scores than girls. It must be emphasized, however, that the sample size in this instance is extremely small. In the comprehensive schools, girls tend to obtain higher mean scores than boys: the most significant difference between mean scores in favour of the girls occurs in the 'skilled' parental occupation category ($p < 0.001$).

2. *Parental occupation.* When scores for both sexes are combined, there is a tendency in each group of schools for high mean scores to coincide with high-status parental occupation and for low mean scores to coincide with low-status parental occupation, but this tendency is not always apparent when the sexes are considered separately. In the small primary schools, for example, mean scores obtained by boys in the 'skilled', 'semi-skilled' and 'unskilled' categories do not differ significantly from one another, but, again, it must be emphasized that the sample size in this instance is extremely small.

3. *School group.* Mean scores for pupils in the small primary schools are significantly higher than those for pupils in the comprehensive schools. Taking the sample as a whole, the differences between mean scores for both boys and girls are significant at the 0·1 per cent level. Within parental occupation categories, significant differences in favour of the pupils in the small primary schools occur at the 0·1 per cent level in the 'professional and clerical' and 'skilled' categories, at the one per cent level in the 'semi-skilled' category, and at the five per cent level in the 'unskilled' category. Mean scores for pupils in the small primary schools are also significantly higher than those for pupils in the large primary schools: with all parental occupation categories combined, the differences between mean scores for both boys and girls are significant at the 0·1 per cent level. Within parental occupation categories, significant differences in favour of the pupils in the small primary schools occur at the 0·1 per cent level for boys in the 'semi-skilled' and 'unskilled' categories, at the one per cent level for girls in the 'skilled' category, and at the five per cent level for boys in the 'professional and clerical' category. Differences between mean scores in the remaining parental occupation groups do not reach a significant level but, in each case, mean scores for pupils in the small primary schools are higher than those for pupils in the large primary schools.

Taking the sample as a whole, mean scores for pupils in the large primary schools are significantly higher than those for pupils in the comprehensive schools. Significant differences in favour of the primary school pupils are concentrated in the higher parental occupation categories: there are no significant differences between mean scores for pupils in the 'semi-skilled' and 'unskilled' categories.

157

TABLE 2.3: *Battery 1 Listening Test. Mean scores by type of school, sex of pupil, and parental occupation.*

TYPE OF SCHOOL SEX OF PUPIL		Professional and Clerical	Skilled	Semi-skilled	Unskilled	TOTAL
Large Primary Boys	N	705	927	603	324	2559
	x̄	23·25	21·04	18·97	16·99	20·65
	SD	7·77	7·54	7·02	6·76	7·67
Large Primary Girls	N	730	860	625	338	2553
	x̄	25·50	23·40	20·55	18·81	22·70
	SD	7·82	7·72	7·23	6·88	7·89
Large Primary Total	N	1435	1787	1228	662	5112
	x̄	24·39	22·18	19·77	17·92	21·67
	SD	7·88	7·72	7·17	6·88	7·85
Small Primary Boys	N	12	25	33	16	86
	x̄	30·16	27·04	25·42	22·37	25·98
	SD	5·66	5·70	7·92	6·94	7·23
Small Primary Girls	N	11	42	29	12	94
	x̄	29·54	28·52	28·62	22·91	27·91
	SD	7·27	5·48	5·41	5·70	6·05
Small Primary Total	N	23	67	62	28	180
	x̄	29·86	27·97	26·91	22·60	27·01
	SD	6·49	5·61	7·04	6·44	6·71
Comprehensive Boys	N	232	351	260	124	967
	x̄	23·68	20·89	19·32	17·36	20·68
	SD	7·67	7·44	7·99	6·90	7·84
Comprehensive Girls	N	278	415	254	150	1097
	x̄	25·54	22·80	21·89	19·35	22·81
	SD	8·03	8·03	8·23	7·26	8·21
Comprehensive Total	N	510	766	514	274	2064
	x̄	24·69	21·92	20·59	18·45	21·81
	SD	7·92	7·82	8·21	7·17	8·11

PARENTAL OCCUPATION (header spanning Professional and Clerical, Skilled, Semi-skilled, Unskilled)

Notes

1. *Sex differences.* In all school groups, mean scores for girls are significantly higher than those for boys: differences between mean scores are significant at the 0·1 per cent level.

2. *Parental occupation.* There is a linear relationship between test score and parental occupation: in all school groups and for pupils of both sexes, high mean scores coincide with high-status parental occupation and low mean scores with low-status parental occupation.

3. *School group.* Mean scores for pupils in the small primary schools are significantly higher than those for pupils in the comprehensive schools. With all parental occupation categories combined, differences between mean scores in favour of the primary school pupils are significant at the 0·1 per cent level for both boys and girls. Within parental occupation categories, significant differences between mean scores in favour of the primary school pupils occur at the 0·1 per cent level in each category except the 'unskilled' category, where they occur at the one per cent level. Mean scores for pupils in the small primary schools are also significantly higher than those for pupils in the large primary schools. With all parental occupation categories combined, differences between mean scores in favour of pupils in the small primary schools are significant at the 0·1 per cent level for both boys and girls. Within parental occupation categories, mean scores for boys in the 'professional and clerical' category, and for both boys and girls in the 'skilled' and 'semi-skilled' categories, differ significantly at the 0·1 per cent level. Mean scores for boys in the 'unskilled' category differ significantly at the one per cent level, while those for girls in the same category differ significantly at the five per cent level. Differences between the mean scores of girls in the 'professional and clerical' category do not reach a significant level, but mean scores for girls in the small schools are higher than those for girls in the large schools.

Taking the sample as a whole, the mean scores obtained by pupils in the large primary schools do not differ significantly from those obtained by pupils in the comprehensive schools.

TABLE 2.4: *Battery 1 Reading Test. Mean scores by type of school, sex of pupil, and parental occupation.*

TYPE OF SCHOOL SEX OF PUPIL		Professional and Clerical	Skilled	Semi-skilled	Unskilled	TOTAL
		PARENTAL OCCUPATION				
Large Primary Boys	N	702	916	597	322	2537
	x̄	29·75	25·86	23·10	20·01	25·55
	SD	11·30	10·30	9·22	7·93	10·57
Large Primary Girls	N	727	850	614	328	2519
	x̄	33·95	29·73	26·07	23·11	29·19
	SD	11·68	11·10	10·29	9·16	11·46
Large Primary Total	N	1429	1766	1211	650	5056
	x̄	31·88	27·72	24·61	21·57	27·36
	SD	11·68	10·86	9·89	8·71	11·18
Small Primary Boys	N	12	25	33	16	86
	x̄	37·16	30·40	31·63	26·31	31·05
	SD	10·70	8·69	11·45	7·91	10·46
Small Primary Girls	N	11	42	28	12	93
	x̄	42·63	36·26	33·46	28·91	35·22
	SD	11·91	10·25	10·04	8·91	10·86
Small Primary Total	N	23	67	61	28	179
	x̄	39·78	34·07	32·47	27·42	33·22
	SD	11·62	10·11	10·86	8·45	10·87
Comprehensive Boys	N	233	335	253	112	933
	x̄	39·96	36·73	31·85	28·85	35·27
	SD	11·89	11·54	12·13	12·31	12·47
Comprehensive Girls	N	272	399	256	145	1072
	x̄	43·84	41·17	37·29	32·60	39·76
	SD	11·28	11·27	12·71	11·70	12·25
Comprehensive Total	N	505	734	509	257	2005
	x̄	42·05	39·14	34·59	30·96	37·67
	SD	11·72	11·61	12·72	12·11	12·55

Notes

1. *Sex differences.* In all school groups, mean scores for girls are significantly higher than those for boys: differences between mean scores are significant at the 0·1 per cent level.

Appendix Two

2. *Parental occupation.* There is a linear relationship between test score and parental occupation: in all school groups and for pupils of both sexes, high mean scores coincide with high-status parental occupation and low mean scores with low-status parental occupation.

3. *School group.* Mean scores for pupils in the comprehensive schools are significantly higher than those for pupils in the small primary schools. With all parental occupation categories combined, differences between mean scores in favour of the comprehensive school pupils are significant at the 0·1 per cent level for both boys and girls. Within parental occupation categories, however, significant differences in favour of the comprehensive school pupils occur only in the 'skilled' (p < 0·001) and 'unskilled' (p < 0·05) categories: there are no significant differences between mean scores for pupils in the 'professional and clerical' and 'semi-skilled' categories. Mean scores for pupils in the comprehensive schools are significantly higher than those for pupils in the large primary schools. With all parental occupation categories combined, and within each separate parental occupation category, differences between mean scores in favour of the comprehensive school pupils are significant at the 0·1 per cent level for both boys and girls. Mean scores for pupils in the small primary schools are also significantly higher than those for pupils in the large primary schools. With all parental occupation categories combined, differences between mean scores in favour of the pupils in the small schools are significant at the 0·1 per cent level for both boys and girls. Within parental occupation categories, mean scores for both boys and girls in the 'semi-skilled' category and for girls in the 'skilled' category differ significantly in favour of the small school pupils at the 0·1 per cent level. Mean scores for boys in the 'unskilled' category differ significantly at the one per cent level. Mean scores for both boys and girls in the 'professional and clerical' category, for girls in the 'unskilled' category, and for boys in the 'skilled' category differ significantly in favour of the small school pupils at the five per cent level.

F

TABLE 2.5: *Battery 1 Writing Test. Mean scores by type of school, sex of pupil, and parental occupation.*

Type of School / Sex of Pupil		Parental Occupation: *Professional and Clerical*	*Skilled*	*Semi-skilled*	*Unskilled*	Total
Large Primary Boys	N	538	677	383	168	1766
	x̄	20·18	16·70	14·04	11·93	16·73
	SD	10·57	9·65	9·26	8·02	10·09
Large Primary Girls	N	585	663	414	168	1830
	x̄	24·94	21·00	18·12	16·33	21·18
	SD	10·45	9·83	9·33	9·54	10·33
Large Primary Total	N	1123	1340	797	336	3596
	x̄	22·66	18·83	16·16	14·13	18·99
	SD	10·78	9·97	9·52	9·08	10·46
Small Primary Boys	N	7	9	20	11	47
	x̄	28·00	19·44	18·75	18·18	20·12
	SD	8·50	10·81	11·77	5·87	10·54
Small Primary Girls	N	8	21	16	8	53
	x̄	33·75	25·33	18·56	15·75	23·11
	SD	12·01	7·59	7·55	7·27	10·16
Small Primary Total	N	15	30	36	19	100
	x̄	31·06	23·56	18·66	17·15	21·71
	SD	10·90	9·09	10·11	6·61	10·45
Comprehensive Boys	N	234	356	266	123	979
	x̄	35·22	30·88	25·60	22·74	29·46
	SD	14·96	14·42	14·35	14·87	15·21
Comprehensive Girls	N	278	414	257	152	1101
	x̄	39·98	37·36	32·39	26·56	35·37
	SD	14·49	14·16	15·28	14·00	15·15
Comprehensive Total	N	512	770	523	275	2080
	x̄	37·80	34·36	28·94	24·85	32·59
	SD	14·90	14·64	15·20	14·52	15·46

Notes

1. *Sex differences.* In all school groups, mean scores for girls are significantly higher than those for boys: differences between mean scores are significant at the 0·1 per cent level.

2. *Parental occupation.* There is a linear relationship between test score and parental occupation: in all school groups and for pupils of both sexes, high mean scores coincide with high-status parental occupation and low mean scores with low-status parental occupation.

3. *School group.* Mean scores for pupils in the comprehensive schools are significantly higher than those for pupils in either group of primary schools. With all parental occupation categories combined, and within each separate parental occupation category, differences between mean scores in favour of the comprehensive school pupils are significant at the 0·1 per cent level for both boys and girls. There are few significant differences between the mean scores obtained by the pupils in the large primary schools and those obtained by the pupils in the small primary schools. Significant differences in favour of the pupils in the small schools occur at the 0·1 per cent level for boys in the 'unskilled' category and at the five per cent level for boys and girls in the 'professional and clerical' category and for girls in the 'skilled' category. Mean scores tend to be higher in the small schools than in the large schools, but differences between means do not reach statistical significance except in the instances cited above.

TABLE 2.6: *Distribution of Battery 1 sample by type of school, sex of pupil, and parental occupation.*

TYPE OF SCHOOL SEX OF PUPIL		Professional and Clerical	Skilled	Semi-skilled	Unskilled	TOTAL
		PARENTAL OCCUPATION				
Large Primary Boys	N	705	927	603	324	2559
	%	27·55	36·23	23·56	12·66	100
Large Primary Girls	N	730	860	625	338	2553
	%	28·59	33·69	24·48	13·24	100
Large Primary Total	N	1435	1787	1228	662	5112
	%	28·07	34·96	24·02	12·95	100
Small Primary Boys	N	12	25	33	16	86
	%	13·95	29·07	38·37	18·61	100
Small Primary Girls	N	11	42	29	12	94
	%	11·70	44·68	30·85	12·77	100
Small Primary Total	N	23	67	62	28	180
	%	12·78	37·22	34·44	15·56	100
Comprehensive Boys	N	237	357	270	127	991
	%	23·92	36·02	27·24	12·82	100
Comprehensive Girls	N	281	419	270	159	1129
	%	24·89	37·11	23·92	14·08	100
Comprehensive Total	N	518	776	540	286	2120
	%	24·44	36·60	25·47	13·49	100

Notes

The small primary schools contain proportionately fewer pupils in the 'professional and clerical' parental occupation category and proportionately more pupils in the 'semi-skilled' and 'unskilled' categories than do either the large primary schools or the comprehensive schools. The social composition of the large primary schools is similar to that of the comprehensive schools.

164

Appendix Two

TABLE 2.7: *Battery 1 Writing Test. Percentage of Cohort 2 pupils tested, absent, or not entered for the test, by French course and parental occupation.*

FRENCH COURSE % TESTED, ABSENT OR NOT ENTERED FOR TEST	PARENTAL OCCUPATION				TOTAL
	Professional and Clerical	*Skilled*	*Semi-skilled*	*Unskilled*	
'En Avant'					
% Tested ..	73·16	69·17	59·64	44·73	64·60
% Absent ..	6·31	6·47	6·63	7·94	6·66
% Not Entered for Test ..	20·53	24·36	33·73	47·33	28·74
'Bonjour Line'					
% Tested ..	86·70	85·00	75·00	69·23	81·97
% Absent ..	6·92	8·00	5·21	7·69	7·10
% Not Entered for Test ..	6·38	7·00	19·79	23·08	10·93
'Parlons Francais'					
% Tested ..	27·27	21·42	15·00	3·03	17·62
% Absent ..	2·27	1·79	0·00	0·00	1·04
% Not Entered for Test ..	70·46	76·79	85·00	96·97	81·34
'Bon Voyage'					
% Tested ..	91·43	97·83	93·33	93·33	94·59
% Absent ..	8·57	2·17	6·67	6·67	5·41
% Not Entered for Test ..	0·00	0·00	0·00	0·00	0·00
All Courses Combined					
% Tested ..	73·26	69·43	59·04	46·03	64·87
% Absent ..	6·26	6·32	6·22	7·53	6·44
% Not Entered for Test ..	20·48	24·25	34·74	46·44	28·69

Notes

Taking the sample as a whole, 64·87 per cent of the pupils in Cohort 2 took the Battery 1 Writing Test, 6·44 per cent were absent on the day of testing, and 28·69 per cent were not entered for the test because they had not been introduced to writing in French before the test period. The number of Cohort 2 pupils following the different French courses at the time of testing was as follows:

'En Avant': 4655 pupils
'Bonjour Line': 549 pupils
'Parlons Francais': 193 pupils
'Bon Voyage': 111 pupils

Except for the small group of pupils following the 'Bon Voyage' course, it is clear that the percentage of pupils taking the Writing test increases with social

165

status: high-status parental occupation is associated with an increasing percentage of pupils taking the Writing test and low-status parental occupation with a decreasing percentage of pupils taking the test. Correspondingly, high-status parental occupation is associated with a decreasing percentage of pupils who had not been introduced to writing in French before the date of testing and low-status parental occupation with an increasing percentage of pupils not introduced to writing in French.

Appendix Two

FIGURE 2.1: *Distribution of RCA scores for Cohort 1 pupils within each parental occupation category.*

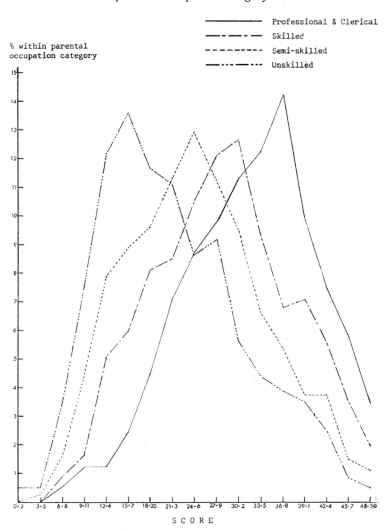

FIGURE 2.2: *Distribution of Battery 1 Speaking test scores for cohort 2 pupils within each parental occupation category.*

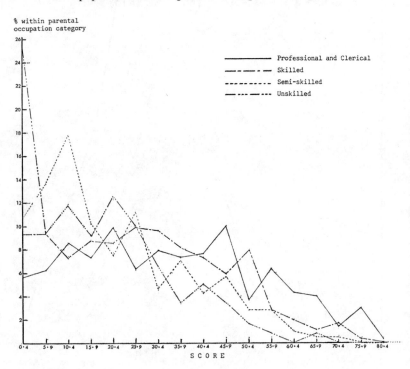

FIGURE 2.3: *Distribution of Battery 1 Listening test scores for cohort 2 pupils within each parental occupation category.*

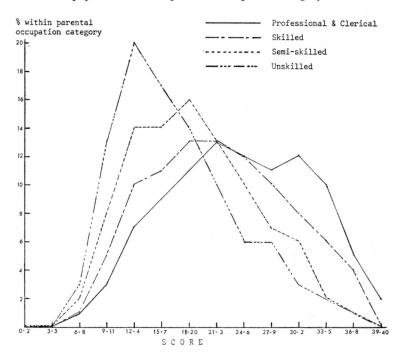

FIGURE 2.4: *Distribution of Battery 1 Reading test scores for cohort 2 pupils within each parental occupation category.*

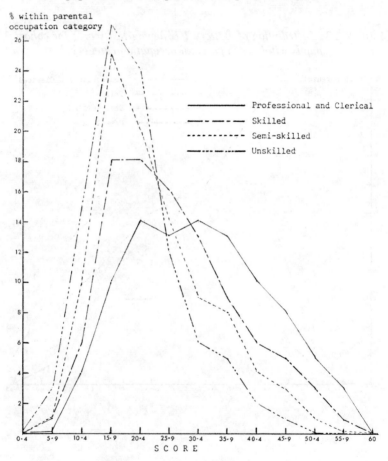

FIGURE 2.5: *Distribution of Battery 1 Writing test scores for cohort 2 pupils within each parental occupation category.*

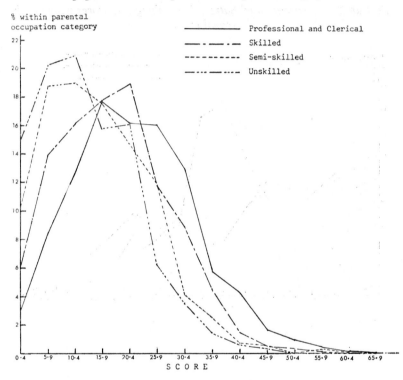

FIGURE 2.6: *Distribution of Battery 1 Speaking test scores within each school group.*

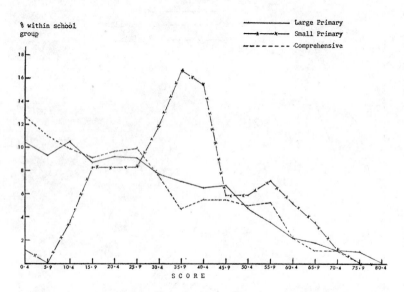

FIGURE 2.7: *Distribution of Battery 1 Listening test scores within each school group.*

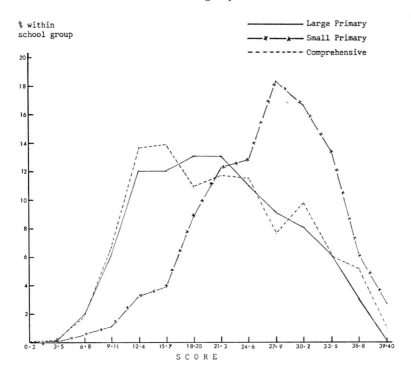

FIGURE 2.8: *Distribution of Battery 1 Reading test scores within each school group.*

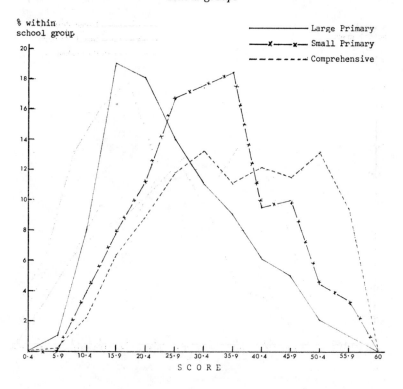

FIGURE 2.9: *Distribution of Battery 1 Writing test scores within each school group.*

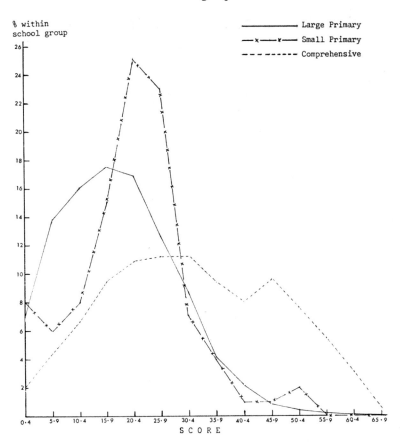

APPENDIX THREE

Pupils' Attitudes Towards Learning French in the Primary School

(Tables 3.1 - 3.42)

Appendix Three

Tables 3.1 to 3.38 show the percentage of pupils in the second cohort who agree with each statement in the attitude questionnaire. The responses are shown distributed by pupils' sex and general attitude towards French. These tables are based on the responses of 3,887 pupils: data obtained from pupils who were absent for all the French group tests, or who were not included in the original experimental sample in September 1965, were excluded from the analysis.

TABLE 3.1: *Item 1. 'I would like to speak many languages'.*

PUPILS WHO LIKE FRENCH			PUPILS WHO DISLIKE FRENCH		
Boys	*Girls*	*Total*	*Boys*	*Girls*	*Total*
82·07%	83·36%	83·35%	57·76%	57·56%	58·94%

Notes

72·29 per cent of the total sample agree with the item statement.

Results of χ^2 tests: significantly more girls than boys agree with the item statement (p < 0·001); significantly more pupils who like French agree with the item statement than do those who dislike French (p < 0·001).

TABLE 3.2: *Item 2. 'Saying something over and over again is the best way to learn it'.*

PUPILS WHO LIKE FRENCH			PUPILS WHO DISLIKE FRENCH		
Boys	*Girls*	*Total*	*Boys*	*Girls*	*Total*
74·41%	81·30%	79·97%	67·64%	75·63%	72·10%

Notes

76·38 per cent of the total sample agree with the item statement.

Results of χ^2 tests: significantly more girls than boys agree with the item statement (p < 0·001); significantly more pupils who like French agree with the item statement than do those who dislike French (p < 0·001).

177

French in the Primary School

TABLE 3.3: *Item 3. 'It would be easier to learn a language if you were taught to read it and speak it at the same time'.*

PUPILS WHO LIKE FRENCH			PUPILS WHO DISLIKE FRENCH		
Boys	*Girls*	*Total*	*Boys*	*Girls*	*Total*
50·00%	47·46%	49·59%	50·14%	49·16%	50·57%

Notes
50·04 per cent of the total sample agree with the item statement.
Results of χ^2 tests: there are no significant differences between groups in response to this item.

TABLE 3.4: *Item 4. 'I am not interested in learning foreign languages'.*

PUPILS WHO LIKE FRENCH			PUPILS WHO DISLIKE FRENCH		
Boys	*Girls*	*Total*	*Boys*	*Girls*	*Total*
20·28%	22·27%	22·25%	38·85%	33·89%	38·71%

Notes
29·72 per cent of the total sample agree with the item statement.
Results of χ^2 tests: significantly more boys than girls agree with the item statement ($p < 0.01$); significantly more pupils who dislike French agree with the item statement than do those who like French ($p < 0.001$).

TABLE 3.5: *Item 5. 'I would like to go to France'.*

PUPILS WHO LIKE FRENCH			PUPILS WHO DISLIKE FRENCH		
Boys	*Girls*	*Total*	*Boys*	*Girls*	*Total*
89·74%	93·19%	92·24%	69·14%	76·75%	73·90%

Notes
83·42 per cent of the total sample agree with the item statement.
Results of χ^2 tests: significantly more girls than boys agree with the item statement ($p < 0.001$); significantly more pupils who like French agree with the item statement than do those who dislike French ($p < 0.001$).

Appendix Three

TABLE 3.6: *Item 6. 'Learning French is a waste of time'.*

PUPILS WHO LIKE FRENCH			PUPILS WHO DISLIKE FRENCH		
Boys	Girls	Total	Boys	Girls	Total
7·66%	6·89%	7·31%	36·22%	30·67%	35·28%

Notes
19·94 per cent of the total sample agree with the item statement.
Results of χ^2 tests: significantly more boys than girls agree with the item statement ($p < 0.001$); significantly more pupils who dislike French agree with the item statement than do those who like French ($p < 0.001$).

TABLE 3.7: *Item 7. 'French is easier than the other subjects that I learn at school'.*

PUPILS WHO LIKE FRENCH			PUPILS WHO DISLIKE FRENCH		
Boys	Girls	Total	Boys	Girls	Total
27·00%	29·40%	28·93%	12·98%	10·78%	12·24%

Notes
21·27 per cent of the total sample agree with the item statement.
Results of χ^2 tests: significantly more girls than boys agree with the item statement ($p < 0.001$); significantly more pupils who like French agree with the item statement than do those who dislike French ($p < 0.001$).

TABLE 3.8: *Item 8. 'It is more difficult to understand the tape-recorder than the teacher'.*

PUPILS WHO LIKE FRENCH			PUPILS WHO DISLIKE FRENCH		
Boys	Girls	Total	Boys	Girls	Total
73·11%	72·90%	75·01%	71·59%	77·59%	76·23%

Notes
75·57 per cent of the total sample agree with the item statement.
Results of χ^2 tests: there are no significant differences between groups in response to this item.

French in the Primary School

TABLE 3.9: *Item 9. 'There are many languages which are more important to learn than French'.*

PUPILS WHO LIKE FRENCH			PUPILS WHO DISLIKE FRENCH		
Boys	*Girls*	*Total*	*Boys*	*Girls*	*Total*
47·40%	35·18%	41·27%	41·40%	59·24%	69·98%

Notes

54·24 per cent of the total sample agree with the item statement.

Results of χ^2 tests: significantly more boys than girls agree with the item statement (p<0·001); significantly more pupils who dislike French agree with the item statement than do those who like French (p<0·001).

TABLE 3.10: *Item 10. 'Every year French gets more interesting'.*

PUPILS WHO LIKE FRENCH			PUPILS WHO DISLIKE FRENCH		
Boys	*Girls*	*Total*	*Boys*	*Girls*	*Total*
83·96%	91·60%	89·42%	40·64%	49·58%	44·79%

Notes

69·04 per cent of the total sample agree with the item statement.

Results of χ^2 tests: significantly more girls than boys agree with the item statement (p<0·001); significantly more pupils who like French agree with the item statement than do those who dislike French (p<0·001).

TABLE 3.11: *Item 11. 'I do not always understand what I am saying when I speak in French'.*

PUPILS WHO LIKE FRENCH			PUPILS WHO DISLIKE FRENCH		
Boys	*Girls*	*Total*	*Boys*	*Girls*	*Total*
61·79%	60·22%	62·36%	72·34%	75·63%	75·40%

Notes

68·33 per cent of the total sample agree with the item statement.

Results of χ^2 tests: there are no significant differences between the sexes in response to this item; significantly more pupils who dislike French agree with the item statement than do those who like French (p<0·001).

Appendix Three

TABLE 3.12: *Item 12. 'I think everyone should learn French at school'.*

PUPILS WHO LIKE FRENCH			PUPILS WHO DISLIKE FRENCH		
Boys	Girls	Total	Boys	Girls	Total
78·18%	81·54%	80·76%	37·91%	43·70%	40·72%

Notes
62·50 per cent of the total sample agree with the item statement.
Results of χ^2 tests: significantly more girls than boys agree with the item statement ($p < 0.001$); significantly more pupils who like French agree with the item statement than do those who dislike French ($p < 0.001$).

TABLE 3.13: *Item 13. 'French is too difficult for me to learn'.*

PUPILS WHO LIKE FRENCH			PUPILS WHO DISLIKE FRENCH		
Boys	Girls	Total	Boys	Girls	Total
9·20%	7·61%	8·42%	39·70%	34·17%	38·81%

Notes
22·21 per cent of the total sample agree with the item statement.
Results of χ^2 tests: significantly more boys than girls agree with the item statement ($p < 0.001$); significantly more pupils who dislike French agree with the item statement than do those who like French ($p < 0.001$).

TABLE 3.14: *Item 14. 'I would like to meet some French people'.*

PUPILS WHO LIKE FRENCH			PUPILS WHO DISLIKE FRENCH		
Boys	Girls	Total	Boys	Girls	Total
90·80%	95·56%	94·32%	62·75%	77·31%	69·54%

Notes
83·03 per cent of the total sample agree with the item statement.
Results of χ^2 tests: significantly more girls than boys agree with the item statement ($p < 0.001$); significantly more pupils who like French agree with the item statement than do those who dislike French ($p < 0.001$).

French in the Primary School

TABLE 3.15: *Item 15. 'Speaking French is easier than reading and writing French'.*

PUPILS WHO LIKE FRENCH			PUPILS WHO DISLIKE FRENCH		
Boys	*Girls*	*Total*	*Boys*	*Girls*	*Total*
74·64%	73·45%	75·73%	66·32%	67·79%	68·77%

Notes
72·55 per cent of the total sample agree with the item statement.
Results of χ^2 tests: there are no significant differences between the sexes in response to this item; significantly more pupils who like French agree with the item statement than do those who dislike French ($p < 0.001$).

TABLE 3.16: *Item 16. 'If I see a French word written down, it helps me to say it'.*

PUPILS WHO LIKE FRENCH			PUPILS WHO DISLIKE FRENCH		
Boys	*Girls*	*Total*	*Boys*	*Girls*	*Total*
62·50%	63·07%	64·31%	56·54%	54·62%	57·02%

Notes
60·97 per cent of the total sample agree with the item statement.
Results of χ^2 tests: there are no significant differences between the sexes in response to this item; significantly more pupils who like French agree with the item statement than do those who dislike French ($p < 0.001$).

TABLE 3.17: *Item 17. 'I get very bored repeating words over and over again in the French lesson'.*

PUPILS WHO LIKE FRENCH			PUPILS WHO DISLIKE FRENCH		
Boys	*Girls*	*Total*	*Boys*	*Girls*	*Total*
47·64%	43·66%	46·09%	77·89%	76·19%	78·94%

Notes
61·08 per cent of the total sample agree with the item statement.
Results of χ^2 tests: significantly more boys than girls agree with the item statement ($p < 0.001$); significantly more pupils who dislike French agree with the item statement than do those who like French ($p < 0.001$).

TABLE 3.18: *Item 18. 'I think English is the best language'.*

PUPILS WHO LIKE FRENCH			PUPILS WHO DISLIKE FRENCH		
Boys	*Girls*	*Total*	*Boys*	*Girls*	*Total*
66·04%	56·18%	61·93%	84·48%	84·87%	86·29%

Notes

73·13 per cent of the total sample agree with the item statement.

Results of χ^2 tests: significantly more boys than girls agree with the item statement ($p < 0.001$); significantly more pupils who dislike French agree with the item statement than do those who like French ($p < 0.001$).

TABLE 3.19: *Item 19. 'I would like to make friends with some French children'.*

PUPILS WHO LIKE FRENCH			PUPILS WHO DISLIKE FRENCH		
Boys	*Girls*	*Total*	*Boys*	*Girls*	*Total*
89·27%	95·48%	93·38%	59·74%	77·31%	67·60%

Notes

81·64 per cent of the total sample agree with the item statement.

Results of χ^2 tests: significantly more girls than boys agree with the item statement ($p < 0.001$); significantly more pupils who like French agree with the item statement than do those who dislike French ($p < 0.001$).

TABLE 3.20: *Item 20. 'French will be useful to me after I leave school'.*

PUPILS WHO LIKE FRENCH			PUPILS WHO DISLIKE FRENCH		
Boys	*Girls*	*Total*	*Boys*	*Girls*	*Total*
91·62%	91·05%	92·29%	60·96%	64·43%	63·68%

Notes

79·28 per cent of the total sample agree with the item statement.

Results of χ^2 tests: significantly more girls than boys agree with the item statement ($p < 0.001$); significantly more pupils who like French agree with the item statement than do those who dislike French ($p < 0.001$).

French in the Primary School

TABLE 3.21: *Item 21. 'I find it difficult to understand the French lesson'.*

PUPILS WHO LIKE FRENCH			PUPILS WHO DISLIKE FRENCH		
Boys	*Girls*	*Total*	*Boys*	*Girls*	*Total*
24·29%	22·03%	23·74%	63·03%	54·76%	62·08%

Notes

41·22 per cent of the total sample agree with the item statement.

Results of χ^2 tests: significantly more boys than girls agree with the item statement ($p < 0.001$); significantly more pupils who dislike French agree with the item statement than do those who like French ($p < 0.001$).

TABLE 3.22: *Item 22. 'I think that it is more important to be able to speak a foreign language than to read and write it'.*

PUPILS WHO LIKE FRENCH			PUPILS WHO DISLIKE FRENCH		
Boys	*Girls*	*Total*	*Boys*	*Girls*	*Total*
76·53%	76·54%	77·79%	71·59%	73·39%	73·98%

Notes

76·06 per cent of the total sample agree with the item statement.

Results of χ^2 tests: there are no significant differences between the sexes in response to this item; significantly more pupils who like French agree with the item statement than do those who dislike French ($p < 0.01$).

TABLE 3.23: *Item 23. 'I would rather have learned another language instead of French'.*

PUPILS WHO LIKE FRENCH			PUPILS WHO DISLIKE FRENCH		
Boys	*Girls*	*Total*	*Boys*	*Girls*	*Total*
30·19%	20·44%	25·09%	68·67%	53·92%	64·75%

Notes

43·20 per cent of the total sample agree with the item statement.

Results of χ^2 tests: significantly more boys than girls agree with the item statement ($p < 0.001$); significantly more pupils who dislike French agree with the item statement than do those who like French ($p < 0.001$).

TABLE 3.24: *Item 24. 'I am afraid to speak French'.*

PUPILS WHO LIKE FRENCH			PUPILS WHO DISLIKE FRENCH		
Boys	*Girls*	*Total*	*Boys*	*Girls*	*Total*
11·32%	13·87%	13·17%	23·33%	26·05%	25·16%

Notes
18·64 per cent of the total sample agree with the item statement.
Results of χ^2 tests: there are no significant differences between the sexes in response to this item; significantly more pupils who dislike French agree with the item statement than do those who like French ($p < 0.001$).

TABLE 3.25: *Item 25. 'I like having a lesson with a tape-recorder'.*

PUPILS WHO LIKE FRENCH			PUPILS WHO DISLIKE FRENCH		
Boys	*Girls*	*Total*	*Boys*	*Girls*	*Total*
45·52%	45·17%	46·50%	34·90%	29·27%	33·30%

Notes
40·44 per cent of the total sample agree with the item statement.
Results of χ^2 tests: there are no significant differences between the sexes in response to this item; significantly more pupils who like French agree with the item statement than do those who dislike French ($p < 0.001$).

TABLE 3.26: *Item 26. 'There are many more important things to learn in school than French'.*

PUPILS WHO LIKE FRENCH			PUPILS WHO DISLIKE FRENCH		
Boys	*Girls*	*Total*	*Boys*	*Girls*	*Total*
72·87%	66·56%	70·98%	90·59%	87·25%	90·78%

Notes
80·08 per cent of the total sample agree with the item statement.
Results of χ^2 tests: significantly more boys than girls agree with the item statement ($p < 0.001$); significantly more pupils who dislike French agree with the item statement than do those who like French ($p < 0.001$).

French in the Primary School

TABLE 3.27: *Item 27. 'French is my favourite lesson'.*

PUPILS WHO LIKE FRENCH			PUPILS WHO DISLIKE FRENCH		
Boys	*Girls*	*Total*	*Boys*	*Girls*	*Total*
25·00%	32·09%	29·85%	3·29%	5·18%	4·10%

Notes
18·01 per cent of the total sample agree with the item statement.
Results of χ^2 tests: significantly more girls than boys agree with the item statement (p<0·001); significantly more pupils who like French agree with the item statement than do those who dislike French (p<0·001).

TABLE 3.28: *Item 28. 'French people should learn English instead of us learning French'.*

PUPILS WHO LIKE FRENCH			PUPILS WHO DISLIKE FRENCH		
Boys	*Girls*	*Total*	*Boys*	*Girls*	*Total*
40·45%	30·74%	35·62%	68·77%	61·20%	67·83%

Notes
50·32 per cent of the total sample agree with the item statement.
Results of χ^2 tests: significantly more boys than girls agree with the item statement (p<0·001); significantly more pupils who dislike French agree with the item statement than do those who like French (p<0·001).

TABLE 3.29: *Item 29. 'I think my parents are pleased that I am learning French'.*

PUPILS WHO LIKE FRENCH			PUPILS WHO DISLIKE FRENCH		
Boys	*Girls*	*Total*	*Boys*	*Girls*	*Total*
93·86%	95·64%	95·79%	74·41%	79·27%	78·99%

Notes
88·21 per cent of the total sample agree with the item statement.
Results of χ^2 tests: significantly more girls than boys agree with the item statement (p<0·001); significantly more pupils who like French agree with the item statement than do those who dislike French (p<0·001).

Appendix Three

TABLE 3.30: *Item 30. 'I don't think I will ever speak French after I leave school'.*

PUPILS WHO LIKE FRENCH			PUPILS WHO DISLIKE FRENCH		
Boys	*Girls*	*Total*	*Boys*	*Girls*	*Total*
20·16%	19·02%	20·30%	50·05%	45·24%	50·50%

Notes
34·05 per cent of the total sample agree with the item statement.
Results of χ^2 tests: significantly more boys than girls agree with the item statement ($p < 0.001$); significantly more pupils who dislike French agree with the item statement than do those who like French ($p < 0.001$).

TABLE 3.31: *Item 31. 'I think that I have learned a great deal of French in the last few years'.*

PUPILS WHO LIKE FRENCH			PUPILS WHO DISLIKE FRENCH		
Boys	*Girls*	*Total*	*Boys*	*Girls*	*Total*
84·67%	90·57%	89·47%	53·15%	61·49%	57·93%

Notes
75·14 per cent of the total sample agree with the item statement.
Results of χ^2 tests: significantly more girls than boys agree with the item statement ($p < 0.001$); significantly more pupils who like French agree with the item statement than do those who dislike French ($p < 0.001$).

TABLE 3.32: *Item 32. 'Only children who do well in English should learn French'.*

PUPILS WHO LIKE FRENCH			PUPILS WHO DISLIKE FRENCH		
Boys	*Girls*	*Total*	*Boys*	*Girls*	*Total*
24·52%	20·13%	22·28%	38·85%	34·87%	38·05%

Notes
29·47 per cent of the total sample agree with the item statement.
Results of χ^2 tests: significantly more boys than girls agree with the item statement ($p < 0.001$); significantly more pupils who dislike French agree with the item statement than do those who like French ($p < 0.001$).

TABLE 3.33: *Item 33. 'Once I hear a French word I can remember it easily'.*

PUPILS WHO LIKE FRENCH			PUPILS WHO DISLIKE FRENCH		
Boys	*Girls*	*Total*	*Boys*	*Girls*	*Total*
40·92%	44·61%	44·92%	23·71%	22·83%	23·96%

Notes

35·26 per cent of the total sample agree with the item statement.

Results of χ^2 tests: significantly more girls than boys agree with the item statement (p<0·001); significantly more pupils who like French agree with the item statement than do those who dislike French (p<0·001).

TABLE 3.34: *Item 34. 'Every year French gets more difficult'.*

PUPILS WHO LIKE FRENCH			PUPILS WHO DISLIKE FRENCH		
Boys	*Girls*	*Total*	*Boys*	*Girls*	*Total*
54·01%	57·53%	57·31%	75·82%	77·73%	78·76%

Notes

67·08 per cent of the total sample agree with the item statement.

Results of χ^2 tests: there are no significant differences between the sexes in response to this item; significantly more pupils who dislike French agree with the item statement than do those who like French (p<0·001).

TABLE 3.35: *Item 35. 'I would like to go on learning French'.*

PUPILS WHO LIKE FRENCH			PUPILS WHO DISLIKE FRENCH		
Boys	*Girls*	*Total*	*Boys*	*Girls*	*Total*
84·55%	89·94%	88·70%	29·16%	37·82%	33·33%

Notes

63·53 per cent of the sample agree with the item statement.

Results of χ^2 tests: significantly more girls than boys agree with the item statement (p<0·001); significantly more pupils who like French agree with the item statement than do those who dislike French (p<0·001).

TABLE 3.36: *Item 36. 'I think that it is more important to read and write a foreign language than to speak it'.*

PUPILS WHO LIKE FRENCH			PUPILS WHO DISLIKE FRENCH		
Boys	*Girls*	*Total*	*Boys*	*Girls*	*Total*
18·04%	15·93%	17·14%	21·82%	21·29%	22·15%

Notes

19·43 per cent of the total sample agree with the item statement.

Results of χ^2 tests: there are no significant differences between the sexes in response to this item; significantly more pupils who dislike French agree with the item statement than do those who like French (p < 0·001).

TABLE 3.37: *Item 37. 'I think that it is silly to learn French'.*

PUPILS WHO LIKE FRENCH			PUPILS WHO DISLIKE FRENCH		
Boys	*Girls*	*Total*	*Boys*	*Girls*	*Total*
18·16%	3·25%	8·94%	28·13%	32·77%	32·68%

Notes

19·09 per cent of the total sample agree with the item statement.

Results of χ^2 tests: significantly more boys than girls agree with the item statement (p < 0·001); significantly more pupils who dislike French agree with the item statement than do those who like French (p < 0·001).

TABLE 3.38: *Item 38. 'I am better at French that at other subjects'.*

PUPILS WHO LIKE FRENCH			PUPILS WHO DISLIKE FRENCH		
Boys	*Girls*	*Total*	*Boys*	*Girls*	*Total*
22·05%	26·62%	25·40%	7·24%	7·14%	7·24%

Notes

17·02 per cent of the total sample agree with the item statement.

Results of χ^2 tests: significantly more girls than boys agree with the item statement (p < 0·001); significantly more pupils who like French agree with the item statement than do those who dislike French (p < 0·001).

TABLE 3.39: *Battery 1 Speaking Test. Mean scores by sex of pupil, attitude towards French, and parental occupation.*

SEX OF PUPIL ATTITUDE TO FRENCH		PARENTAL OCCUPATION				TOTAL
		Professional and Clerical	Skilled	Semi-skilled	Unskilled	
Boys who like French	N	57	47	47	24	175
	x̄	35·70	32·87	25·82	15·33	29·49
	SD	11·41	8·30	11·35	9·69	10·97
Boys who dislike French	N	59	64	39	22	184
	x̄	27·84	23·95	16·41	22·04	23·37
	SD	10·23	9·25	7·75	10·07	9·59
Girls who like French	N	81	105	56	28	270
	x̄	40·95	33·08	24·98	22·89	32·70
	SD	11·27	10·70	8·77	10·31	11·12
Girls who dislike French	N	37	47	24	13	121
	x̄	29·54	22·70	22·62	16·38	24·09
	SD	9·16	8·51	7·57	9·34	8·86
All pupils who like French	N	138	152	103	52	445
	x̄	38·78	33·01	25·36	19·40	31·44
	SD	11·43	9·85	9·77	10·39	11·10
All pupils who dislike French	N	96	111	63	35	305
	x̄	28·50	23·42	18·77	19·94	23·66
	SD	9·81	8·96	7·82	9·85	9·29

Notes

Taking the sample as a whole, the differences between mean scores for boys and girls liking or disliking French reach a high level of significance ($p < 0.001$). Taking each parental occupation category separately, differences between mean scores for both boys and girls in the 'professional and clerical' and 'skilled' categories and for boys only in the 'semi-skilled' category reach the same high level of significance. Differences between mean scores for girls in the 'semi-skilled' and 'unskilled' categories do not reach significance. Differences between mean scores for boys in the 'unskilled' category reach a low level of significance ($p < 0.05$), but these differences are in the opposite direction from those already cited: in this particular instance, pupils who like French obtain a lower mean score than do those who dislike French. The number of pupils involved, however, is very small.

Appendix Three

TABLE 3.40: *Battery 1 Listening Test. Mean scores by sex of pupil, attitude towards French, and parental occupation.*

SEX OF PUPIL ATTITUDE TO FRENCH		Professional and Clerical	Skilled	Semi-skilled	Unskilled	TOTAL
		PARENTAL OCCUPATION				
Boys who like French	N	216	268	190	98	772
	x̄	27·04	24·01	20·62	18·07	23·27
	SD	7·22	7·28	7·06	7·31	7·83
Boys who dislike French	N	281	355	231	120	987
	x̄	22·19	20·20	17·96	17·29	19·89
	SD	6·98	6·83	6·29	6·99	7·00
Girls who like French	N	313	392	289	138	1132
	x̄	28·06	25·14	22·27	20·63	24·67
	SD	7·14	7·36	7·00	7·35	7·66
Girls who dislike French	N	185	220	165	84	654
	x̄	24·96	21·72	20·01	18·77	21·83
	SD	7·37	7·59	6·16	6·27	7·36
All pupils who like French	N	529	660	479	236	1904
	x̄	27·64	24·68	21·62	19·56	24·10
	SD	7·19	7·35	7·07	7·44	7·76
All pupils who dislike French	N	466	575	396	204	1641
	x̄	23·29	20·78	18·81	17·90	20·66
	SD	7·26	7·17	6·32	6·74	7·21

Notes

Taking the sample as a whole, the differences between mean scores for both boys and girls liking or disliking French reach a high level of significance ($p < 0.001$). Taking each parental occupation category separately, differences between mean scores for both boys and girls reach the same high level of significance in every instance except in that of the 'unskilled' category. In the latter category, differences between mean scores for girls reach a lower level of significance ($p < 0.05$); differences between mean scores for boys do not reach a significant level.

191

TABLE 3.41: *Battery 1 Reading Test. Mean scores by sex of pupil, attitude towards French, and parental occupation.*

SEX OF PUPIL ATTITUDE TO FRENCH		PARENTAL OCCUPATION				TOTAL
		Professional and Clerical	*Skilled*	*Semi-skilled*	*Unskilled*	
Boys who like French	N	217	262	189	99	767
	x̄	35·11	28·66	25·14	21·38	28·68
	SD	11·12	11·07	9·80	8·40	11·46
Boys who dislike French	N	277	353	227	120	977
	x̄	27·25	24·76	21·89	20·76	24·31
	SD	10·61	9·26	8·27	8·08	9·61
Girls who like French	N	314	380	284	132	1110
	x̄	37·22	32·06	27·79	25·31	31·62
	SD	11·23	11·53	10·37	9·68	11·72
Girls who dislike French	N	183	220	160	83	646
	x̄	32·00	27·47	25·76	23·20	27·78
	SD	11·52	10·48	9·02	8·38	10·63
All pupils who like French	N	531	642	473	231	1877
	x̄	36·36	30·67	26·73	23·62	30·42
	SD	11·33	11·47	10·23	9·36	11·70
All pupils who dislike French	N	460	573	387	203	1623
	x̄	29·14	25·80	23·49	21·76	25·69
	SD	11·22	9·84	8·80	8·29	10·17

Notes

Taking the sample as a whole, the differences between mean scores of both boys and girls liking or disliking French reach a high level of significance ($p < 0.001$). Taking each parental occupation category separately, differences between mean scores for both boys and girls in the 'professional and clerical' and 'skilled' categories and for boys only in the 'semi-skilled' category reach the same high level of significance. Differences between mean scores for girls in the 'semi-skilled' category reach a lower level of significance ($p < 0.05$). Differences between mean scores for both boys and girls in the 'unskilled' category do not reach a significant level.

Appendix Three

TABLE 3.42: *Battery 1 Writing Test. Mean scores by sex of pupil, attitude towards French, and parental occupation.*

SEX OF PUPIL ATTITUDE TO FRENCH		PARENTAL OCCUPATION				TOTAL
		Professional and Clerical	*Skilled*	*Semi-skilled*	*Unskilled*	
Boys who like French	N	163	184	102	45	494
	x̄	23·30	18·44	16·61	14·11	19·27
	SD	10·87	10·12	10·00	8·35	10·66
Boys who dislike French	N	212	243	151	57	663
	x̄	17·93	15·49	12·99	12·50	15·44
	SD	9·77	8·88	8·73	8·13	9·30
Girls who like French	N	238	292	183	64	777
	x̄	26·63	22·69	19·08	18·50	22·70
	SD	10·23	9·57	9·31	9·56	10·18
Girls who dislike French	N	152	167	107	51	477
	x̄	23·40	18·74	18·34	15·15	19·75
	SD	10·20	9·35	8·30	8·29	9·69
All pupils who like French	N	401	476	285	109	1271
	x̄	25·28	21·05	18·20	16·68	21·37
	SD	10·62	10·00	9·63	9·33	10·51
All pupils who dislike French	N	364	410	258	108	1140
	x̄	20·21	16·81	15·21	13·75	17·25
	SD	10·31	9·21	8·95	8·31	9·70

Notes

Taking the sample as a whole, the differences between mean scores of both boys and girls liking or disliking French reach a high level of significance ($p < 0.001$). Taking each parental occupation category separately, differences between mean scores for boys in the 'professional and clerical' category and for girls in the 'skilled' category reach the same high level of significance. Differences between mean scores for boys in the 'skilled' and 'semi-skilled' categories and for girls only in the 'professional and clerical' category are somewhat less significant ($p < 0.01$). Differences between mean scores for girls in the 'unskilled' category reach a lower level of significance ($p < 0.05$); differences between mean scores for boys in the 'unskilled' category and for girls in the 'semi-skilled' category do not reach a significant level.

G

French in the Primary School:
the Viewpoint of the Primary Head

(Tables 4.1 - 4.4)

TABLE 4.1: *Battery 1 Speaking Test. Mean scores by attitude of head, sex of pupil, and parental occupation.*

ATTITUDE OF HEAD SEX OF PUPIL		PARENTAL OCCUPATION				TOTAL
		Professional and Clerical	*Skilled*	*Semi-skilled*	*Unskilled*	
Unfavourable Head Boys	N	84	75	78	38	275
	x̄	29·21	26·58	19·55	15·71	23·89
	SD	10·50	8·53	10·26	10·37	10·13
Favourable Head Boys	N	66	77	35	24	202
	x̄	33·92	30·45	24·08	18·29	29·03
	SD	10·93	9·02	7·30	7·30	9·48
Unfavourable Head Girls	N	74	105	56	29	264
	x̄	30·05	26·80	23·92	18·51	26·19
	SD	9·50	9·41	7·92	8·75	9·25
Favourable Head Girls	N	77	97	45	28	247
	x̄	43·75	31·37	23·48	22·78	32·82
	SD	9·38	10·09	8·00	8·90	10·16
Unfavourable Head Total	N	158	180	134	67	539
	x̄	29·60	26·71	21·38	16·92	25·02
	SD	10·02	8·98	9·20	9·62	9·72
Favourable Head Total	N	143	174	80	52	449
	x̄	39·21	30·96	23·75	20·71	31·12
	SD	10·39	9·57	7·67	8·21	9·88

Notes

Mean scores of pupils in schools where the head has a favourable attitude towards teaching French to the whole ability range are higher than those of pupils in schools where the head has an unfavourable attitude. Differences between mean scores are significant at the 0·1 per cent level over the sample as a whole. Differences between mean scores within the 'professional and clerical' and 'skilled' parental occupation categories are significant for girls at the 0·1 per cent level and for boys at the one per cent level. Differences between mean scores within the 'semi-skilled' parental occupation category are significant for boys at the one per cent level, but mean scores for girls do not differ significantly. There are no significant differences between the mean scores of pupils in the 'unskilled' parental occupation category.

TABLE 4.2: *Battery 1 Listening Test. Mean scores by attitude of head, sex of pupil, and parental occupation.*

ATTITUDE OF HEAD SEX OF PUPIL		PARENTAL OCCUPATION				TOTAL
		Professional and Clerical	*Skilled*	*Semi-skilled*	*Unskilled*	
Unfavourable Head Boys	N	385	517	360	205	1467
	x̄	23·22	20·54	18·60	16·19	20·16
	SD	7·68	7·53	6·67	6·48	7·58
Favourable Head Boys	N	320	410	243	119	1092
	x̄	23·28	21·66	19·49	18·37	21·29
	SD	7·87	7·49	7·48	7·00	7·74
Unfavourable Head Girls	N	360	454	339	178	1331
	x̄	24·86	22·97	20·16	17·61	22·05
	SD	7·76	7·71	7·02	6·03	7·74
Favourable Head Girls	N	370	406	286	160	1222
	x̄	26·11	23·88	21·01	20·15	23·40
	SD	7·82	7·70	7·44	7·49	7·97
Unfavourable Head Total	N	745	971	699	383	2798
	x̄	24·01	21·67	19·36	16·85	21·06
	SD	7·76	7·71	6·88	6·31	7·72
Favourable Head Total	N	690	816	529	279	2314
	x̄	24·80	22·76	20·31	19·39	22·40
	SD	7·97	7·67	7·50	7·34	7·93

Notes

Mean scores of pupils in schools where the head has a favourable attitude towards teaching French to the whole ability range are higher than those of pupils in schools where the head has an unfavourable attitude. Differences between mean scores are significant at the 0·1 per cent level over the sample as a whole. Mean scores in the 'professional and clerical' parental occupation category differ significantly for girls at the five per cent level, but do not differ significantly for boys. In the 'skilled' parental occupation category, mean scores for boys differ significantly at the five per cent level, but do not differ significantly for girls. There are no significant differences between the mean scores of pupils in the 'semi-skilled' parental occupation category. In the 'unskilled' category, mean scores differ significantly for girls at the 0·1 per cent level and for boys at the one per cent level.

Appendix Four

TABLE 4.3: *Battery 1 Reading Test. Mean scores by attitude of head, sex of pupil, and parental occupation.*

ATTITUDE OF HEAD SEX OF PUPIL		Professional and Clerical	Skilled	Semi-skilled	Unskilled	TOTAL
		PARENTAL OCCUPATION				
Unfavourable Head	N	383	512	361	199	1455
Boys	x̄	29·40	25·41	23·08	19·38	25·06
	SD	11·48	10·64	9·38	7·93	10·74
Favourable Head	N	319	404	236	123	1082
Boys	x̄	30·15	26·43	23·13	21·03	26·19
	SD	11·06	9·80	8·97	7·82	10·31
Unfavourable Head	N	357	450	343	174	1324
Girls	x̄	32·74	29·73	25·83	22·24	28·55
	SD	11·80	11·31	9·68	8·88	11·32
Favourable Head	N	370	400	271	154	1195
Girls	x̄	35·10	29·71	26·36	24·08	29·89
	SD	11·43	10·84	10·99	9·36	11·58
Unfavourable Head	N	740	962	704	373	2779
Total	x̄	31·01	27·43	24·42	20·71	26·72
	SD	11·76	11·17	9·63	8·51	11·15
Favourable Head	N	689	804	507	277	2277
Total	x̄	32·81	28·06	24·86	22·72	28·14
	SD	11·53	10·46	10·23	8·84	11·15

Notes

Mean scores of pupils in schools where the head has a favourable attitude towards teaching French to the whole ability range are higher than those of pupils in schools where the head has an unfavourable attitude. Differences between mean scores are significant at the 0·1 per cent level over the sample as a whole. Mean scores in the 'professional and clerical' parental occupation category differ significantly for girls at the one per cent level, but do not differ significantly for boys. Differences between mean scores within each of the other parental occupation categories do not reach a significant level, but there is a general tendency for pupils in schools where the head has a favourable attitude to obtain higher mean scores than those in schools where the head has an unfavourable attitude.

TABLE 4.4: *Battery 1 Writing Test. Mean scores by attitude of head, sex of pupil, and parental occupation.*

ATTITUDE OF HEAD SEX OF PUPIL		PARENTAL OCCUPATION				TOTAL
		Professional and Clerical	*Skilled*	*Semi-skilled*	*Unskilled*	
Unfavourable Head	N	254	327	180	75	836
Boys	x̄	18·74	16·44	14·97	13·48	16·56
	SD	9·42	9·79	9·32	8·82	9·64
Favourable Head	N	284	350	203	93	930
Boys	x̄	21·43	16·93	13·20	10·67	16·86
	SD	11·27	9·48	9·12	7·05	10·43
Unfavourable Head	N	253	321	198	78	850
Girls	x̄	22·63	20·28	17·96	16·35	20·08
	SD	9·17	9·43	8·76	9·47	9·43
Favourable Head	N	332	342	216	90	980
Girls	x̄	26·63	21·65	18·24	16·31	22·09
	SD	10·82	10·07	9·72	9·59	10·85
Unfavourable Head	N	507	648	378	153	1686
Total	x̄	20·68	18·34	16·54	14·94	18·33
	SD	9·50	9·81	9·15	9·27	9·70
Favourable Head	N	616	692	419	183	1910
Total	x̄	24·23	19·26	15·80	13·44	19·55
	SD	11·33	10·06	9·76	8·86	10·96

Notes

Mean scores of pupils in schools where the head has a favourable attitude towards teaching French to the whole ability range are higher than those of pupils in schools where the head has an unfavourable attitude. Differences between mean scores are significant at the 0·1 per cent level over the sample as a whole. Differences between mean scores within the 'professional and clerical' parental occupation category are significant for girls at the 0·1 per cent level and for boys at the one per cent level. Differences between mean scores within the 'skilled' and 'semi-skilled' parental occupation categories do not reach a significant level. In the 'unskilled' category, there are no significant differences between the mean scores for girls; mean scores for boys in this category tend to be slightly higher in schools where the head has an unfavourable attitude than in those where the head has a favourable attitude, but the differences between the two groups of scores only reach significance at the five per cent level.

APPENDIX FIVE

The HMI Evaluation of the
Primary Stage of the Pilot Scheme

(Tables 5.1 - 5.5)

TABLE 5.1: *The fluency of the class: results of χ^2 tests.*

VARIABLE 2	d.f.	χ^2	SIGNIFICANCE LEVEL	COMMENTS
Pupils' pronunciation	1	25·887	***	In more HF classes pupils had 'very good' or 'good' pronunciation. In more LF classes pupils had 'reasonable' or 'poor' pronunciation.
Pupils' intonation	1	29·942	***	In more HF classes pupils had 'very good' or 'good' intonation. In more LF classes pupils had 'reasonable' or 'poor' intonation.
Pupils' accuracy	1	7·793	**	In more HF classes pupils made 'occasional' mistakes. In more LF classes pupils made 'frequent' mistakes.
Pupils' audibility	1	11·399	***	In more HF classes pupils were 'clearly audible'. In more LF classes pupils were 'audible' or 'barely audible'.
Pupils' 'French manner'	2	30·388	***	In more HF classes pupils 'frequently' imitated the teacher's 'French manner'. In more LF classes pupils did so 'occasionally' or 'not at all'.
Pupils' opportunity to speak French	2	11·941	**	In more HF classes pupils had 'plenty of individual practice'. In more LF classes pupils had 'mostly group practice' or 'mostly whole-class practice'.
Pupils' active participation in French lesson	2	25·011	***	In more HF classes 'all' pupils actively participated in the French lesson. In more LF classes 'most' or 'some' did so.
Pupils' responsiveness to French lesson	2	23·741	***	In more HF classes pupils were 'very responsive'. In more LF classes pupils were 'quite responsive' or 'not very responsive'.
Pupils' ability to use language skills in new situations	3	24·849	***	In more HF classes pupils gave 'a lot' of evidence of their ability to use language skills in new situations. In more LF classes pupils gave 'little' or 'no' evidence of such ability.
Teacher's fluency	2	18·224	***	More teachers of HF classes were 'very fluent' or 'fluent'. More teachers of LF classes were 'fairly fluent' or 'hesitant'.
Teacher's pronunciation	2	9·180	*	More teachers of HF classes had 'very good' or 'good' pronunciation. More teachers of LF classes had 'reasonable' or 'poor' pronunciation.

TABLE 5.1. (cont.)

VARIABLE 2	d.f.	χ^2	SIGNIFICANCE LEVEL	COMMENTS
Teacher's intonation	2	11·815	**	More teachers of HF classes had 'very good' or 'good' intonation. More teachers of LF classes had 'reasonable' or 'poor' intonation.
Teacher's 'French manner'	2	28·554	***	More teachers of HF classes 'conveyed a feeling of French-ness' 'completely' or 'to a considerable extent'. More teachers of LF classes conveyed 'French-ness' 'to some extent' or 'not at all'.
Teacher's skill with A/V equipment	1	10·194	**	More teachers of HF classes were 'very competent with A/V equipment'. More teachers of LF classes were 'competent' or 'not very competent' with A/V equipment.
Extent to which French lesson oral	2	16·145	***	In more HF classes the French lesson was 'entirely' oral. In more LF classes there was 'occasional' or 'systematic' use of the written word.
Extent to which lesson conducted in French	1	7·868	**	In more HF classes no English was used by teacher or pupils. In more LF classes there was 'occasional' or 'frequent' use of English by teacher and pupils.
Use of activities to reinforce oral skills	3	18·017	***	More teachers of HF classes made 'imaginative and effective use' of activities. More teachers of LF classes used activities 'without much confidence' or 'not at all'.
Extent to which aims of French lesson achieved	2	18·832	***	In more HF classes the aims of the French lesson were achieved 'completely'. In more LF classes the aims of the French lesson were only 'partially' achieved.

Notes

1. Variable 1 in Table 5.1 is the rated fluency of the class. 'Highly fluent' (HF) classes are those rated 'very fluent' or 'fluent'. 'Less fluent' (LF) classes are those rated 'fairly fluent', 'hesitant' or 'very hesitant'.

2. All non-significant variables have been omitted from Table 5.1.

3. Levels of significance are shown as follows: $*p<0.05$; $**p<0.01$; $***p<0.001$.

French in the Primary School

TABLE 5.2: *The responsiveness of the class to the French lesson: results of χ^2 tests.*

VARIABLE 2	d.f.	χ^2	SIGNIFICANCE LEVEL	COMMENTS
Pupils' fluency	3	25·923	***	In more HR classes pupils were 'very fluent' or 'fluent'. In more LR classes pupils were 'fairly fluent' or 'hesitant'.
Pupils' pronunciation	1	8·139	**	In more HR classes pupils had 'good' pronunciation. In more LR classes pupils had 'reasonable' pronunciation.
Pupils' intonation	1	12·102	***	In more HR classes pupils had 'very good' or 'good' intonation. In more LR classes pupils had 'reasonable' or 'poor' intonation.
Pupils' audibility	1	30·412	***	In more HR classes pupils were 'clearly audible'. In more LR classes pupils were 'audible' or 'barely audible'.
Pupils' 'French manner'	2	20·925	***	In more HR classes pupils 'frequently' imitated the teacher's 'French manner'. In more LR classes pupils did so 'occasionally' or 'not at all'.
Pupils' active participation in French lesson	2	38·529	***	In more HR classes 'all' pupils actively participated in the French lesson. In more LR classes 'most' or 'some' did so.
Pupils' ability to use language skills in new situations	3	23·293	***	In more HR classes pupils gave 'a lot' of evidence of their ability to use language skills in new situations. In more LR classes pupils gave 'little' evidence of such ability.
Teacher's fluency	2	11·374	**	More teachers of HR classes were 'very fluent' or 'fluent'. More teachers of LR classes were 'fairly fluent'.
Teacher's pronunciation	2	7·570	*	More teachers of HR classes had 'very good' or 'good' pronunciation. More teachers of LR classes had 'reasonable' or 'poor' pronunciation.
Teacher's intonation	2	6·193	*	More teachers of HR classes had 'very good' or 'good' intonation. More teachers of LR classes had 'reasonable' or 'poor' intonation.

TABLE 5.2. (cont.)

VARIABLE 2	d.f.	χ^2	SIGNIFICANCE LEVEL	COMMENTS
Teacher's 'French manner'	2	22·469	***	More teachers of HR classes 'conveyed a feeling of French-ness' 'completely' or 'to a considerable extent'. More teachers of LR classes conveyed 'French-ness' 'to some extent' or 'not at all'.
Teacher's skill with A/V equipment	1	12·979	***	More teachers of HR classes were 'very competent' with A/V equipment. More teachers of LR classes were 'competent' or 'not very competent' with A/V equipment.
Use of activities to reinforce oral skills	3	18·411	***	More teachers of HR classes made 'imaginative and effective use' of activities. More teachers of LR classes only made use of activities 'where the course suggested them'.
Extent to which aims of French lesson achieved	2	25·622	***	In more HR classes the aims of the French lesson were achieved 'completely'. In more LR classes the aims of the French lesson were only 'partially' achieved.

Notes

1. Variable 1 in Table 5.2 is the rated responsiveness of the class to the French lesson. 'Highly responsive' (HR) classes are those rated 'very responsive'. 'Less responsive' (LR) classes are those rated 'quite responsive' or 'not very responsive' or 'unresponsive'.

2. All non-significant variables have been omitted from Table 5.2.

TABLE 5.3: *The use of English in the French class: results of χ^2 tests.*

VARIABLE 2	d.f.	χ^2	SIGNIFICANCE LEVEL	COMMENTS
Pupils' fluency	3	14·808	**	In more NE classes pupils were 'very fluent' or 'fluent'. In more E classes pupils were 'fairly fluent' or 'hesitant'.
Pupils' intonation	1	6·428	*	In more NE classes pupils had 'very good' or 'good' intonation. In more E classes pupils had 'reasonable' or 'poor' intonation.
Pupils' accuracy	1	6·827	**	In more NE classes pupils made 'occasional' mistakes. In more E classes pupils made 'frequent' mistakes.
Pupils' 'French manner'	2	12·486	**	In more NE classes pupils 'frequently' imitated the teacher's 'French manner'. In more E classes pupils did so 'occasionally' or 'not at all'.
Pupils' active participation in French lesson	2	16·235	***	In more NE classes 'all' pupils actively participated in the French lesson. In more E classes 'some' pupils did so.
Pupils' ability to use language skills in new situations	3	12.695	**	In more NE classes pupils gave 'a lot' of evidence of their ability to use language skills in new situations. In more E classes pupils showed 'none' of such ability.
Teacher's fluency	2	7·819	*	More teachers of NE classes were 'very fluent' or 'fluent'. More teachers of E classes were 'fairly fluent' or 'hesitant'.
Teacher's 'French manner'	2	18·177	***	More teachers of NE classes 'conveyed a feeling of French-ness' 'completely'. More teachers of E classes conveyed 'French-ness' ' to some extent' or 'not at all'.
Extent to which aims of French lesson achieved	2	6·069	*	In more NE classes the aims of the French lesson were achieved 'completely'. In more E classes the aims of the French lesson were only 'partially' achieved.

Notes

1. Variable 1 in Table 5.3. is the extent to which English is used in the French class. 'Non-English' (NE) classes are those in which no English is used by teacher or pupils during the French lesson. 'English' (E) classes are those in which English is used 'occasionally' or 'frequently' by teacher and pupils.

2. All non-significant variables have been omitted from Table 5.3.

TABLE 5.4: *The improved fluency of the class: results of χ^2 tests.*

VARIABLE 2	d.f.	χ^2	SIGNIFICANCE LEVEL	COMMENTS
Pupils' pronunciation	4	58·465	***	In more HP and MP classes pupils' pronunciation showed 'marked' or 'some' improvement. In more LP classes pupils' pronunciation showed 'no improvement' or 'regression'.
Pupils' intonation	4	68·478	***	In more HP and MP classes pupils' intonation showed 'marked' or 'some' improvement. In more LP classes pupils' intonation showed 'no improvement' or 'regression'.
Pupils' accuracy	4	75·642	***	In more HP and MP classes pupils' accuracy in speaking French showed 'marked' or 'some' improvement. In more LP classes pupils' accuracy showed 'no improvement' or 'regression'.
Pupils' audibility	4	46·676	***	In more HP and MP classes pupils' audibility in speaking French showed 'marked' or 'some' improvement. In more LP classes pupils' audibility showed 'no improvement' or 'regression'.
Pupils' confidence	4	83·898	***	In more HP and MP classes pupils' confidence in speaking French showed 'marked' or 'some' improvement. In more LP classes pupils' confidence showed 'no improvement' or 'regression'.
Pupils' enthusiasm for French	4	44·494	***	In more HP and MP classes pupils showed 'marked' or 'some' increase in their enthusiasm for French. In more LP classes pupils showed no increase in enthusiasm or a falling-off of enthusiasm.
Opportunity for class to practise French	4	32·218	***	In more HP and MP classes opportunities for the class to practise French had increased. In more LP classes such opportunities had remained the same or had decreased.

TABLE 5.4. (Cont.)

VARIABLE 2	d.f.	χ^2	SIGNIFICANCE LEVEL	COMMENTS
Opportunity for individual pupil to practise French	4	25·014	***	In more HP and MP classes opportunities for the individual pupil to practise French had increased. In more LP classes such opportunities had remained the same or had decreased.
Opportunity for slower pupils to participate in French lesson	2	14·594	***	In more HP and MP classes opportunities for the slower pupils to participate in the French lesson had increased. In more LP classes such opportunities had remained the same or had decreased.
Introduction of written French	2	7·764	*	In more HP and MP classes the introduction of written French had produced 'a beneficial effect'. In more LP classes the introduction of written French had produced 'an adverse effect' or 'no effect'.
Teacher's command of French	4	21·635	***	More teachers of HP and MP classes showed 'marked' or 'some' improvement in their command of French. More teachers of LP classes showed 'no improvement' or 'regression' in their command of French.
Teacher's enthusiasm for French	4	33·738	***	More teachers of HP and MP classes showed 'marked' or 'some' increase in their enthusiasm for French. More teachers of LP classes showed no increase in enthusiasm or a falling-off of enthusiasm.

Notes

1. Variable 1 in Table 5.4. is rated improvement in the fluency of the class. 'High-progress' (HP) classes are those reported to be showing marked improvement in fluency. 'Moderate-progress' (MP) classes are those reported to be showing some improvement in fluency. 'Low-progress' (LP) classes are those reported to be showing no improvement in fluency or regression from a previous standard of performance.

2. All non-significant variables have been omitted from Table 5.4.

Appendix Five

TABLE 5.5: *The increased enthusiasm of the class for French: results of* χ^2 *tests.*

VARIABLE 2	d.f.	χ^2	SIGNIFICANCE LEVEL	COMMENTS
Pupils' fluency	4	44·494	***	In more HE and ME classes pupils' fluency showed 'marked' or 'some' improvement. In more UE classes pupils' fluency showed 'no improvement' or 'regression'.
Pupils' pronunciation	4	23·950	***	In more HE and ME classes pupils' pronunciation showed 'marked' or 'some' improvement. In more UE classes pupils' pronunciation showed 'no improvement' or 'regression'.
Pupils' intonation	4	45·531	***	In more HE and ME classes pupils' intonation showed 'marked' or 'some' improvement. In more UE classes pupils' intonation showed 'no improvement' or 'regression'.
Pupils' accuracy	4	53·995	***	In more HE and ME classes pupils' accuracy in speaking French showed 'marked' or 'some' improvement. In more UE classes pupils' accuracy showed 'no improvement' or 'regression'.
Pupils' audibility	4	56·578	***	In more HE and ME classes pupils' audibility in speaking French showed 'marked' or 'some' improvement. In more UE classes pupils' audibility showed 'no improvement' or 'regression'.
Pupils' confidence	4	83·898	***	In more HE and ME classes pupils' confidence in speaking French showed 'marked' or 'some' improvement. In more UE classes pupils' confidence showed 'no improvement' or 'regression'.
Opportunity for class to practise French	4	68·671	***	In more HE and ME classes opportunities for the class to practise French had increased. In more UE classes such opportunities had remained the same or had decreased.

TABLE 5.5. (Cont.)

VARIABLE 2	d.f.	χ^2	SIGNIFICANCE LEVEL	COMMENTS
Opportunity for individual pupil to practise French	4	68·671	***	In more HE and ME classes opportunities for the individual pupil to practise French had increased. In more UE classes such opportunities had remained the same or had decreased.
Opportunity for slower pupils to participate in French lesson	2	30·796	***	In more HE and ME classes opportunities for the slower pupils to participate in the French lesson had increased. In more UE classes such opportunities had remained the same or had decreased.
Introduction of written French	2	15·984	***	In more HE and ME classes the introduction of written French had produced 'a beneficial effect'. In more UE classes the introduction of written French had produced 'an adverse effect' or 'no effect'.
Teacher's command of French	4	20·881	***	More teachers of HE and ME classes showed 'marked' or 'some' improvement in their command of French. More teachers of UE classes showed 'no improvement' or 'regression' in their command of French.
Teacher's enthusiasm for French	4	38·106	***	More teachers of HE and ME classes showed 'marked' or 'some' increase in their enthusiasm for French. More teachers of UE classes showed no increase in enthusiasm or a falling-off of enthusiasm.

Notes

1. Variable 1 in Table 5.5. is the rated increase in the enthusiasm of the class for French. 'Highly enthusiastic' (HE) classes are those reported to be showing a marked increase in their enthusiasm for French. 'Moderately enthusiastic' (ME) classes are those reported to be showing some increase in their enthusiasm for French. 'Unenthusiastic' (UE) classes are those reported to be showing no increase in enthusiasm for French or a falling-off of enthusiasm.
2. All non-significant variables have been omitted from Table 5.5.

APPENDIX SIX

Achievement in French in the Secondary School

(Tables 6.1 - 6.5; Figures 6.1 - 6.6)

TABLE 6.1: *Cohort 1. Distribution of sample by type of school, sex of pupil, and parental occupation.*

		PARENTAL OCCUPATION					
TYPE OF SCHOOL SEX OF PUPIL		Profess-ional	Clerical	Skilled	Semi-skilled	Un-skilled	TOTAL
Secondary Modern Boys	N	83	146	474	283	185	1171
	%	7·09	12·47	40·48	24·17	15·80	100
Secondary Modern Girls	N	78	155	482	308	191	1214
	%	6·43	12·77	39·70	25·37	15·73	100
Secondary Modern Total	N	161	301	956	591	376	2385
	%	6·75	12·62	40·08	24·78	15·77	100
Grammar Boys	N	122	103	160	52	30	467
	%	26·12	22·06	34·26	11·13	6·42	100
Grammar Girls	N	112	173	209	79	37	610
	%	18·36	28·36	34·26	12·95	6·06	100
Grammar Total	N	234	276	369	131	67	1077
	%	21·73	25·63	34·26	12·16	6·22	100
Comprehensive Boys	N	36	35	97	33	16	217
	%	16·59	16·13	44·70	15·21	7·37	100
Comprehensive Girls	N	45	44	79	48	19	235
	%	19·15	18·72	33·62	20·43	8·09	100
Comprehensive Total	N	81	79	176	81	35	452
	%	17·92	17·48	38·94	17·92	7·74	100
All Other Types Boys	N	12	20	53	87	31	203
	%	5·91	9·85	26·11	42·86	15·27	100
All Other Types Girls	N	9	29	39	68	38	183
	%	4·92	15·85	21·31	37·16	20·77	100
All Other Types Total	N	21	49	92	155	69	386
	%	5·44	12·69	23·83	40·16	17·88	100
All Types Combined Boys	N	253	304	784	455	262	2058
	%	12·29	14·77	38·10	22·11	12·73	100
All Types Combined Girls	N	244	401	809	503	285	2242
	%	10·88	17·89	36·08	22·44	12·71	100
All Types Combined Total	N	497	705	1593	958	547	4300
	%	11·56	16·40	37·05	22·28	12·72	100

Appendix Six

The three main types of secondary school differ significantly from one another in their social composition. The secondary modern schools in the sample take in proportionately fewer pupils in the 'professional' and 'clerical' parental occupation categories, but proportionately more in the 'semi-skilled' and 'unskilled' categories, than do the grammar or the comprehensive schools. The grammar schools in the sample take in proportionately more pupils in the 'clerical' parental occupation category, but proportionately fewer in the 'semi-skilled' and 'skilled' categories, than do the comprehensive schools.

TABLE 6.2: *Battery 2 Speaking Test. Mean scores by type of school, sex of pupil, and parental occupation.*

TYPE OF SCHOOL SEX OF PUPIL		PARENTAL OCCUPATION				TOTAL
		Professional and Clerical	*Skilled*	*Semi-skilled*	*Unskilled*	
Secondary Modern Boys	N	25	51	25	19	120
	x̄	56·92	43·00	41·88	46·42	46·20
	SD	26·25	14·99	17·30	14·16	19·11
Secondary Modern Girls	N	31	55	26	17	129
	x̄	55·03	55·74	57·61	49·52	55·13
	SD	22·42	21·28	26·24	22·93	22·97
Secondary Modern Total	N	56	106	51	36	249
	x̄	55·87	49·61	49·90	47·88	50·83
	SD	24·22	19·58	23·66	18·88	21·66
Grammar Boys	N	27	19	5	1	52
	x̄	84·85	76·15	58·20	61·00	78·65
	SD	15·45	19·30	6·40	0·00	18·23
Grammar Girls	N	22	21	9	3	55
	x̄	85·40	74·38	70·00	69·66	77·81
	SD	14·85	21·54	16·87	12·28	19·01
Grammar Total	N	49	40	14	4	107
	x̄	85·10	75·22	65·78	67·50	78·22
	SD	15·19	20·52	15·15	11·28	18·64
Comprehensive Boys	N	6	15	4	2	27
	x̄	70·33	66·80	58·25	57·50	65·62
	SD	23·45	16·91	23·44	31·49	21·32
Comprehensive Girls	N	12	8	5	1	26
	x̄	79·00	63·25	80·60	53·00	73·46
	SD	15·75	21·21	27·89	0·00	21·79
Comprehensive Total	N	18	23	9	3	53
	x̄	76·11	65·56	70·66	56·00	69·47
	SD	19·12	18·60	28·28	25·80	21·90
All Other Types Boys	N	2	4	8	4	18
	x̄	57·00	51·75	37·62	49·00	45·44
	SD	14·99	13·40	12·17	19·96	16·52
All Other Types Girls	N	4	6	9	2	21
	x̄	64·75	56·00	69·22	41·50	61·95
	SD	10·42	18·56	19·48	7·49	19·00
All Other Types Total	N	6	10	17	6	39
	x̄	62·16	54·30	54·35	46·50	54·33
	SD	12·68	16·82	22·79	17·23	19·70

TABLE 6.2. (cont.)

PARENTAL OCCUPATION

TYPE OF SCHOOL SEX OF PUPIL		*Professional and Clerical*	*Skilled*	*Semi-skilled*	*Unskilled*	TOTAL
All Types Combined	N	60	89	42	26	217
Boys	x̄	70·83	54·48	44·57	48·23	56·33
	SD	25·15	21·59	17·81	17·31	23·61
All Types Combined	N	69	90	49	23	231
Girls	x̄	69·44	60·77	64·36	51·60	63·21
	SD	23·18	22·55	25·06	21·63	23·79
All Types Combined	N	129	179	91	49	448
Total	x̄	70·09	57·64	55·23	49·81	59·88
	SD	24·13	22·30	24·12	19·53	23·95

Notes

1. *Sex differences.* With all school groups and parental occupation categories combined, there is a significant difference ($p < 0.01$) between mean scores in favour of the girls. Within the different types of school, however, significant differences in favour of the girls only occur in the secondary modern schools and in the 'all other types' group of schools. There are no significant differences between mean scores for boys and girls in the grammar schools or in the comprehensive schools.

2. *Parental occupation.* When scores for pupils of both sexes and in all types of secondary school are combined, there is a linear relationship between test score and parental occupation: high mean scores coincide with high-status parental occupation and low mean scores with low-status parental occupation. Differences between mean scores are significant at the 0·1 per cent level. When each type of school is considered separately, however, differences between mean scores for pupils in the various parental occupation categories reach the one per cent level of significance in the grammar schools, but fail to reach a significant level in any other type of school.

3. *School type.* There are obvious differences in the test performance of pupils in the different types of secondary school. Mean scores obtained by grammar school pupils are significantly higher than those obtained by comprehensive school pupils; both are significantly higher than those obtained by secondary modern school pupils. Mean scores obtained by pupils in secondary modern schools do not differ significantly from those obtained by pupils in the 'all other types' group of schools.

TABLE 6.3: *Battery 2 Listening Test. Mean scores by type of school, sex of pupil, and parental occupation.*

TYPE OF SCHOOL SEX OF PUPIL		PARENTAL OCCUPATION				TOTAL
		Professional and Clerical	*Skilled*	*Semi-skilled*	*Unskilled*	
Secondary Modern Boys	N	222	458	267	180	1127
	x̄	16·80	15·80	15·01	14·04	15·53
	SD	5·24	4·94	4·86	4·74	5·03
Secondary Modern Girls	N	228	464	300	187	1179
	x̄	17·52	17·49	15·96	15·64	16·81
	SD	5·68	5·34	5·17	5·01	5·38
Secondary Modern Total	N	450	922	567	367	2306
	x̄	17·17	16·65	15·51	14·86	16·19
	SD	5·48	5·21	5·05	4·94	5·25
Grammar Boys	N	218	155	47	30	450
	x̄	26·38	24·99	23·42	24·60	25·47
	SD	6·08	5·62	5·47	4·60	5·86
Grammar Girls	N	280	204	79	33	596
	x̄	26·88	24·68	24·27	24·06	25·62
	SD	5·74	5·76	5·21	5·87	5·81
Grammar Total	N	498	359	126	63	1046
	x̄	26·66	24·81	23·96	24·31	25·56
	SD	5·89	5·70	5·32	5·31	5·83
Comprehensive Boys	N	71	96	32	15	214
	x̄	22·15	20·93	15·18	15·46	20·09
	SD	6·22	6·71	3·94	6·63	6·73
Comprehensive Girls	N	88	76	48	18	230
	x̄	25·04	20·01	18·66	16·44	21·37
	SD	6·42	6·73	6·82	4·82	7·17
Comprehensive Total	N	159	172	80	33	444
	x̄	23·75	20·52	17·27	16·00	20·76
	SD	6·49	6·73	6·08	5·73	6·99
All Other Types Boys	N	30	51	84	30	195
	x̄	14·60	15·45	16·00	16·10	15·65
	SD	4·66	4·16	4·53	4·54	4·49
All Other Types Girls	N	36	39	68	36	179
	x̄	18·27	17·33	18·16	17·05	17·78
	SD	4·74	4·39	5·57	5·31	5·14
All Other Types Total	N	66	90	152	66	374
	x̄	16·60	16·26	16·96	16·62	16·67
	SD	5·05	4·36	5·14	5·00	4·93

TABLE 6.3. (cont.)

		PARENTAL OCCUPATION				
TYPE OF SCHOOL SEX OF PUPIL		*Professional and Clerical*	*Skilled*	*Semi-skilled*	*Unskilled*	TOTAL
All Types Combined	N	541	760	430	255	1986
Boys	x̄	21·24	18·30	16·14	15·61	18·29
	SD	7·33	6·50	5·46	5·89	6·78
All Types Combined	N	632	783	495	274	2184
Girls	x̄	22·76	19·60	17·85	16·89	19·78
	SD	7·25	6·36	6·17	5·81	6·86
All Types Combined	N	1173	1543	925	529	4170
Total	x̄	22·06	18·96	17·05	16·27	19·07
	SD	7·32	6·47	5·91	5·88	6·86

Notes

1. *Sex differences.* With all school groups and parental occupation categories combined, there is a significant difference ($p < 0.001$) between mean scores in favour of the girls. Within the different types of school, but with all parental occupation categories combined, significant differences in favour of the girls only occur in the secondary modern schools and in the 'all other types' group of schools: these differences are significant at the 0·1 per cent level. In the comprehensive schools, significant differences in favour of the girls occur at the one per cent level in the 'professional and clerical' and 'semi-skilled' parental occupation categories, but the differences between the sexes are not significant when all parental occupation categories are combined. There are no significant differences between boys' and girls' mean scores in the grammar schools.

2. *Parental occupation.* When scores for pupils of both sexes and in all types of secondary school are combined, there is a linear relationship between test score and parental occupation: high mean scores coincide with high-status parental occupation and low mean scores with low-status parental occupation. Differences between mean scores are significant at the 0·1 per cent level. When each type of school is considered separately, mean scores for pupils in the various parental occupation categories differ significantly at the 0·1 per cent level in the secondary modern, comprehensive, and grammar schools, but do not differ significantly in the 'all other types' group of schools. Within the grammar and comprehensive schools, mean scores for pupils in the 'unskilled' category do not differ significantly from those for pupils in the 'semi-skilled' category.

3. *School type.* There are obvious differences in the test performance of pupils in the different types of secondary school. Mean scores obtained by grammar school pupils are significantly higher than those obtained by comprehensive school pupils; both are significantly higher than those obtained by secondary modern school pupils. Mean scores obtained by pupils in secondary modern schools do not differ significantly from those obtained by pupils in the 'all other types' group of schools.

TABLE 6.4: *Battery 2 Reading Test. Mean scores by type of school, sex of pupil, and parental occupation.*

TYPE OF SCHOOL SEX OF PUPIL		Professional and Clerical	Skilled	Semi-skilled	Unskilled	TOTAL
		PARENTAL OCCUPATION				
Secondary Modern	N	225	469	280	183	1157
Boys	x̄	17·68	15·30	14·78	14·13	15·45
	SD	6·77	5·92	5·55	5·77	6·10
Secondary Modern	N	229	466	301	189	1185
Girls	x̄	20·82	18·68	17·06	16·72	18·37
	SD	7·47	7·33	6·56	6·69	7·21
Secondary Modern	N	454	935	581	372	2342
Total	x̄	19·26	16·99	15·96	15·45	16·93
	SD	7·30	6·87	6·20	6·39	6·84
Grammar	N	216	147	47	27	437
Boys	x̄	32·78	30·85	27·27	30·85	31·42
	SD	6·63	7·33	7·07	4·83	7·04
Grammar	N	283	208	79	37	607
Girls	x̄	34·62	31·25	30·79	32·13	32·82
	SD	6·31	6·80	6·56	6·47	6·74
Grammar	N	499	355	126	64	1044
Total	x̄	33·82	31·08	29·48	31·59	32·23
	SD	6·52	7·02	6·97	5·87	6·90
Comprehensive	N	71	95	32	16	214
Boys	x̄	27·01	24·38	17·68	14·68	23·53
	SD	9·45	9·79	7·28	6·30	9·92
Comprehensive	N	89	78	48	19	234
Girls	x̄	31·76	24·37	21·52	18·57	26·12
	SD	8·24	9·46	8·56	7·76	9·88
Comprehensive	N	160	173	80	35	448
Total	x̄	29·65	24·38	19·98	16·80	24·88
	SD	9·11	9·64	8·28	7·39	9·98
All Other Types	N	32	52	84	30	198
Boys	x̄	17·75	17·17	15·23	15·46	16·18
	SD	5·96	6·25	5·34	5·20	5·77
All Other Types	N	38	38	65	37	178
Girls	x̄	20·86	19·13	19·18	17·40	19·16
	SD	7·58	7·53	7·86	7·69	7·78
All Other Types	N	70	90	149	67	376
Total	x̄	19·44	18·00	16·95	16·53	17·59
	SD	7·06	6·89	6·85	6·76	6·96

TABLE 6.4. (cont.)

		PARENTAL OCCUPATION				
TYPE OF SCHOOL SEX OF PUPIL		Professional and Clerical	Skilled	Semi-skilled	Unskilled	TOTAL
All Types Combined Boys	N	544	763	443	256	2006
	x̄	24·89	19·56	16·40	16·08	19·86
	SD	10·00	9·25	6·97	7·60	9·44
All Types Combined Girls	N	639	790	493	282	2204
	x̄	28·46	22·57	19·98	18·96	23·24
	SD	9·65	9·22	8·52	8·59	9·80
All Types Combined Total	N	1183	1553	936	538	4210
	x̄	26·82	21·09	18·28	17·59	21·63
	SD	9·97	9·36	8·03	8·26	9·77

Notes

1. *Sex differences.* When all school groups are combined, there are significant differences between mean scores in favour of the girls within each parental occupation category: these differences are all significant at the 0·1 per cent level. Within the different types of school, but with all parental occupation categories combined, significant differences between mean scores in favour of the girls reach the 0·1 per cent level in the secondary modern schools and in the schools of the 'all other types' group; in the grammar schools and the comprehensive schools, these differences are significant at the one per cent level. Significant differences in favour of the girls are concentrated in the 'professional and clerical' and 'semi-skilled' parental occupation categories in the grammar and comprehensive schools.

2. *Parental occupation.* When scores for pupils of both sexes and in all types of secondary school are combined, there is a linear relationship between test score and parental occupation: high mean scores coincide with high-status parental occupation and low mean scores with low-status parental occupation. Differences between mean scores are significant at the 0·1 per cent level. When each type of school is considered separately, mean scores for pupils in the various parental occupation categories differ significantly at the 0·1 per cent level in the secondary modern, comprehensive, and grammar schools and at the 5 per cent level in the 'all other types' group of schools. In this latter group of schools and in the secondary modern schools, mean scores for pupils in the 'unskilled' category do not differ significantly from those for pupils in the 'semi-skilled' category.

3. *School type.* There are obvious differences in the test performance of pupils in the different types of secondary school. Mean scores obtained by grammar school pupils are significantly higher than those obtained by comprehensive school pupils; both are significantly higher than those obtained by secondary modern school pupils. Mean scores obtained by pupils in secondary modern schools do not differ significantly from those obtained by pupils in the 'all other types' group of schools.

TABLE 6.5: *Battery 2 Writing Test. Mean scores by type of school, sex of pupil, and parental occupation.*

TYPE OF SCHOOL SEX OF PUPIL		*Professional and Clerical*	*Skilled*	*Semi-skilled*	*Unskilled*	TOTAL
			PARENTAL OCCUPATION			
Secondary Modern Boys	N	226	458	274	180	1138
	x̄	14·42	10·73	8·83	8·95	10·72
	SD	12·32	9·48	7·91	9·30	9·96
Secondary Modern Girls	N	224	465	295	185	1169
	x̄	19·72	16·13	12·72	12·85	15·44
	SD	12·78	11·77	10·76	10·41	11·81
Secondary Modern Total	N	450	923	569	365	2307
	x̄	17·06	13·45	10·85	10·93	13·11
	SD	12·83	11·03	9·69	10·07	11·18
Grammar Boys	N	222	155	51	29	457
	x̄	44·40	37·80	31·50	33·75	40·05
	SD	14·69	15·67	13·69	10·42	15·41
Grammar Girls	N	277	205	78	37	597
	x̄	48·42	41·52	40·11	42·27	44·58
	SD	13·21	12·67	12·32	12·72	13·38
Grammar Total	N	499	360	129	66	1054
	x̄	46·63	39·92	36·71	38·53	42·62
	SD	14·03	14·16	13·55	12·50	14·47
Comprehensive Boys	N	70	96	33	14	213
	x̄	31·74	26·18	14·81	13·07	25·38
	SD	17·28	18·00	11·48	12·43	17·76
Comprehensive Girls	N	88	77	45	19	229
	x̄	37·82	25·31	20·06	15·73	28·29
	SD	16·21	16·64	16·27	12·07	17·96
Comprehensive Total	N	158	173	78	33	442
	x̄	35·13	25·79	17·84	14·60	26·89
	SD	16·96	17·41	14·67	12·29	17·92
All Other Types Boys	N	32	52	81	29	194
	x̄	16·65	11·88	9·70	9·86	11·45
	SD	10·85	10·45	9·55	9·80	10·36
All Other Types Girls	N	38	38	65	37	178
	x̄	19·71	16·73	16·95	14·62	17·01
	SD	10·82	13·63	13·13	11·88	12·64
All Other Types Total	N	70	90	146	66	372
	x̄	18·31	13·93	12·93	12·53	14·11
	SD	10·94	12·14	11·84	11·27	11·84

TABLE 6.5. (cont.)

PARENTAL OCCUPATION

TYPE OF SCHOOL SEX OF PUPIL		*Professional and Clerical*	*Skilled*	*Semi-skilled*	*Unskilled*	TOTAL
All Types Combined	N	550	761	439	252	2002
Boys	x̄	28·86	18·27	12·07	12·13	19·05
	SD	19·68	16·58	11·81	12·47	17·45
All Types Combined	N	627	785	483	278	2173
Girls	x̄	34·94	23·69	18·40	17·20	24·93
	SD	18·91	16·72	15·47	14·82	18·22
All Types Combined	N	1177	1546	922	530	4175
Total	x̄	32·10	21·02	15·39	14·79	22·11
	SD	19·51	16·87	14·21	13·98	18·09

Notes

1. *Sex differences.* When all school groups are combined, there are significant differences between mean scores in favour of the girls within each parental occupation category: these differences are all significant at the 0·1 per cent level. Within the different types of school, but with all parental occupation categories combined, significant differences between mean scores in favour of the girls reach the 0·1 per cent level in the grammar schools, the secondary modern schools, and the schools of the 'all other types' group; in the comprehensive schools, boys' and girls' mean scores do not differ significantly.

2. *Parental occupation.* When scores for pupils of both sexes and in all types of secondary school are combined, there is a linear relationship between test score and parental occupation: high mean scores coincide with high-status parental occupation and low mean scores with low-status parental occupation. Differences between mean scores are significant at the 0·1 per cent level. When each type of school is considered separately, mean scores for pupils in the various parental occupation categories differ significantly at the 0·1 per cent level in the secondary modern, comprehensive, and grammar schools and at the one per cent level in the 'all other types' group of schools. Mean scores for pupils in the 'unskilled' category in each of these types of school do not, however, differ significantly from those for pupils in the 'semi-skilled' category.

3. *School type.* There are obvious differences in the test performance of pupils in the different types of secondary school. Mean scores obtained by grammar school pupils are significantly higher than those obtained by comprehensive school pupils; both are significantly higher than those obtained by secondary modern school pupils. Mean scores obtained by pupils in secondary modern schools do not differ significantly from those obtained by pupils in the 'all other types' group of schools.

FIGURE 6.1: *Distribution of Battery 2 Listening test scores for cohort 1 pupils within each parental occupation category.*

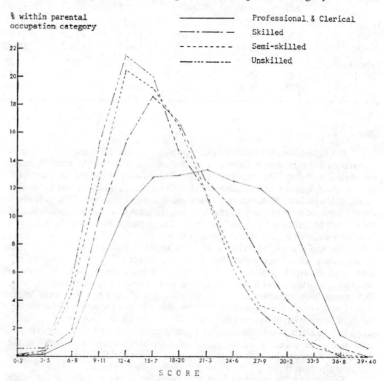

FIGURE 6.2: *Distribution of Battery 2 Reading test scores for cohort 1 pupils within each parental occupation category.*

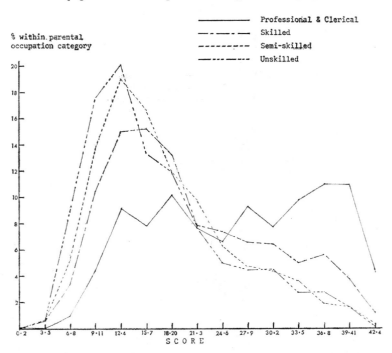

FIGURE 6.3: *Distribution of Battery 2 Writing test scores for cohort 1 pupils within each parental occupation category.*

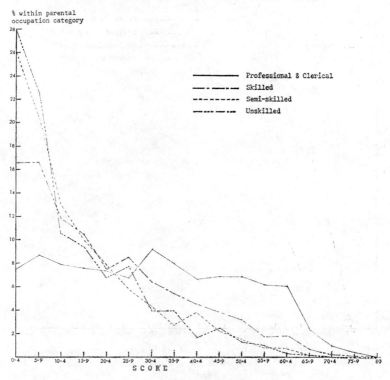

FIGURE 6.4: *Distribution of Battery 2 Listening test scores within each school group.*

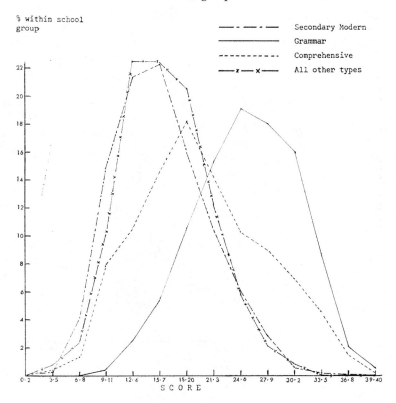

FIGURE 6.5: *Distribution of Battery 2 Reading test scores within each school group.*

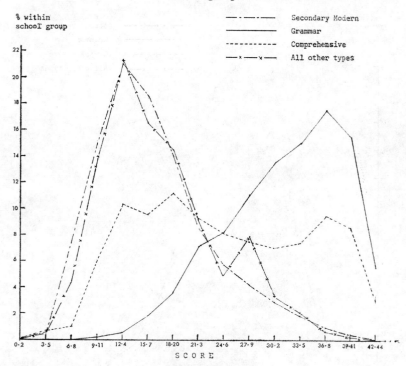

Appendix Six

FIGURE 6.6: *Distribution of Battery 2 Writing test scores within each school group.*

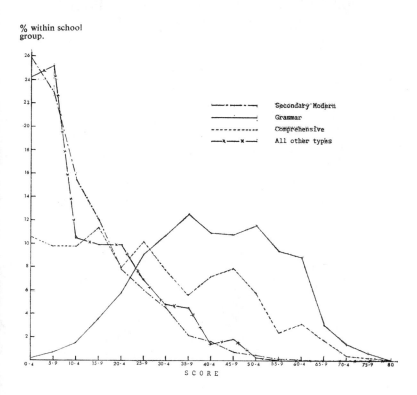

H

APPENDIX SEVEN

Pupils´ Attitudes Towards Learning French in the Secondary School

(Tables 7.1 - 7.36)

Tables 7.1 to 7.28 show the percentage of pupils in the first experimental cohort who agree with each statement in the attitude questionnaire. The responses are shown distributed by pupils' sex and general attitude towards French, within the different types of secondary school. These tables are based on the responses of 3,898 pupils: data obtained from pupils who were absent for the French group tests were excluded from the analysis.

TABLE 7.1: *Item 1. 'I would like to speak many languages'.*

TYPE OF SCHOOL	PUPILS WHO LIKE FRENCH			PUPILS WHO DISLIKE FRENCH		
	Boys	*Girls*	*Total*	*Boys*	*Girls*	*Total*
Secondary Modern	76·23%	79·36%	78·11%	49·27%	47·37%	48·46%
Grammar	79·61%	85·12%	82·82%	45·75%	64·16%	55·52%
Comprehensive	80·00%	83·97%	82·28%	40·81%	47·43%	43·75%
All School Types	77·90%	81·87%	80·24%	47·83%	51·17%	49·32%

Notes

66.67 per cent of the total sample agree with the item statement.

Results of χ^2 tests: within each type of school, significantly more pupils who like French agree with the item statement than do those who dislike French ($p < 0.001$). Significantly different responses are obtained from pupils in the different types of school ($p < 0.001$): 74·55 per cent of the grammar school pupils, 67·11 per cent of the comprehensive school pupils and 63·01 per cent of the secondary modern school pupils agree with the item statement. Significantly more girls than boys agree with the item statement: the differences between the sexes are more significant for grammar school pupils ($p < 0.001$) and secondary modern school pupils ($p < 0.01$) than for comprehensive school pupils ($p < 0.05$).

H*

TABLE 7.2: *Item 2. 'I would like to go to France'.*

TYPE OF SCHOOL	PUPILS WHO LIKE FRENCH			PUPILS WHO DISLIKE FRENCH		
	Boys	*Girls*	*Total*	*Boys*	*Girls*	*Total*
Secondary Modern	90·53%	92·84%	91·92%	67·53%	73·59%	70·11%
Grammar	91·42%	94·93%	93·45%	79·08%	84·48%	81·95%
Comprehensive	93·04%	92·94%	92·98%	65·30%	81·01%	72·31%
All School Types	91·17%	93·56%	92·58%	69·17%	76·82%	72·60%

Notes

83·80 per cent of the total sample agree with the item statement.

Results of χ^2 tests: within each type of school, significantly more pupils who like French agree with the item statement than do those who dislike French ($p < 0.001$). Significantly different responses are obtained from pupils in the different types of school ($p < 0.001$): 89·96 per cent of the grammar school pupils, 84·82 per cent of the comprehensive school pupils and 80·81 per cent of the secondary modern school pupils agree with the item statement. Significantly more girls than boys agree with the item statement: the differences between the sexes are more significant for secondary modern pupils ($p < 0.001$) than for pupils in grammar or comprehensive schools ($p < 0.05$).

TABLE 7.3: *Item 3. 'I am not interested in learning foreign languages'.*

TYPE OF SCHOOL	PUPILS WHO LIKE FRENCH			PUPILS WHO DISLIKE FRENCH		
	Boys	*Girls*	*Total*	*Boys*	*Girls*	*Total*
Secondary Modern	26·52%	30·71%	29·03%	37·11%	40·40%	38·50%
Grammar	15·27%	14·05%	14·85%	38·56%	28·65%	33·33%
Comprehensive	18·42%	22·07%	20·52%	33·39%	44·30%	41·57%
All School Types	21·75%	24·00%	23·08%	37·59%	38·13%	37·83%

Notes

29·55 per cent of the total sample agree with the item statement.

Results of χ^2 tests: within each type of school, significantly more pupils who dislike French agree with the item statement than do those who like French ($p < 0.001$). Significantly different responses are obtained from pupils in the different types of school ($p < 0.001$): 33·84 per cent of the secondary modern school pupils, 28·92 per cent of the comprehensive school pupils and 20·44 per cent of the grammar school pupils agree with the item statement. Differences between the sexes in response to this item are very slight: in the grammar schools, proportionately fewer girls than boys agree with the item statement ($p < 0.05$), but no significant differences between the sexes in response to this item are found in the other types of school.

TABLE 7.4: *Item 4. 'Learning French is a waste of time'.*

TYPE OF SCHOOL	PUPILS WHO LIKE FRENCH			PUPILS WHO DISLIKE FRENCH		
	Boys	*Girls*	*Total*	*Boys*	*Girls*	*Total*
Secondary Modern	3·65%	3·75%	3·71%	57·88%	45·27%	52·54%
Grammar	2·88%	0·45%	1·47%	40·13%	24·41%	31·79%
Comprehensive	4·34%	1·92%	2·95%	48·97%	34·17%	42·37%
All School Types	3·47%	2·41%	2·85%	54·09%	39·39%	47·52%

Notes

22·45 per cent of the total sample agree with the item statement.

Results of χ^2 tests: within each type of school, significantly more pupils who dislike French agree with the item statement than do those who like French (p<0·001). Significantly different responses are obtained from pupils in the different types of school (p<0·001): 28·56 per cent of the secondary modern school pupils, 18·52 per cent of the comprehensive school pupils and 10·64 per cent of the grammar school pupils agree with the item statement. Significantly more boys than girls agree with the item statement: the differences between the sexes are more significant for grammar and secondary modern pupils (p<0·001) than for comprehensive pupils (p<0·01).

TABLE 7.5: *Item 5. 'I find French easier than other subjects'.*

TYPE OF SCHOOL	PUPILS WHO LIKE FRENCH			PUPILS WHO DISLIKE FRENCH		
	Boys	*Girls*	*Total*	*Boys*	*Girls*	*Total*
Secondary School	28·19%	32·94%	31·03%	7·12%	4·32%	5·93%
Grammar	34·40%	35·03%	34·77%	6·71%	1·73%	4·03%
Comprehensive	26·54%	20·52%	23·10%	3·06%	2·53%	2·82%
All School Types	30·16%	32·17%	31·35%	6·63%	3·54%	5·24%

Notes

19·84 per cent of the total sample agree with the item statement.

Results of χ^2 tests: within each type of school, significantly more pupils who like French agree with the item statement than do those who dislike French (p<0·001). Significantly different responses are obtained from pupils in the different types of school (p<0·001): 25·46 per cent of the grammar school pupils, 18·21 per cent of the secondary modern school pupils and 14·96 per cent of the comprehensive school pupils agree with the item statement. In the secondary modern schools, significantly more girls than boys agree with the item statement (p<0·01); no significant differences between the sexes in response to this item are found in the other types of school.

TABLE 7.6: *Item 6. 'It is more difficult to understand the tape-recorder than the teacher'.*

TYPE OF SCHOOL	PUPILS WHO LIKE FRENCH			PUPILS WHO DISLIKE FRENCH		
	Boys	*Girls*	*Total*	*Boys*	*Girls*	*Total*
Secondary School	86·32%	89·51%	88·23%	81·59%	85·96%	83·45%
Grammar	89·17%	90·57%	89·98%	90·78%	84·48%	87·42%
Comprehensive	79·13%	85·89%	83·02%	84·69%	83·54%	84·18%
All School Types	86·39%	89·43%	88·18%	83·40%	85·37%	84·29%

Notes

86·47 per cent of the total sample agree with the item statement.

Results of χ^2 tests: there are few significant differences between groups in response to this item. Boys who like French do not differ significantly from those who dislike French in the extent to which they agree with the item statement; proportionately more girls who like French agree with the item statement than do those who dislike French, but the differences between these two groups only reach significance when all school types are combined ($p < 0.01$). Significantly different responses are obtained from pupils in the different types of school ($p < 0.01$): 89·20 per cent of the grammar school pupils, 85·80 per cent of the secondary modern school pupils and 83·48 per cent of the comprehensive school pupils agree with the item statement. In the secondary modern schools, significantly more girls than boys agree with the item statement ($p < 0.01$); no significant differences between the sexes in response to this item are found in the other types of school.

TABLE 7.7: *Item 7. 'There are many languages which are more important to learn than French'.*

TYPE OF SCHOOL	PUPILS WHO LIKE FRENCH			PUPILS WHO DISLIKE FRENCH		
	Boys	Girls	Total	Boys	Girls	Total
Secondary Modern	42·98%	29·05%	34·61%	68·08%	51·68%	61·11%
Grammar	29·73%	15·24%	21·24%	58·50%	45·61%	51·57%
Comprehensive	23·21%	22·72%	22·93%	57·29%	58·22%	57·71%
All School Types	35·81%	23·58%	28·56%	65·44%	50·99%	58·95%

Notes

41·91 per cent of the total sample agree with the item statement.

Results of χ^2 tests: within each type of school, significantly more pupils who dislike French agree with the item statement than do those who like French ($p < 0.001$). Significantly different responses are obtained from pupils in the different types of school ($p < 0.001$): 48·13 per cent of the secondary modern school pupils, 36·73 per cent of the comprehensive school pupils and 30·36 per cent of the grammar school pupils agree with the item statement. In the secondary modern schools and in the grammar schools, significantly more boys than girls agree with the item statement ($p < 0.001$). There are no significant differences between the sexes in response to this item among comprehensive school pupils.

TABLE 7.8: *Item 8. 'French gets more interesting all the time'.*

TYPE OF SCHOOL	PUPILS WHO LIKE FRENCH			PUPILS WHO DISLIKE FRENCH		
	Boys	Girls	Total	Boys	Girls	Total
Secondary Modern	66·88%	74·31%	71·34%	15·29%	12·57%	14·14%
Grammar	60·31%	58·46%	59·24%	9·93%	12·13%	11·11%
Comprehensive	64·28%	66·44%	65·53%	19·38%	10·81%	15·69%
All School Types	64·22%	68·02%	66·46%	14·86%	12·30%	13·72%

Notes

43·28 per cent of the total sample agree with the item statement.

Results of χ^2 tests: within each type of school, significantly more pupils who like French agree with this item than do those who dislike French ($p < 0.001$). There are no significant differences between pupils in the different types of school in response to this item. In the secondary modern schools, significantly more girls than boys agree with the item statement ($p < 0.001$); there are no significant differences between the sexes in response to this item in the other types of school.

231

French in the Primary School

TABLE 7.9: *Item 9. 'I do not always understand what I am saying when I speak in French'.*

TYPE OF SCHOOL	PUPILS WHO LIKE FRENCH			PUPILS WHO DISLIKE FRENCH		
	Boys	*Girls*	*Total*	*Boys*	*Girls*	*Total*
Secondary Modern	64·88%	64·50%	64·65%	77·02%	66·66%	72·61%
Grammar	49·05%	51·60%	50·53%	73·50%	80·34%	77·16%
Comprehensive	53·09%	56·12%	54·85%	68·68%	79·74%	73·59%
All School Types	57·81%	59·11%	58·57%	75·58%	71·11%	73·57%

Notes

65·16 per cent of the total sample agree with the item statement.

Results of χ^2 tests: within each type of school, significantly more pupils who dislike French agree with the item statement than do those who like French ($p < 0.001$). Significantly different responses are obtained from pupils in the different types of school ($p < 0.001$): 68·71 per cent of the secondary modern school pupils, 62·33 per cent of the comprehensive school pupils and 58·55 per cent of the grammar school pupils agree with the item statement. In the secondary modern schools, significantly more boys than girls agree with the item statement ($p < 0.001$); there are no significant differences between the sexes in response to this item in the other types of school.

TABLE 7.10: *Item 10. 'I think everyone should start learning French in the Primary School'.*

TYPE OF SCHOOL	PUPILS WHO LIKE FRENCH			PUPILS WHO DISLIKE FRENCH		
	Boys	*Girls*	*Total*	*Boys*	*Girls*	*Total*
Secondary Modern	80·90%	88·95%	85·72%	42·42%	50·19%	45·71%
Grammar	85·75%	88·30%	87·23%	47·68%	62·06%	55·38%
Comprehensive	85·21%	91·66%	88·92%	47·95%	53·84%	50·56%
All School Types	83·16%	89·06%	86·64%	43·84%	53·28%	48·06%

Notes

69·74 per cent of the total sample agree with the item statement.

Results of χ^2 tests: within each type of school, significantly more pupils who like French agree with the item statement than do those who dislike French ($p < 0.001$). Significantly different responses are obtained from pupils in the different types of school ($p < 0.001$): 77·62 per cent of the grammar school pupils, 73·82 per cent of the comprehensive school pupils and 65·38 per cent of the secondary modern school pupils agree with the item statement. Significantly more girls than boys agree with the item statement: the differences between the sexes are more significant for secondary modern school pupils ($p < 0.001$) and for grammar school pupils ($p < 0.01$) than for comprehensive school pupils ($p < 0.05$).

TABLE 7.11: *Item 11. 'I find French more difficult than other subjects'.*

TYPE OF SCHOOL	PUPILS WHO LIKE FRENCH			PUPILS WHO DISLIKE FRENCH		
	Boys	*Girls*	*Total*	*Boys*	*Girls*	*Total*
Secondary Modern	56·34%	45·33%	49·78%	85·81%	87·40%	86·48%
Grammar	40·76%	37·64%	38·95%	82·23%	87·28%	84·92%
Comprehensive	46·90%	46·75%	46·81%	90·81%	91·02%	90·90%
All School Types	49·66%	42·89%	45·68%	85·75%	87·74%	86·64%

Notes

63·69 per cent of the total sample agree with the item statement.

Results of χ^2 tests: within each type of school, significantly more pupils who dislike French agree with the item statement than do those who like French (p < 0·001). Significantly different responses are obtained from pupils in the different types of school (p < 0·001): 68·51 per cent of the secondary modern school pupils, 64·33 per cent of the comprehensive school pupils and 52·89 per cent of the grammar school pupils agree with the item statement. In the secondary modern schools, significantly more boys than girls agree with the item statement (p < 0·001). There are no significant differences between the sexes in response to this item in the other types of school.

TABLE 7.12: *Item 12. 'I would like to get to know some French people'.*

TYPE OF SCHOOL	PUPILS WHO LIKE FRENCH			PUPILS WHO DISLIKE FRENCH		
	Boys	*Girls*	*Total*	*Boys*	*Girls*	*Total*
Secondary Modern	83·39%	91·78%	88·04%	42·25%	66·20%	52·47%
Grammar	79·67%	93·77%	87·90%	45·33%	71·51%	59·31%
Comprehensive	83·33%	88·23%	86·14%	41·23%	68·35%	53·40%
All School Types	81·56%	92·03%	87·75%	42·64%	67·63%	53·87%

Notes

72·89 per cent of the total sample agree with the item statement.

Results of χ^2 tests: within each type of school, significantly more pupils who like French agree with the item statement than do those who dislike French (p < 0·001). Significantly different responses are obtained from pupils in the different types of school (p < 0·001): 79·26 per cent of the grammar school pupils, 73·13 per cent of the comprehensive school pupils and 69·96 per cent of the secondary modern school pupils agree with the item statement. Within each type of school, significantly more girls than boys agree with the item statement (p < 0·001).

TABLE 7.13: *Item 13. 'I prefer speaking French to reading and writing it'.*

TYPE OF SCHOOL	PUPILS WHO LIKE FRENCH			PUPILS WHO DISLIKE FRENCH		
	Boys	*Girls*	*Total*	*Boys*	*Girls*	*Total*
Secondary Modern	68·60%	60·28%	63·62%	52·25%	44·81%	49·09%
Grammar	73·56%	67·89%	70·28%	61·84%	56·32%	58·89%
Comprehensive	72·17%	62·82%	66·78%	62·88%	36·70%	51·13%
All School Types	70·80%	63·16%	66·29%	54·91%	46·59%	51·17%

Notes

59·66 per cent of the total sample agree with the item statement.

Results of χ^2 tests: within each type of school, significantly more pupils who like French agree with the item statement than do those who dislike French. The differences between groups are more significant for secondary modern and grammar school pupils ($p < 0.001$) than for comprehensive school pupils ($p < 0.01$). Significantly different responses are obtained from pupils in the different types of school ($p < 0.001$): 66·82 per cent of the grammar school pupils, 60·62 per cent of the comprehensive school pupils and 56·23 per cent of the secondary modern school pupils agree with the item statement. In the comprehensive schools, significantly more boys than girls agree with the item statement ($p < 0.01$). The same trend is present, but to a less significant extent ($p < 0.05$), in the secondary modern schools. There are no significant differences between the sexes in response to this item among grammar school pupils.

TABLE 7.14: *Item 14. 'I think English is the best language'.*

TYPE OF SCHOOL	PUPILS WHO LIKE FRENCH			PUPILS WHO DISLIKE FRENCH		
	Boys	*Girls*	*Total*	*Boys*	*Girls*	*Total*
Secondary Modern	78·30%	65·20%	70·48%	90·42%	85·88%	88·49%
Grammar	72·81%	66·43%	69·12%	85·13%	85·05%	85·09%
Comprehensive	67·54%	66·88%	67·16%	84·84%	89·74%	87·00%
All School Types	75·00%	65·81%	69·60%	88·99%	86·08%	87·69%

Notes

77·60 per cent of the total sample agree with the item statement.

Results of χ^2 tests: within each type of school, significantly more pupils who dislike French agree with the item statement than do those who like French ($p < 0.001$). Significantly different responses are obtained from pupils in the different types of school ($p < 0.01$): 79·69 per cent of the secondary modern school pupils, 75·11 per cent of the comprehensive school pupils and 74 per cent of the grammar school pupils agree with the item statement. In the secondary modern schools, significantly more boys than girls agree with the item statement ($p < 0.001$). There are no significant differences between the sexes in response to this item in the other types of school.

TABLE 7.15: *Item 15. 'French will be useful to me after I leave school'.*

TYPE OF SCHOOL	PUPILS WHO LIKE FRENCH			PUPILS WHO DISLIKE FRENCH		
	Boys	*Girls*	*Total*	*Boys*	*Girls*	*Total*
Secondary Modern	76·85%	79·88%	78·65%	32·84%	33·00%	32·91%
Grammar	81·90%	85·31%	83·90%	38·66%	54·11%	46·87%
Comprehensive	83·18%	77·92%	80·14%	34·02%	36·36%	35·05%
All School Types	79·42%	81·49%	80·64%	33·90%	38·11%	35·79%

Notes

60·87 per cent of the total sample agree with the item statement.

Results of χ^2 tests: within each type of school, significantly more pupils who like French agree with the item statement than do those who dislike French ($p < 0.001$). Significantly different responses are obtained from pupils in the different types of school ($p < 0.001$): 72·64 per cent of the grammar school pupils, 62·35 per cent of the comprehensive school pupils and 55·25 per cent of the secondary modern school pupils agree with the item statement. In the secondary modern schools, significantly more girls than boys agree with the item statement ($p < 0.001$). The same trend is present, but to a less significant extent ($p < 0.01$), in the grammar schools. There are no significant differences between the sexes in response to this item among comprehensive school pupils.

TABLE 7.16: *Item 16. 'I would rather have learned another language instead of French'.*

TYPE OF SCHOOL	PUPILS WHO LIKE FRENCH			PUPILS WHO DISLIKE FRENCH		
	Boys	*Girls*	*Total*	*Boys*	*Girls*	*Total*
Secondary Modern	29·69%	19·33%	23·47%	69·67%	64·42%	67·44%
Grammar	16·77%	14·38%	15·38%	67·33%	58·62%	62·65%
Comprehensive	19·29%	16·12%	17·47%	58·94%	62·33%	60·46%
All School Types	23·80%	17·26%	19·94%	68·20%	62·87%	65·81%

Notes

40·08 per cent of the total sample agree with the item statement.

Results of χ^2 tests: within each type of school, significantly more pupils who dislike French agree with the item statement than do those who like French ($p < 0.001$). Significantly different responses are obtained from pupils in the different types of school ($p < 0.001$): 45·89 per cent of the secondary modern school pupils, 34·24 per cent of the comprehensive school pupils and 29·76 per cent of the grammar school pupils agree with the item statement. In the secondary modern schools, significantly more boys than girls agree with the item statement ($p < 0.001$). The same trend is present, but to a less significant extent ($p < 0.05$), in the grammar schools. There are no significant differences between the sexes in response to this item among comprehensive school pupils.

TABLE 7.17: *Item 17. 'I am afraid to speak French'.*

TYPE OF SCHOOL	PUPILS WHO LIKE FRENCH			PUPILS WHO DISLIKE FRENCH		
	Boys	Girls	Total	Boys	Girls	Total
Secondary Modern	16·05%	19·62%	18·18%	24·63%	33·00%	28·20%
Grammar	10·47%	13·48%	12·21%	22·22%	30·23%	26·46%
Comprehensive	11·50%	10·32%	10·82%	29·89%	45·56%	36·93%
All School Types	13·49%	16·41%	15·21%	24·78%	33·68%	28·77%

Notes

21·17 per cent of the total sample agree with the item statement.

Results of χ^2 tests: within each type of school, significantly more pupils who dislike French agree with the item statement than do those who like French ($p < 0.001$). Significantly different responses are obtained from pupils in the different types of school ($p < 0.001$): 23·29 per cent of the secondary modern school pupils, 21·17 per cent of the comprehensive school pupils and 16·54 per cent of the grammar school pupils agree with the item statement. In the secondary modern schools, significantly more girls than boys agree with the item statement ($p < 0.05$). The same tendency is apparent in the other types of school, but the differences between the sexes do not reach a significant level.

TABLE 7.18: *Item 18. 'There are many more important things to learn in school than French'.*

TYPE OF SCHOOL	PUPILS WHO LIKE FRENCH			PUPILS WHO DISLIKE FRENCH		
	Boys	Girls	Total	Boys	Girls	Total
Secondary Modern	80·69%	73·47%	76·36%	94·79%	94·70%	94·75%
Grammar	79·28%	63·29%	70·02%	95·39%	89·59%	92·30%
Comprehensive	66·96%	68·18%	67·66%	96·96%	88·60%	93·25%
All School Types	78·45%	69·42%	73·12%	95·12%	92·91%	94·13%

Notes

82·41 per cent of the total sample agree with the item statement.

Results of χ^2 tests: within each type of school, significantly more pupils who dislike French agree with the item statement than do those who like French ($p < 0.001$). Significantly different responses are obtained from pupils in the different types of school ($p < 0.001$): 85·76 per cent of the secondary modern school pupils, 77·92 per cent of the comprehensive school pupils and 76·86 per cent of the grammar school pupils agree with the item statement. In the secondary modern and the grammar schools, significantly more boys than girls agree with the item statement ($p < 0.001$). There are no significant differences between the sexes in response to this item among comprehensive school pupils.

Appendix Seven

TABLE 7.19: *Item 19. 'French is my favourite subject'.*

TYPE OF SCHOOL	PUPILS WHO LIKE FRENCH			PUPILS WHO DISLIKE FRENCH		
	Boys	*Girls*	*Total*	*Boys*	*Girls*	*Total*
Secondary Modern	13·30%	22·57%	18·84%	1·59%	0·38%	1·07%
Grammar	8·62%	12·18%	10·69%	0	0	0
Comprehensive	12·28%	12·90%	12·63%	0	0	0
All School Types	11·53%	17·87%	15·27%	1·16%	0·26%	0·76%

Notes
8·88 per cent of the total sample agree with the item statement.
Results of χ^2 tests: within each type of school, significantly more pupils who like French agree with the item statement than do those who dislike French ($p < 0.001$). There are no significant differences between school groups in response to this item. In the secondary modern schools, significantly more girls than boys agree with the item statement ($p < 0.001$). There are no significant differences between the sexes in response to this item in the other types of school.

TABLE 7.20: *Item 20. 'French people should learn English instead of us learning French'.*

TYPE OF SCHOOL	PUPILS WHO LIKE FRENCH			PUPILS WHO DISLIKE FRENCH		
	Boys	*Girls*	*Total*	*Boys*	*Girls*	*Total*
Secondary Modern	45·77%	29·32%	35·86%	72·60%	67·79%	70·55%
Grammar	27·24%	14·96%	20·08%	65·97%	52·94%	58·91%
Comprehensive	24·77%	21·56%	22·93%	67·70%	65·33%	66·66%
All School Types	36·57%	23·56%	28·86%	71·05%	64·17%	67·96%

Notes
46·07 per cent of the total sample agree with the item statement.
Results of χ^2 tests: within each type of school, significantly more pupils who dislike French agree with the item statement than do those who like French ($p < 0.001$). Significantly different responses are obtained from pupils in the different types of school ($p < 0.001$): 53·58 per cent of the secondary modern school pupils, 40·04 per cent of the comprehensive school pupils and 31·85 per cent of the grammar school pupils agree with the item statement. In the secondary modern and the grammar schools, significantly more boys than girls agree with the item statement ($p < 0.001$). There are no significant differences between the sexes in response to this item among comprehensive school pupils.

I

TABLE 7.21: *Item 21. 'I think my parents are pleased that I am learning French'.*

TYPE OF SCHOOL	PUPILS WHO LIKE FRENCH			PUPILS WHO DISLIKE FRENCH		
	Boys	Girls	Total	Boys	Girls	Total
Secondary Modern	92·01%	95·13%	93·88%	60·77%	63·09%	61·76%
Grammar	96·42%	98·38%	97·57%	72·79%	81·54%	77·63%
Comprehensive	99·09%	97·40%	98·11%	62·76%	71·62%	66·66%
All School Types	94·48%	96·52%	95·69%	62·85%	68·22%	65·29%

Notes

82·65 per cent of the total sample agree with the item statement.

Results of χ^2 tests: within each type of school, significantly more pupils who like French agree with the item statement than do those who dislike French ($p < 0.001$). Significantly different responses are obtained from pupils in the different types of school ($p < 0.001$): 91·77 per cent of the grammar school pupils, 85·91 per cent of the comprehensive school pupils and 77·82 per cent of the secondary modern school pupils agree with the item statement. In the secondary modern schools, significantly more girls than boys agree with the item statement ($p < 0.001$). The same trend is present in the grammar schools, but to a less significant extent ($p < 0.05$). There are no significant differences between the sexes in response to this item among comprehensive school pupils.

TABLE 7.22: *Item 22. 'I prefer reading and writing French to speaking it'.*

TYPE OF SCHOOL	PUPILS WHO LIKE FRENCH			PUPILS WHO DISLIKE FRENCH		
	Boys	Girls	Total	Boys	Girls	Total
Secondary Modern	31·89%	39·97%	36·73%	38·16%	47·15%	42·02%
Grammar	23·79%	28·77%	26·68%	32·66%	39·53%	36·33%
Comprehensive	23·68%	35·29%	30·33%	34·34%	53·84%	42·93%
All School Types	28·00%	35·63%	32·50%	36·86%	46·11%	41·03%

Notes

36·23 per cent of the total sample agree with the item statement.

Results of χ^2 tests: within each type of school, significantly more pupils who dislike French agree with the item statement than do those who like French ($p < 0.01$). Significantly different responses are obtained from pupils in the different types of school ($p < 0.001$): 39·41 per cent of the secondary modern school pupils, 35·36 per cent of the comprehensive school pupils and 29·60 per cent of the grammar school pupils agree with the item statement. In the secondary modern schools, significantly more girls than boys agree with the item statement ($p < 0.001$). The same trend is present in the comprehensive schools, but to a less significant extent ($p < 0.01$). A similar tendency is apparent in the grammar schools, but the differences between the sexes do not reach a significant level.

Appendix Seven

TABLE 7.23: *Item 23. 'I don't think I will ever speak French after I leave school'.*

TYPE OF SCHOOL	PUPILS WHO LIKE FRENCH			PUPILS WHO DISLIKE FRENCH		
	Boys	*Girls*	*Total*	*Boys*	*Girls*	*Total*
Secondary Modern	41·28%	33·57%	36·65%	51·18%	43·30%	47·80%
Grammar	18·26%	19·58%	19·03%	58·27%	55·81%	56·96%
Comprehensive	24·77%	25·00%	24·90%	53·60%	60·25%	56·57%
All School Types	30·97%	27·76%	29·07%	52·59%	47·88%	50·47%

Notes
38·47 per cent of the total sample agree with the item statement.
Results of χ^2 tests: within each type of school, significantly more pupils who dislike French agree with the item statement than do those who like French ($p < 0.001$). Significantly different responses are obtained from pupils in the different types of school ($p < 0.001$): 42·34 per cent of the secondary modern school pupils, 37·50 per cent of the comprehensive school pupils and 30·49 per cent of the grammar school pupils agree with the item statement. In the secondary modern schools, significantly more boys than girls agree with the item statement ($p < 0.001$). There are no significant differences between the sexes in response to this item in the other types of school.

TABLE 7.24: *Item 24. 'If you are no good at French, you should be allowed to drop it'.*

TYPE OF SCHOOL	PUPILS WHO LIKE FRENCH			PUPILS WHO DISLIKE FRENCH		
	Boys	*Girls*	*Total*	*Boys*	*Girls*	*Total*
Secondary Modern	64·95%	58·84%	61·30%	86·62%	84·57%	85·75%
Grammar	84·71%	76·09%	79·70%	94·73%	91·95%	93·25%
Comprehensive	72·80%	73·07%	72·96%	93·87%	92·30%	93·18%
All School Types	72·87%	66·40%	69·06%	88·69%	87·04%	87·95%

Notes
77·34 per cent of the total sample agree with the item statement.
Results of χ^2 tests: within each type of school, significantly more pupils who dislike French agree with the item statement than do those who like French ($p < 0.001$). Significantly different responses are obtained from pupils in the different types of school ($p < 0.001$): 83·81 per cent of the grammar school pupils, 80·94 per cent of the comprehensive school pupils and 73·71 per cent of the secondary modern school pupils agree with the item statement. In the secondary modern schools, significantly more boys than girls agree with the item statement ($p < 0.001$). The same trend is present in the grammar schools, but to a less significant extent ($p < 0.01$). There are no significant differences between the sexes in response to this item among comprehensive school pupils.

239

French in the Primary School

TABLE 7.25: *Item 25. 'It is easier to remember French words if you see them written down'.*

TYPE OF SCHOOL	PUPILS WHO LIKE FRENCH			PUPILS WHO DISLIKE FRENCH		
	Boys	*Girls*	*Total*	*Boys*	*Girls*	*Total*
Secondary Modern	74·03%	82·56%	79·13%	70·39%	74·80%	72·27%
Grammar	78·13%	81·23%	79·94%	75·67%	79·31%	77·63%
Comprehensive	78·94%	84·61%	82·22%	71·71%	74·35%	72·88%
All School Types	76·09%	82·36%	79·79%	71·86%	75·78%	73·35%

Notes
76·97 per cent of the total sample agree with the item statement.
Results of χ^2 tests: there is a general tendency for more pupils who like French to agree with the item statement than do those who dislike French, but the differences between these two groups rarely reach a significant level. There are no significant differences between school groups in response to this item. In the secondary modern schools, significantly more girls than boys agree with the item statement ($p < 0.001$). There are no significant differences between the sexes in response to this item in the other types of school.

TABLE 7.26: *Item 26. 'French gets more difficult all the time'.*

TYPE OF SCHOOL	PUPILS WHO LIKE FRENCH			PUPILS WHO DISLIKE FRENCH		
	Boys	*Girls*	*Total*	*Boys*	*Girls*	*Total*
Secondary Modern	60·64%	59·65%	60·05%	86·93%	88·47%	87·59%
Grammar	54·48%	54·16%	54·30%	88·66%	89·53%	89·13%
Comprehensive	58·92%	65·80%	62·92%	88·77%	87·01%	88·00%
All School Types	58·26%	58·54%	58·42%	87·40%	88·56%	87·92%

Notes
71·36 per cent of the total sample agree with the item statement.
Results of χ^2 tests: within each type of school, significantly more pupils who dislike French agree with the item statement than do those who like French ($p < 0.001$). Significantly different responses are obtained from pupils in the different types of school ($p < 0.001$): 74·05 per cent of the secondary modern school pupils, 72·85 per cent of the comprehensive school pupils and 64·82 per cent of the grammar school pupils agree with the item statement. In the secondary modern schools, significantly more boys than girls agree with the item statement ($p < 0.05$). There are no significant differences between the sexes in response to this item in the other types of school.

240

Appendix Seven

TABLE 7.27: *Item 27. 'I would like to go on learning French next year'.*

TYPE OF SCHOOL	PUPILS WHO LIKE FRENCH			PUPILS WHO DISLIKE FRENCH		
	Boys	Girls	Total	Boys	Girls	Total
Secondary Modern	74·45%	81·36%	78·59%	12·02%	17·18%	14·23%
Grammar	91·31%	94·23%	93·02%	22·60%	29·65%	26·41%
Comprehensive	90·17%	84·21%	86·74%	13·40%	20·77%	16·66%
All School Types	82·37%	86·09%	84·56%	13·83%	20·36%	16·78%

Notes

54·83 per cent of the total sample agree with the item statement.

Results of χ^2 tests: within each type of school, significantly more pupils who like French agree with the item statement than do those who dislike French ($p < 0.001$). Significantly different responses are obtained from pupils in the different types of school ($p < 0.001$): 73·09 per cent of the grammar school pupils, 58·90 per cent of the comprehensive school pupils and 45·79 per cent of the secondary modern school pupils agree with the item statement. In the secondary modern schools, significantly more girls than boys agree with the item statement ($p < 0.001$). The same trend is present in the grammar schools, but to a less significant extent ($p < 0.05$). There are no significant differences between the sexes in response to this item among comprehensive school pupils.

TABLE 7.28: *Item 28. 'I like learning French more now than I did in the Primary School'.*

TYPE OF SCHOOL	PUPILS WHO LIKE FRENCH			PUPILS WHO DISLIKE FRENCH		
	Boys	Girls	Total	Boys	Girls	Total
Secondary Modern	76·20%	80·02%	78·49%	19·82%	25·00%	22·02%
Grammar	74·75%	73·53%	74·03%	27·63%	22·15%	24·83%
Comprehensive	76·10%	79·73%	78·19%	27·55%	30·66%	28·90%
All School Types	75·68%	77·80%	76·94%	21·91%	24·96%	23·26%

Notes

53·41 per cent of the total sample agree with the item statement.

Results of χ^2 tests: within each type of school, significantly more pupils who like French agree with the item statement than do those who dislike French ($p < 0.001$). Significantly different responses are obtained from pupils in the different types of school ($p < 0.001$): 59·34 per cent of the grammar school pupils, 58·76 per cent of the comprehensive school pupils and 49·76 per cent of the secondary modern school pupils agree with the item statement. In the secondary modern schools, significantly more girls than boys agree with the item statement ($p < 0.001$). The same trend is present in the comprehensive schools, but to a less significant extent ($p < 0.05$). There are no significant differences between the sexes in response to this item among grammar school pupils.

TABLE 7.29: *Battery 2 Speaking Test. Mean scores by type of school, sex of pupil, attitude towards French, and parental occupation.*

TYPE OF SCHOOL SEX OF PUPIL ATTITUDE TO FRENCH		PARENTAL OCCUPATION				TOTAL
		Professional and Clerical	*Skilled*	*Semi-skilled*	*Unskilled*	
Secondary Modern	N	42	69	30	18	159
Pupils who like	x̄	60·80	56·59	57·90	57·50	58·05
French	SD	24·38	19·13	24·17	20·53	21·84
Secondary Modern	N	14	35	20	18	87
Pupils who dislike	x̄	41·07	37·42	37·95	38·27	38·31
French	SD	16·47	11·15	17·66	10·34	13·75
Grammar	N	42	29	7	1	79
Pupils who like	x̄	87·57	81·55	63·71	71·00	83·03
French	SD	14·12	18·02	16·47	0·00	17·20
Grammar	N	8	11	7	3	29
Pupils who dislike	x̄	73·87	58·54	67·85	66·33	65·82
French	SD	15·24	17·09	13·38	12·81	16·55
Comprehensive	N	16	16	5	2	39
Pupils who like	x̄	80·06	71·68	87·20	71·00	77·07
French	SD	15·51	16·95	21·65	17·99	18·00
Comprehensive	N	2	7	4	1	14
Pupils who dislike	x̄	44·50	51·57	40·00	26·00	45·42
French	SD	15·49	14·06	22·91	0·00	18·37
All Boys who	N	45	49	17	10	121
like French	x̄	75·37	62·97	52·05	54·60	65·36
	SD	23·43	22·61	21·32	19·79	24·11
All Boys who	N	13	35	16	12	76
dislike French	x̄	57·23	43·20	37·31	42·66	44·27
	SD	26·41	14·73	12·47	11·18	17·65
All Girls who	N	55	65	25	11	156
like French	x̄	74·92	66·63	69·36	63·81	69·79
	SD	22·56	20·52	24·25	19·87	22·20
All Girls who	N	11	18	15	10	54
dislike French	x̄	46·45	44·61	53·13	40·20	46·53
	SD	13·43	17·58	25·71	17·78	20·07
All Pupils who	N	100	114	42	21	277
like French	x̄	75·13	65·06	62·35	59·42	67·85
	SD	22·96	21·52	24·62	20·36	23·16
All Pupils who	N	24	53	31	22	130
dislike French	x̄	52·29	43·67	44·96	41·54	45·21
	SD	22·12	15·77	21·51	14·61	18·73

Notes

In view of the small numbers involved, the distribution of scores within school groups is not shown separately for boys and girls. Taken over all school groups, the differences between mean scores for pupils liking or disliking French reach a high level of significance ($p < 0.001$) for girls in the 'professional and clerical' parental occupation category and for both boys and girls in the 'skilled' category. Differences between mean scores for girls in the 'unskilled' category reach a lower level of significance ($p < 0.01$), as do those for boys in the 'professional and clerical' and 'semi-skilled' categories ($p < 0.05$). Differences between mean scores for boys in the 'unskilled' category and for girls in the 'semi-skilled' category do not reach a significant level. In the grammar schools, pupils in the 'semi-skilled' category who dislike French obtain a higher mean score than do those who like French, but it must be emphasised that the number of pupils involved is very small. This result is, in fact, due to the unusually high scores obtained by 4 girls who dislike French.

TABLE 7.30: *Battery 2 Listening Test. Mean scores by type of school, sex of pupil, attitude towards French, and parental occupation.*

| TYPE OF SCHOOL SEX OF PUPIL ATTITUDE TO FRENCH | | PARENTAL OCCUPATION | | | | TOTAL |
		Professional and Clerical	Skilled	Semi-skilled	Unskilled	
Secondary Modern	N	108	168	109	70	455
Boys who like	x̄	17·65	17·60	16·91	15·72	17·16
French	SD	5·51	5·46	4·99	4·61	5·28
Secondary Modern	N	115	284	157	111	667
Boys who dislike	x̄	15·97	14·78	13·84	12·96	14·46
French	SD	4·82	4·29	4·39	4·49	4·54
Secondary Modern	N	142	292	149	97	680
Girls who like	x̄	18·52	18·44	16·79	15·97	17·75
French	SD	5·57	5·49	5·49	5·11	5·55
Secondary Modern	N	87	172	151	89	499
Girls who dislike	x̄	15·88	15·92	15·08	15·26	15·54
French	SD	5·44	4·60	4·71	4·89	4·85
Grammar	N	165	104	25	13	307
Boys who like	x̄	27·26	26·23	25·48	26·30	26·72
French	SD	5·86	5·48	5·76	3·47	5·68
Grammar	N	54	52	23	17	146
Boys who dislike	x̄	23·57	22·73	21·17	23·29	22·86
French	SD	5·84	5·30	3·93	4·93	5·34
Grammar	N	209	144	55	20	428
Girls who like	x̄	27·90	25·53	25·49	25·95	26·70
French	SD	5·44	5·52	4·81	5·60	5·52
Grammar	N	74	59	24	13	170
Girls who dislike	x̄	24·18	22·52	21·50	21·15	23·00
French	SD	5·57	5·79	5·00	5·03	5·65
Comprehensive	N	40	52	17	5	114
Boys who like	x̄	24·52	23·40	16·35	14·80	22·36
French	SD	6·03	6·37	4·12	7·70	6·81
Comprehensive	N	31	43	13	10	97
Boys who dislike	x̄	19·09	18·23	14·00	15·80	17·69
French	SD	4·99	5·80	2·98	5·99	5·54

244

TABLE 7.30. (cont.)

TYPE OF SCHOOL SEX OF PUPIL ATTITUDE TO FRENCH		PARENTAL OCCUPATION				TOTAL
		Professional and Clerical	*Skilled*	*Semi-skilled*	*Unskilled*	
Comprehensive	N	72	44	26	12	154
Girls who like	x̄	25·70	22·00	21·11	16·66	23·16
French	SD	6·19	7·08	7·01	5·03	7·06
Comprehensive	N	16	33	21	6	76
Girls who dislike	x̄	22·00	17·03	15·66	16·00	17·61
French	SD	6·49	5·19	5·38	4·32	5·96
All Pupils who	N	736	804	381	217	2138
like French	x̄	24·05	21·06	18·93	17·44	21·34
	SD	7·14	6·66	6·41	6·20	7·11
All Pupils who	N	377	643	389	246	1655
dislike French	x̄	19·16	16·79	15·33	15·13	16·74
	SD	6·51	5·54	5·10	5·60	5·88

Notes

Taken over all school groups, the differences between mean scores for boys liking or disliking French reach a high level of significance ($p < 0.001$) in each parental occupation category. The differences between mean scores for girls liking or disliking French, taken over all school groups, are highly significant ($p < 0.001$) in the 'professional and clerical', 'skilled' and 'semi-skilled' parental occupation categories, but are less significant ($p < 0.05$) in the 'unskilled' category.

French in the Primary School

TABLE 7.31: *Battery 2 Reading Test. Mean scores by type of school, sex of pupil, attitude towards French, and parental occupation.*

TYPE OF SCHOOL SEX OF PUPIL ATTITUDE TO FRENCH		PARENTAL OCCUPATION				TOTAL
		Professional and Clerical	Skilled	Semi-skilled	Unskilled	
Secondary Modern Boys who like French	N	109	172	112	72	465
	x̄	19·77	17·83	16·66	15·95	17·71
	SD	6·76	6·75	6·34	6·76	6·79
Secondary Modern Boys who dislike French	N	116	291	167	112	686
	x̄	15·61	13·87	13·74	12·92	13·98
	SD	6·07	4·83	4·66	4·67	5·06
Secondary Modern Girls who like French	N	144	292	148	97	681
	x̄	22·64	20·32	18·42	18·18	20·09
	SD	7·76	7·63	6·65	7·24	7·57
Secondary Modern Girls who dislike French	N	86	174	153	91	504
	x̄	17·73	15·92	15·74	15·24	16·05
	SD	5·70	5·87	6·20	5·67	5·96
Grammar Boys who like French	N	164	99	25	12	300
	x̄	33·89	32·10	30·48	33·08	32·98
	SD	6·33	7·08	6·75	3·88	6·64
Grammar Boys who dislike French	N	53	49	23	15	140
	x̄	29·35	28·53	24·17	29·06	28·18
	SD	6·44	7·29	5·93	4·78	6·77
Grammar Girls who like French	N	211	147	55	23	436
	x̄	36·22	32·53	32·20	34·26	34·36
	SD	5·48	6·40	6·05	5·86	6·18
Grammar Girls who dislike French	N	75	60	24	14	173
	x̄	30·36	27·96	27·58	28·64	29·00
	SD	6·19	6·62	6·56	5·89	6·48
Comprehensive Boys who like French	N	40	50	17	6	113
	x̄	30·87	28·58	20·70	15·50	27·51
	SD	8·64	8·16	7·18	6·60	9·22
Comprehensive Boys who dislike French	N	31	44	13	10	98
	x̄	21·96	19·90	14·46	14·20	19·25
	SD	8·05	9·38	5·86	6·06	8·74

246

TABLE 7.31. (cont.)

TYPE OF SCHOOL SEX OF PUPIL ATTITUDE TO FRENCH		PARENTAL OCCUPATION				TOTAL
		Professional and Clerical	*Skilled*	*Semi-skilled*	*Unskilled*	
Comprehensive	N	73	45	26	12	156
Girls who like	x̄	32·94	28·22	24·73	19·50	29·17
French	SD	7·84	8·79	8·51	8·20	9·25
Comprehensive	N	16	34	21	7	78
Girls who dislike	x̄	26·75	19·00	17·42	17·00	19·98
French	SD	8·56	7·56	6·93	6·67	8·32
All Pupils who	N	741	805	383	222	2151
like French	x̄	30·03	24·42	21·20	19·93	25·32
	SD	9·33	9·46	8·78	9·19	9·99
All Pupils who	N	377	652	401	249	1679
dislike French	x̄	21·95	17·49	16·14	15·79	17·92
	SD	8·93	7·92	6·79	7·17	8·13

Notes

Taken over all school groups, the differences between mean scores for boys liking or disliking French are highly significant ($p < 0.001$) in the 'professional and clerical', 'skilled' and 'semi-skilled' parental occupation categories, but are slightly less significant ($p < 0.01$) in the 'unskilled' category. The differences between mean scores for girls liking or disliking French, taken over all school groups, reach a high level of significance ($p < 0.001$) in each parental occupation category.

TABLE 7.32: *Battery 2 Writing Test. Mean scores by type of school, sex of pupil, attitude towards French, and parental occupation.*

TYPE OF SCHOOL SEX OF PUPIL ATTITUDE TO FRENCH		PARENTAL OCCUPATION				TOTAL
		Professional and Clerical	*Skilled*	*Semi-skilled*	*Unskilled*	
Secondary Modern Boys who like French	N x̄ SD	110 18·18 13·12	172 14·10 10·69	107 10·93 8·97	70 12·30 11·09	459 14·06 11·33
Secondary Modern Boys who dislike French	N x̄ SD	116 10·71 10·32	280 8·80 8·03	166 7·75 6·97	111 6·85 7·14	673 8·55 8·19
Secondary Modern Girls who like French	N x̄ SD	139 23·05 13·26	295 19·00 12·10	148 15·39 11·83	95 15·67 12·13	677 18·58 12·60
Secondary Modern Girls who dislike French	N x̄ SD	86 14·18 9·74	170 11·21 9·23	147 10·04 8·77	89 9·92 7·14	492 11·15 8·97
Grammar Boys who like French	N x̄ SD	168 46·87 14·72	102 41·42 15·85	26 38·23 12·28	13 40·00 8·43	309 44·05 15·05
Grammar Boys who dislike French	N x̄ SD	55 37·43 12·47	54 31·50 13·47	26 25·34 11·89	16 28·68 9·03	151 32·30 13·20
Grammar Girls who like French	N x̄ SD	207 51·92 12·16	144 43·22 12·57	54 42·59 12·22	23 46·43 12·01	428 47·52 13·03
Grammar Girls who dislike French	N x̄ SD	73 39·61 11·47	60 37·13 11·72	24 34·54 10·62	14 35·42 10·76	171 37·69 11·54
Comprehensive Boys who like French	N x̄ SD	40 37·65 15·44	52 32·92 16·50	17 18·76 13·20	5 17·80 13·36	114 31·80 16·97
Comprehensive Boys who dislike French	N x̄ SD	30 24·00 16·31	43 18·48 16·47	14 9·64 7·63	9 10·44 11·04	96 18·16 15·86

TABLE 7.32. (cont.)

TYPE OF SCHOOL SEX OF PUPIL ATTITUDE TO FRENCH		Professional and Clerical	Skilled	Semi-skilled	Unskilled	TOTAL
		PARENTAL OCCUPATION				
Comprehensive Girls who like French	N	72	44	24	12	152
	x̄	40·12	31·29	26·29	18·16	33·65
	SD	16·47	15·36	18·15	12·94	17·63
Comprehensive Girls who dislike French	N	16	34	20	7	77
	x̄	28·43	17·00	12·55	11·57	17·72
	SD	12·83	14·74	9·88	9·00	14·05
All Pupils who like French	N	736	809	376	218	2139
	x̄	38·34	26·66	20·46	19·47	29·86
	SD	19·06	17·40	16·40	16·16	19·17
All Pupils who dislike French	N	376	641	397	246	1660
	x̄	22·84	15·09	11·68	11·27	15·46
	SD	16·76	14·11	11·10	11·07	14·37

Notes
Taken over all school groups, differences between mean scores for both boys and girls liking or disliking French reach a high level of significance ($p < 0.001$) in each parental occupation category.

TABLE 7.33: *Battery 2 Speaking Test. Mean scores by sex of pupil, contact with France, and parental occupation.*

SEX OF PUPIL CONTACT WITH FRANCE		PARENTAL OCCUPATION				TOTAL
		Professional and Clerical	*Skilled*	*Semi-skilled*	*Unskilled*	
Boys who have visited France	N	17	15	3	1	36
	x̄	70·35	55·66	41·66	61·00	61·58
	SD	22·62	24·25	10·21	0·00	23·69
Boys who have not visited France	N	42	74	40	23	179
	x̄	70·35	54·24	44·20	48·26	55·01
	SD	26·57	21·34	18·70	18·05	23·54
Girls who have visited France	N	21	12	8	4	45
	x̄	72·38	69·00	81·62	69·00	72·82
	SD	19·24	24·95	19·83	11·97	20·39
Girls who have not visited France	N	47	78	41	18	184
	x̄	69·04	59·51	61·00	48·61	61·21
	SD	25·65	22·21	25·08	22·65	24·30

Notes

Taking the sample as a whole, mean scores for pupils who have visited France are significantly higher than those for pupils who have not visited France. Differences between mean scores are significant at the 0·1 per cent level. Differences between mean scores do not reach a significant level within the different types of secondary school, but it must be noted that the sample size in this instance is extremely small.

TABLE 7.34: *Battery 2 Listening Test. Mean scores by sex of pupil, contact with France, and parental occupation.*

		PARENTAL OCCUPATION				
SEX OF PUPIL CONTACT WITH FRANCE		Professional and Clerical	Skilled	Semi-skilled	Unskilled	TOTAL
Boys who have	N	150	129	53	20	352
visited France	x̄	23·48	19·41	17·24	16·90	20·67
	SD	7·72	7·06	6·13	7·44	7·65
Boys who have not	N	380	613	372	226	1591
visited France	x̄	20·45	18·17	16·00	15·57	17·84
	SD	7·04	6·36	5·35	5·75	6·48
Girls who have	N	156	109	62	26	353
visited France	x̄	23·75	21·40	19·37	18·38	21·86
	SD	7·20	6·74	5·91	5·16	6·95
Girls who have not	N	473	667	428	243	1811
visited France	x̄	22·60	19·33	17·58	16·73	19·42
	SD	7·21	6·26	6·19	5·90	6·79

Notes
Taking the sample as a whole, mean scores for pupils who have visited France are significantly higher than those for pupils who have not visited France. Differences between mean scores for the sample as a whole and for boys and girls separately are significant at the 0·1 per cent level. Differences between mean scores in favour of pupils who have visited France are significant at the 0·1 per cent level for comprehensive school pupils and at the 5 per cent level for secondary modern school pupils. The differences between mean scores for grammar school pupils do not reach a significant level, but there is a positive tendency for pupils who have visited France to obtain higher scores than those who have not.

TABLE 7.35: *Battery 2 Reading Test. Mean scores by sex of pupil, contact with France, and parental occupation.*

			PARENTAL OCCUPATION			
SEX OF PUPIL CONTACT WITH FRANCE		*Professional and Clerical*	*Skilled*	*Semi-skilled*	*Unskilled*	TOTAL
Boys who have visited France	N	152	128	56	21	357
	x̄	28·07	21·99	17·92	16·28	23·61
	SD	9·55	9·60	8·04	8·13	10·14
Boys who have not visited France	N	380	615	381	226	1602
	x̄	23·82	19·19	16·29	16·20	19·18
	SD	9·92	9·14	6·87	7·66	9·12
Girls who have visited France	N	157	116	63	26	362
	x̄	29·99	25·72	22·41	20·61	26·63
	SD	8·97	9·47	8·43	8·63	9·57
Girls who have not visited France	N	479	667	425	251	1822
	x̄	28·12	22·06	19·66	18·78	22·64
	SD	9·80	9·09	8·49	8·59	9·72

Notes

Taking the sample as a whole, mean scores for pupils who have visited France are significantly higher than those for pupils who have not visited France. Differences between mean scores for the sample as a whole and for boys and girls separately are significant at the 0·1 per cent level. Differences between mean scores in favour of pupils who have visited France are significant at the 0·1 per cent level for secondary modern school pupils and at the one per cent level for comprehensive school pupils. The differences between mean scores for grammar school pupils do not reach a significant level, but there is a positive tendency for pupils who have visited France to obtain higher scores than those who have not.

TABLE 7.36: *Battery 2 Writing Test. Mean scores by sex of pupil, contact with France, and parental occupation.*

		PARENTAL OCCUPATION				
SEX OF PUPIL CONTACT WITH FRANCE		*Professional and Clerical*	*Skilled*	*Semi-skilled*	*Unskilled*	TOTAL
Boys who have visited France	N	151	123	54	19	347
	x̄	36·19	22·21	13·55	14·42	26·52
	SD	19·02	18·26	14·09	13·20	19·89
Boys who have not visited France	N	387	618	382	224	1611
	x̄	26·41	17·78	11·94	12·22	17·70
	SD	19·46	16·32	11·65	12·57	16·65
Girls who have visited France	N	154	113	58	25	350
	x̄	37·92	30·01	23·51	18·48	31·59
	SD	17·77	18·04	16·60	14·24	18·53
Girls who have not visited France	N	471	665	421	248	1805
	x̄	34·40	22·71	17·69	17·04	23·81
	SD	19·33	16·22	15·27	15·02	18·00

Notes
Taking the sample as a whole, mean scores for pupils who have visited France are significantly higher than those for pupils who have not visited France. Differences between mean scores for the sample as a whole and for boys and girls separately are significant at the 0·1 per cent level. Differences between mean scores in favour of pupils who have visited France are significant at the 0·1 per cent level for comprehensive and secondary modern school pupils and at the five per cent level for grammar school pupils.

APPENDIX NINE

The HMI Evaluation of the
Secondary Stage of the Pilot Scheme

(Tables 9.1 - 9.3)

TABLE 9.1: *The fluency of the class: results of χ^2 tests.*

VARIABLE 2	d.f.	YEAR 1		YEAR 2		COMMENTS
		χ^2	Significance Level	χ^2	Significance Level	
Pupils' response to French	4	106·563	***	69·407	***	In more HF classes the pupils' response to the French lesson was 'good'. In more MF and LF classes the pupils' response was 'fair' or 'poor'.
Pupils' attitude towards learning French	4	38·506	***	80·125	***	In more HF classes the pupils' attitude towards learning French was 'highly enthusiastic'. In more LF classes the pupils' attitude was 'unenthusiastic'.
Pupils' ability to speak in French	2	64·191	***	48·975	***	In more HF classes speaking skills were being developed 'fully'. In more MF and LF classes speaking skills were being developed 'to some extent' or 'not at all'.
Pupils' oral reading	2	40·956	***	17·583	***	In more HF classes pupils' oral reading was being developed 'fully'. In more MF and LF classes oral reading was being developed 'to some extent' or 'not at all'.
Pupils' reading comprehension	2	16·040	***	11·295	**	In more HF classes pupils' reading comprehension was being developed 'fully'. In more MF and LF classes reading comprehension was being developed 'to some extent' or 'not at all'.
Pupils' ability to write in French	2	21·117	***	10·175	**	In more HF classes pupils' ability to write in French was being developed 'fully'. In more MF and LF classes writing skills were being developed 'to some extent' or 'not at all'.

TABLE 9.1. (Cont.)

VARIABLE 2	d.f.	YEAR 1		YEAR 2		COMMENTS
		χ^2	Significance Level	χ^2	Significance Level	
Pupils' knowledge of cultural background	2	14·408	***	6·078	*	In more HF classes pupils' knowledge of cultural background was being developed 'fully'. In more MF and LF classes knowledge of cultural background was being developed 'to some extent' or 'not at all'.
Teacher's linguistic competence	4	36·344	***	22·004	***	More teachers of HF classes had 'excellent' or 'good" linguistic skills. More teachers of MF and LF classes were rated 'average', 'fair' or 'poor' in this respect.
Teacher's skill with A/V equipment	4	25·232	***	15·192	**	More teachers of HF classes were rated 'excellent' or 'good' in their handling of A/V equipment. More teachers of MF and LF classes were rated 'average', 'fair' or 'poor' in this respect.
Teacher's overall competence	4	52·341	***	30·666	***	More teachers of HF classes were rated 'excellent' or 'good' for overall competence. More teachers of MF and LF classes were rated 'average', 'fair' or 'poor' in this respect.
Teacher's attitude towards Pilot Scheme pupils	2	17·352	***	3·753	NS	In Year 1 more teachers of HF classes had a favourable attitude towards teaching Pilot Scheme pupils and more teachers of MF and LF classes had a non-committal or unfavourable attitude. In Year 2 the classes did not differ significantly according to the teacher's attitude.

TABLE 9.1. (Cont.)

VARIABLE 2	d.f.	YEAR 1		YEAR 2		COMMENTS
		χ^2	*Significance Level*	χ^2	*Significance Level*	
Effects of primary French	2	38·585	***	32·021	***	In more HF classes pupils appeared to have benefited 'a great deal' from their primary French course. In more MF and LF classes pupils appeared to have benefited 'to some extent' or 'not at all'.
Overall impression of French lesson	2	33·672	***	28·519	***	In more HF classes a favourable impression of the French lesson was reported. In more MF and LF classes an unfavourable impression was reported.
School type	4	9·449	NS	21·910	***	In Year 1 there were no significant differences between classes according to school type. In Year 2 more HF classes were in grammar schools, more MF classes were in comprehensive schools and more LF classes were in secondary modern schools.

Notes

1. Variable 1 in Table 9.1 is the rated fluency of the French class. 'Highly fluent' (HF) classes are those rated 'good' for overall fluency. 'Moderately fluent' (MF) classes are those rated 'fair'. 'Less fluent' (LF) classes are those rated 'poor'.

2. The analysis of the questionnaire data was carried out separately for classes visited during 1967-68 ('Year 1') and for those visited during 1968-69 ('Year 2'). During Year 1 reports were received of visits to 135 first cohort French classes; during Year 2 reports were received of visits to 129 such classes.

3. All variables which proved non-significant in both Year 1 and Year 2 have been omitted from Table 9.1.

4. Levels of significance are shown as follows: NS non significant; $*p < 0.05$; $**p < 0.01$; $***p < 0.001$.

TABLE 9.2: *The responsiveness of the class to the French lesson: results of χ^2 tests.*

VARIABLE 2	d.f.	YEAR 1		YEAR 2		COMMENTS
		χ^2	Significance Level	χ^2	Significance Level	
Pupils' overall fluency	4	106·563	***	69·406	***	In more HR classes the pupils' overall fluency was 'good'. In more MR and LR classes the pupils' overall fluency was 'fair' or 'poor'.
Pupils' attitude towards learning French	4	74·744	***	102·825	***	In more HR classes the pupils' attitude towards learning French was 'highly enthusiastic' or 'enthusiastic'. In more LR classes the pupils' attitude was 'unenthusiastic'.
Pupils' ability to speak in French	2	53·090	***	31·622	***	In more HR classes speaking skills were being developed 'fully'. In more MR and LR classes speaking skills were being developed 'to some extent' or 'not at all'.
Pupils' oral reading	2	27·170	***	10·893	**	In more HR classes pupils' oral reading was being developed 'fully'. In more MR and LR classes oral reading was being developed 'to some extent' or 'not at all'.
Pupils' reading comprehension	2	4·790	NS	7·485	*	In Year 1 there were no significant differences between classes with regard to the development of reading comprehension. In Year 2 reading comprehension was being developed 'fully' or 'to some extent' in more HR classes, but 'not at all' in more MR and LR classes.

TABLE 9.2. (Cont.)

VARIABLE 2	d.f.	YEAR 1		YEAR 2		COMMENTS
		χ^2	*Significance Level*	χ^2	*Significance Level*	
Pupils' ability to write in French	2	13·597	**	10·767	**	In more HR and MR classes pupils' ability to write in French was being developed 'fully' or 'to some extent'. In more LR classes this ability was not being developed at all.
Pupils' knowledge of cultural background	2	11·638	**	6·963	*	In more HR and MR classes pupils' knowledge of cultural background was being developed 'fully' or 'to some extent'. In more LR classes this knowledge was not being developed at all.
Teacher's linguistic competence	4	46·568	***	22·874	***	More teachers of HR classes had 'excellent' or 'good' linguistic skills. More teachers of MR and LR classes were rated 'average', 'fair', or 'poor' in this respect.
Teacher's skill with A/V equipment	4	41·086	***	33·068	***	More teachers of HR classes were rated 'excellent' or 'good' in their handling of A/V equipment. More teachers of MR and LR classes were rated 'average', 'fair' or 'poor' in this respect.
Teacher's overall competence	4	67·109	***	41·684	***	More teachers of HR classes were rated 'excellent' or 'good' for overall competence. More teachers of MR and LR classes were rated 'average', 'fair' or 'poor' in this respect.

TABLE 9.2. (Cont.)

VARIABLE 2	d.f.	YEAR 1		YEAR 2		COMMENTS
		χ^2	Signific-ance Level	χ^2	Signific-ance Level	
Teacher's attitude towards Pilot Scheme pupils	2	8·652	*	7·878	*	More teachers of HR classes had a favourable attitude towards teaching Pilot Scheme pupils. More teachers of MR and LR classes had a non-committal or unfavourable attitude.
Effects of primary French course	2	42·502	***	31·681	***	In more HR classes pupils appeared to have benefited 'a great deal' from their primary French course. In more MR classes pupils had benefited 'to some extent'. In more LR classes pupils did not appear to have benefited at all.
Overall impression of French lesson	2	43·778	***	45·390	***	In more HR classes a favourable impression of the French lesson was reported. In more LR classes an unfavourable impression was reported.

Notes
1. Variable 1 in Table 9.2. is the rated responsiveness of the class to the French lesson. 'Highly responsive' (HR) classes are those rated 'good' for their general response. 'Moderately responsive' (MR) classes are those rated 'fair'. 'Less responsive' (LR) classes are those rated 'poor'.
2. All variables which proved non-significant in both Year 1 and Year 2 have been omitted from Table 9.2.

TABLE 9.3: *Pupils' attitudes towards learning French: results of χ^2 tests.*

VARIABLE 2	d.f.	YEAR 1		YEAR 2		COMMENTS
		χ^2	Signific- ance Level	χ^2	Signific- ance Level	
Pupils' response to French lesson	4	74·744	***	102·825	***	In more HE classes the pupils' response to the French lesson was 'good'. In more ME and UE classes the pupils' response was 'fair' or 'poor'.
Pupils' overall fluency	4	38·506	***	80·125	***	In more HE classes the pupils' overall fluency was 'good'. In more ME and UE classes the pupils' overall fluency was 'fair' or 'poor'.
Pupils' ability to speak in French	2	33·756	***	42·055	***	In more HE classes speaking skills were being developed 'fully'. In more ME and UE classes speaking skills were being developed 'to some extent' or 'not at all'.
Pupils' oral reading	2	23·705	***	17·037	***	In more HE classes pupils' oral reading was being developed 'fully'. In more ME and UE classes oral reading was being developed 'to some extent' or 'not at all'.
Pupils' ability to write in French	2	2·400	NS	14·510	***	In Year 1 there were no significant differences between classes with regard to the development of written skills. In Year 2 written skills were being developed 'fully' or 'to some extent' in more HE and ME classes, but 'not at all' in more UE classes.
Pupils' knowledge of cultural background	2	23·376	***	6·343	*	In more HE and ME classes knowledge of cultural background was being developed 'fully' or 'to some extent'. In more UE classes this knowledge was not being developed at all.

TABLE 9.3. (Cont.)

VARIABLE 2	d.f.	YEAR 1		YEAR 2		COMMENTS
		χ^2	Significance Level	χ^2	Significance Level	
Teacher's linguistic competence	4	37·584	***	27·995	***	More teachers of HE classes had 'excellent' or 'good' linguistic skills. More teachers of ME and UE classes were rated 'average', 'fair' or 'poor' in this respect.
Teacher's skill with A/V equipment	4	37·606	***	37·791	***	More teachers of HE classes were rated 'excellent' or 'good' in their handling of A/V equipment. More teachers of ME and UE classes were rated 'average', 'fair' or 'poor' in this respect.
Teacher's overall competence	4	73·130	***	42·733	***	More teachers of HE classes were rated 'excellent' or 'good' for overall competence. More teachers of ME and UE classes were rated 'average', 'fair' or 'poor' in this respect.
Teacher's attitude towards Pilot Scheme pupils	2	17·262	***	7·986	*	More teachers of HE classes had a favourable attitude towards teaching Pilot Scheme pupils. More teachers of ME and UE classes had a non-committal or unfavourable attitude.
Effects of primary French course	2	8·660	*	42·332	***	In more HE classes pupils appeared to have benefited 'a great deal' from their primary French course. In more ME and UE classes pupils had benefited 'to some extent' or 'not at all'.
Overall impression of French lesson	2	58·771	***	42·931	***	In more HE classes a favourable impression of the French lesson was reported. In more UE classes an unfavourable impression was reported.

Notes

1. Variable 1 in Table 9.3 is the rated attitude of the class towards learning French. 'Highly enthusiastic' (HE) classes are those described in these terms. 'Moderately enthusiastic' (ME) classes are those described as 'enthusiastic'. 'Unenthusiastic' (UE) classes are those so described.

2. All variables which proved non-significant in both Year 1 and Year 2 have been omitted from Table 9.3.

Index